PRESIDENTIAL PORK

D1259079

PRESIDENTIAL PORK

WHITE HOUSE INFLUENCE OVER THE DISTRIBUTION OF FEDERAL GRANTS

JOHN HUDAK

BROOKINGS INSTITUTION PRESS
Washington, D.C.

Copyright © 2014
THE BROOKINGS INSTITUTION
1775 Massachusetts Avenue, N.W., Washington, D.C. 20036
www.brookings.edu

Library of Congress Cataloging-in-Publication data

Hudak, John Joseph.
    Presidential pork : White House influence over the distribution of federal grants / John Hudak.
        pages   cm
    Includes bibliographical references and index.
    ISBN 978-0-8157-2520-6 (pbk. : alk. paper)
    1. Grants-in-aid—United States. 2. Executive power—United States. 3. United States—Appropriations and expenditures. 4. Government spending policy—United States. 5. Presidents—United States—Decision making. I. Title.
    HJ275.2.H84 2014
    336.3'9—dc23   2013048161

9 8 7 6 5 4 3 2 1

Printed on acid-free paper

Typeset in Adobe Garamond

Composition by Cynthia Stock
Silver Spring, Maryland

Printed by R. R. Donnelley
Harrisonburg, Virginia

Contents

Acknowledgments

I could probably double the size of this work if I devoted the space necessary to those who deserved an acknowledgment. I realize that at every stage of my life and my career I stand on the shoulders of those who came before me and those around me. A force in American politics for whom I have the greatest respect—Hillary Rodham Clinton—once titled a book *It Takes a Village*. Secretary Clinton, though focused on a much more critical issue, could easily have applied that title to the development of a research project. This project came about because of some of the most caring, talented, patient, and understanding villagers, and it reflects their character as much as it displays my own work. Below, I shall insufficiently tip my hat.

Presidential Pork, begun when I was at Vanderbilt, is due substantially to the guidance, training, support, and time of Dave Lewis. The ideas and originality in this book, while my own, were nurtured by his efforts. His always welcomed (even though occasionally stressful) critique, feedback, suggestions, and revisions contributed substantially to my writing, and I cannot even imagine the book without this valued guidance. As a mentor and a friend, he helped to ensure this work was of high quality. My success as a scholar has been and will be due in large part to his role.

In addition to Dave, other colleagues at Vanderbilt supported this project in ways for which I will be eternally grateful. Bruce Oppenheimer, John Geer, Josh Clinton, and Kevin Stack provided insightful comments. Suzanne Globetti and Marc Hetherington helped to improve my work and level my sanity during different periods of my career. My positive experience in the

Department of Political Science was due in large part to the leadership of Neal Tate. I cannot adequately put into words what a force and a role model Neal was to the department and to me personally. His death was a loss to the department, to the university, to the discipline, and I am fortunate to have worked with him. I am grateful to have had the opportunity to call him and others named here colleagues.

This research was supported by the National Science Foundation, the Vanderbilt University Social Science Dissertation Fellowship, the Vanderbilt University Graduate School and Department of Political Science, the Center for the Study of Democratic Institutions, and the Brookings Institution. I have also received incredibly helpful feedback at conferences and elsewhere from Larry Bartels, Matthew Beckmann, John Gasper, Laurel Harbridge, Jon Hiskey, Cindy Kam, George Krause, Andrew Reeves, Bert Rockman, Mitch Seligson, Zeynep Somer-Topcu, Justin Vaughn, Adam Warber, Alan Wiseman, and the participants in the Conference on Federal Spending, hosted by Nate Monroe (University of California–Merced).

I would be remiss if I did not thank the tremendous and careful feedback from Katie Dunn Tenpas and Brandon Rottinghaus. This book is much improved by their detailed suggestions and recommendations. I owe them a debt of gratitude, as does every individual who reads this book, for making the journey from cover to cover a smoother one.

I must also thank the individuals—who must remain nameless—who agreed to be interviewed for the portion of the research that ultimately became chapter 7 of this book. Their time, information, and expertise proved profoundly insightful and aided dramatically in this contribution. They taught me much about the executive branch of American government, but also how to deal with the personalities and characters that populate the Washington establishment.

Beyond the formal and faculty acknowledgments of support and assistance for this project, I have a host of others who have helped me immensely. Virginia Hettinger made sure that an undergraduate at the University of Connecticut was prepared, confident, and eager to become a social scientist. While many people helped along the way, I can surely say Virginia is singularly responsible for starting me on that path.

As this project was conceived and grew, I had the privilege of working alongside peers and colleagues who have made my life as a researcher more enriching. Specifically, Stacy Clifford, Evan Haglund, Jason Husser, Grace Jensen, Gbemende Johnson, Mason Moseley, Carrie Russell, Jen Selin, and Steve Utych have been incredible colleagues with whom I am lucky to have worked.

This book began during my time at Vanderbilt and was completed at the Brookings Institution. I would be remiss if I did not thank my colleagues in Governance Studies who helped along the way, including Darrell West, Sarah Binder, Stephanie Dahle, Christine Jacobs, Elaine Kamarck, Tom Mann, and Phil Wallach. I am also indebted to the research assistance of Ashley Gabriele, Grace Wallack, Lucy Arnold, and Brian Boessenecker.

A few other friends and colleagues have helped me in ways that deserve specific acknowledgment. Jennifer Anderson and Jenna Lukasik always provided advice, support, feedback, coffee breaks, and conference experiences, and their friendship kept me sane as *Presidential Pork* matured. Jennifer also showed me how laborious a research project can be and truly put my own into perspective.

Sarah Hinde Case provided feedback, friendship, and help whenever I needed it. Whether our daily conversations involved politics or policy, daily events or distractions, work or wine, she has been a dear friend, a source of enormous support, and I surely would not have crossed the finish line without her.

Brian Faughnan has read as much of this book as anyone. His ability to show (or at least feign) interest in this project is impressive. Many of the ideas in this book have been developed, expanded, and refined through casual and formal conversations, constant trips for coffee, and occasional libations. Brian has been a great friend and colleague and someone to whom I am greatly indebted.

I depend on the support of an incredible family that has supported me over time and is responsible for my becoming the person and scholar I am today. Mom, Dad, Gram, Aunt Peg, Uncle Diz, Michelle, and Tennessee parents—Sam and Sue—have been incredible forces in my life and I owe them everything. They are among the most important members of my village, and I am fortunate to have each of them in my life.

Finally, my wife, Emily, has been a source of constant strength, motivation, encouragement, happiness, and sanity. She (and a pug named Mooshu), more than anyone else, has endured the ups and downs, the confidence and worry, the brightest hours and darkest days. Her patience is astonishing; her love is unending. I am lucky to have her in my life, and this achievement is as much hers as it is mine.

PRESIDENTIAL PORK

1

Introduction

On the other hand, if the money is being spent as it needs to be spent—to rebuild our roads and our bridges and our schools, and making sure that we are putting in place the kinds of infrastructure foundations that are necessary for economic growth over the long term—then I think all of us will benefit and our voters and our constituents, the people we work for, are going to be extraordinarily grateful.
—Barack Obama, March 12, 2009[1]

Many administrations have sought to maximize their control of the machinery of government for political gain, dispatching Cabinet secretaries bearing government largess to battleground states in the days before elections. But [Karl] Rove . . . pursued the goal far more systematically than his predecessors . . . enlisting political appointees at every level of government in a permanent campaign.
—*Washington Post*, August 19, 2007[2]

In late 2008 and early 2009, the United States rapidly entered a profound economic recession. In concert with Congress, the Bush and Obama administrations crafted legislation intended to stem economic losses and restart the economy on a path toward growth, employment, and stability. That legislation, which became the American Recovery and Reinvestment Act of 2009, was signed into law on February 19, 2009.[3] The White House stated that the act was "a nationwide effort to create jobs, jumpstart growth and transform our economy to compete in the 21st century"[4] and that it would

1. Obama (2009c).
2. Solomon, MacGillis, and Cohen (2007).
3. P.L. 111-5.
4. Obama (2009a).

"provide immediate tax relief to families and businesses, while investing in priorities like health care, education, energy, and infrastructure."[5]

The Recovery Act (or ARRA) ultimately provided $282 billion in tax relief, $274 billion in discretionary funding through grants and contracts, and $284 billion in entitlement program funding.[6] Although the legislation attempted to serve a universal goal—to rehabilitate the flailing economy—the means by which the Obama administration sought to achieve that goal was controversial. During negotiations on the bill and even after its passage, criticism percolated within the two parties and branches of government as well as in the media. Concerns over the structure and content of the bill included issues such as the role of politics in the economic recovery and the exercise and expansion of executive power in policymaking.

As the quote from President Obama at the start of this chapter illustrates, one goal of the Recovery Act was to improve economic growth. However, the president went on to explain that he sought benefits of his own from the legislation—benefits from the people who elected him. In describing the Recovery Act, he notes in explicitly electoral terms, "our voters, our constituents, the people we work for, are going to be extraordinarily grateful." The president is clear that he sees the Recovery Act as a means of connecting with "our voters"—a shared concern and experience of legislators and presidents alike. He wants "good public policy" that will stabilize the economy, create jobs, and invest in the future. However, any discussion of satisfying "voters" and "constituents" alludes to a shift away from policy interests and toward the electoral dynamics of legislation. The Recovery Act provided a way to make voters happy, and happy voters reelect the party in power.

President Obama was not alone in recognizing that the Recovery Act was an opportunity for the White House to claim credit. Vice President Joe Biden remarked of the law, "We've sent money out to renovate a school in a particular city, in a particular state—it will be up there [on the recovery.gov website]. All the press will see it on the website. The neighbors and the community will see it."[7] The Recovery Act was a multipronged tool. It was enacted to save the economy from a deepening recession, and it served to make sure that the president's constituents gave him credit for delivering money to their areas.

This book unites two fundamental tenets in the study of American government: that presidents are powerful players in domestic policy affairs and that

---

5. Obama (2009b).
6. "The Recovery Act" (www.recovery.gov/About/Pages/The_Act.aspx).
7. Biden (2009).

elected officials are motivated by elections. Neither tenet is especially controversial in itself. Scholars, members of the media, and ordinary citizens view such claims as a description of standard attributes of the U.S. political system.

However, rarely are the two ideas combined to inform research on the U.S. presidency. The research presented in this book does exactly that. Central to the argument is a single, simple claim: presidents engage in pork barrel politics. That is, presidents manipulate the distribution of federal funds to advance their electoral interests. Presidents, like their counterparts in Congress, are election-driven individuals. Yet, unlike individual legislators, presidents and their appointees have discretionary authority over the distribution of hundreds of billions of federal dollars each year. Presidents therefore have both the motive and means to politicize spending for electoral purposes. This perspective offers critical insights into presidential behavior and power.

To explore these ideas, this book asks two central questions. First, do presidents engage in pork barrel politics? While presidents may have the motive and means, it is essential to determine—rather than assume—that they do. Second, if presidents do engage in such behavior, how exactly do they do it? The U.S. government is extensive, and annual spending decisions number in the millions. What tools, techniques, and mechanisms do presidents employ to make federal spending responsive to their electoral goals?

Directing federal funds to key constituencies is a traditional legislative practice long relied on to advance electoral interests. Legislators direct funds—often in the form of congressional earmarks—back home in order to "claim credit" with their voters.[8] However, the phrase "presidential earmarks," less commonly heard than its congressional counterpart, illustrates the executive branch's desire to use spending in politically and electorally expedient ways. The president's electorally strategic distribution of funds, though often underreported, is not invisible. A 2006 *Wall Street Journal* article declares, "Presidents like pork, too." It proceeds to explain that "the president's earmarks are harder—if not impossible—to tally" and that "once federal agencies get funding from Congress, [the president's] appointees are fairly free to steer sums to places, programs and vendors as the administration decides."[9]

This book challenges the common claims that spending power and the drive for electoral success are predominantly congressional phenomena. In fact, this book argues that more than any representatives or senators,

---

8. In his 1974 book *Congress: The Electoral Connection*, David Mayhew notes that credit claiming—demonstrating one's value to constituents by taking credit for good deeds—is a critical electoral tool for members of Congress.

9. Calmes (2006).

presidents engage in pork barrel politics in a comprehensive and systematic way. Through its state-centered, winner-take-all design, the Electoral College creates incentives that make federal spending an appealing campaign tool for the executive branch. In order to implement such an electoral strategy, presidents must extract discretionary spending power from Congress and structure the executive branch to be responsive to their interests. The following chapters focus on one type of discretionary spending, the federal grant, first to show that presidents do engage in pork barrel politics and second to show precisely how they do it.

Presidential Pork: Why Does It Matter?

Studying presidential pork—and federal spending in general—helps answer what Harold Lasswell called a fundamental question of politics: *Who gets what, when, and how?*[10] This question concerns not just academics or politicians but also citizens, who have two basic requests of their government: one for their share of government goods and services and the other for accountability regarding the distribution of the remainder. The study of presidential influence over fund distribution helps citizens understand whether they and their communities are receiving sufficient or insufficient streams of government revenue.

A republican government provides for an electorate that is well informed with regard to the behavior of its representatives. One key function of the U.S. government involves spending—which, because citizens have come to rely on the government for a host of public goods and services, has grown dramatically. Knowledge about government spending allows citizens to judge the performance of officials and the appropriateness of their decisions. In fact, when citizens are dissatisfied with the functioning of government (in terms of spending or any other administrative actions), a thorough understanding of the process provides the foundation for reforming the system. Reforms both address perceived problems and provide solutions that are consistent with citizen demands and expectations.

Moreover, as federal budgets grow into the trillions of dollars—a consequence of increased citizen demands—the government accounts for a nontrivial portion of economic activity in the United States. The U.S. government also plays a profound economic role abroad. Information regarding the processes that govern and ultimately determine economic activity is critical

10. Laswell (1936).

for all economic actors and markets in general. Increased information and transparency allow consumers and producers to develop clearer expectations and improve decisionmaking.

Finally, spending is not simply a matter of dollars and cents. It is policy. As funds are transferred, policy is created, molded, and implemented. Spending affects access to and quality of health care, the performance of the agriculture and manufacturing sectors, advances in scientific research, the effectiveness of education, the safety of consumer products, the construction of highways and buildings, and the enforcement of laws—to name only a few policy areas. Citizens feel the effects of federal spending on a daily basis. The forces, biases, interests, and politics that influence the distribution of government funds have a substantial impact on public policy and American society. Evaluating the existence and extent of presidential pork barrel politics better informs citizens about their relationship to their government.

Presidential Pork: Where Does It Come From?

The common perception is that pork barrel politicking is a strictly congressional practice, undertaken by legislators who are motivated primarily by elections and who, more important, hold the purse strings of government. The media, scholars, and citizens often think of Congress as the only branch of government in charge of federal spending. To be sure, Congress influences a substantial stream of federal funding and claims credit for its distribution. But Congress is not alone in that endeavor. Presidents and their surrogates in federal agencies oversee the allocation of huge portions of federal largesse.

To understand pork barrel politics, it is important to discuss briefly the different types of federal spending and to identify where allocation decisions are made. Some federal spending—such as that for Social Security and Medicare, among other programs—is considered "mandatory." It is essentially automatic spending, whereby Congress does not need to determine funding levels or allocation mechanisms every year. Other types of spending— "nonmandatory"—require annual approval of appropriations.[11] For programs that fall in the latter category, Congress or the president or both have

---

11. Often this spending is called "discretionary." However, for the purposes of this book, that terminology is likely to be confusing. The focus of the empirical analysis is "discretionary federal grants," which specifically denotes grants over which the executive branch has discretionary authority. In common parlance, discretionary spending is intended to subsume all spending that is not "mandatory" and includes spending over which Congress, rather than the executive branch, asserts greater control. The distinction is an important one.

substantial discretion regarding the level of spending and allocation of funds. It is this type of spending that facilitates pork barrel politics because political actors are able to manipulate the distribution of dollars for electoral gain.

While nonmandatory spending is the source of pork barrel politics, differences exist within this category. Such spending often includes rent on buildings, employee travel costs, employee salaries, and other internal expenses of the bureaucracy, but it also includes money that the government distributes throughout the nation. The use of those funds, often in the form of grants, contracts, loans, and cooperative agreements, is more malleable. They are intended to be sent to recipients throughout the fifty states, and political actors battle for their fair share (as need would demand) or more than their fair share (as politics would encourage) for their constituents.

Who, then, controls nonmandatory spending? That is a fundamental question in the study of political pork and one that this book engages directly in answering. Congress has a strong hold on determining distribution in some areas of spending. Studies by Lee and by Lee and Oppenheimer show that in certain areas, such as formula funding and block grant funding, legislators—particularly senators from small states—are able to bring home substantial sums.[12] Formulas or other distribution schemes often are negotiated in congressional committees and subcommittees, and legislators, particularly those critical to building coalitions, ensure that legislation is laden with local benefits. Presidents play a role in the negotiations, but spending decisions rest largely with Congress.

In other areas—such as contracts and, especially relevant to this book, competitive discretionary grants—presidents and their appointees wield significant power over allocation decisions. Congress appropriates funding for contracts and grants every year, but the power to distribute the funding is transferred to the executive branch for a variety of reasons, including time constraints and lack of expertise. (A broader discussion of delegation can be found in chapter 2.) However, regardless of the reasons, the president, White House staff, political appointees, and federal agency staff all play critical roles in doling out tremendous sums of money each year.

How much do federal grants matter? Federal grants are often viewed as relatively small, discrete allocations of money to help build a school, for example, or to equip a police department or install a sewer system. However, federal grant making involves much more than that. In addition to including almost every area of domestic policy, it involves substantial sums of money.

---

12. Lee (2000); Lee (2003); Lee and Oppenheimer (1999).

For example, this book examines competitive discretionary grants (hereafter called "discretionary grants" or simply "grants") from 1996 to 2011. These grants (in real dollars) totaled well over $100 billion each year, came from all fifteen cabinet departments and dozens of independent agencies and commissions, and funded projects in all fifty states.

Presidents have myriad means of influencing distribution from this pot of federal grant dollars. They have, for example, an army of hand-selected political appointees serving in almost every agency in the federal government. Those individuals influence the administration of policy and the development of programming (for grants, that includes items like eligibility and evaluation criteria), manage personnel, manage communication within agencies, and help translate the interests of the executive branch's principal—the president—down to millions of agents. Presidents also rely on powerful White House institutions like the Office of Management and Budget, the Office of Presidential Personnel, and the Office of Cabinet Affairs to ensure that policy—especially spending policy—reflects the priorities of the president. What results is a federal grants process that offers presidents and their appointees numerous opportunities to influence the distribution of funds and thereby a variety of outcomes.

Despite the amount of discretionary funding allocated by the executive branch and the number of opportunities that it has to influence the allocation process, it is often overlooked as the public, the media, and academics focus on congressional ribbon cutting and earmarking. This book focuses on discretionary federal funding, examining how presidents exercise their spending authority and who reaps the benefits.

The Analytical Framework

That presidents engage in pork barrel politics—manipulating federal spending for electoral gain—is not a clear-cut claim. There exist alternative explanations of how federal funds are allocated. Those who study the topic and observers of the process often argue that other, nonpresidential forces act on fund distribution, and any rigorous examination of presidential pork must refute or account for alternative theories. The two dominant alternatives concern *congressional control* and *policy need*.

As mentioned above, a basic public expectation of members of Congress is that they deliver federal funds back home. While political scientist David Mayhew was among a group of scholars who wrote about pork barrel politics, research on the topic long predates his classic 1974 study, *Congress: The*

Electoral Connection, and research since then has offered empirical support for the congressional desire for pork. Another force in the distribution of federal funds is local policy need. Programs are designed to provide relief to those in need or to provide a service that is lacking. The literature on political influence on the allocation of government funds does not argue that political interests alone explain allocations. Instead, politics contributes to the distribution of funding, while needy recipients still benefit from federal programming.

An empirical approach to political influence that integrates different funding forces is valid on its face. While the general public and even the media expect some level of political influence on public policy, there is an expectation of balance. The definition of "balance" is, of course, subject to interpretation. However, political scandals emerge when balance is perceived to be upset—improperly tipped in favor of one side or another—and the system ultimately readjusts. In many ways, political influence over funding—whether congressional, presidential, or other—occurs at the margins. As part of that balance, the targeting of funds to key constituencies cannot be seen as egregious—something that might raise eyebrows. Instead, it must be modest in scope, yet meaningful in effect. I do not identify or define balance; instead, I assume that it exists and let its existence guide the analytical framework. Rather than argue that presidential influence is the exclusive determinant of federal spending, I assert that it is a (largely unexplored) part of the story. By assessing (simultaneously or in tandem) presidential control, congressional control, and policy need, the book presents more confident results while controlling for the major moving parts in the federal funding machinery.

Explanations of the forces that drive the distribution of funds often are seen as competing. However, one explanation need not and should not exclude all others. In fact, theoretically, politically, and statutorily, exclusivity is hard to justify. Instead, all forces must be examined as part of the same interconnected process. Competition among Congress, the president, and the states needs to exist. Grant making is a fixed-sum game whereby one dollar allocated for presidential electoral purposes is one dollar less to promote congressional interests or policy need. However, all three forces have a role to play, and this book assesses each empirically. That said, I do not focus on the role of Congress or the role of state-level needs. The title of the book is *Presidential Pork* because at its core, it is about presidential power and how presidential electoral interests and behavior influence spending policy.

This book presents a two-step empirical process to illustrate presidential power over federal spending. After showing that federal discretionary grants are distributed, in part, to advance presidents' electoral interests, I examine precisely how presidents engage in such behavior. After evaluating internal executive branch processes, I transition from demonstrating correlation between presidential interests and fund distribution to offering an explanation of the causes of the relationship.

Outline of the Book

Chapter 2 challenges existing views of presidential interests and behavior by developing the idea of "the election-driven president" who uses the powers of his office, such as spending authority, to advance his electoral interests. The chapter also explains how and why the president's role has been overlooked and notes the theoretical and empirical weaknesses in previous research that failed to account for the presidential role.

Chapter 3 offers the first empirical assessment of whether presidents engage in pork barrel politics. I analyze federal discretionary grant allocations from 1996 to 2008, assessing whether presidents direct funds to key electoral constituencies: the swing states. I find such a bias in the distribution of grants to exist even after controlling for congressional interests and policy need.

In chapter 4 the same data as the previous chapter—grant allocations from 1996 to 2008—are used to examine agency-level allocations. The analysis shows more precisely how the component parts of the bureaucracy aid and abet presidential pork barrel politicking. In addition, by examining differences in structure and personnel across agencies, it allows for identification of the mechanisms of presidential influence and political control over federal spending. Together chapters 3 and 4 provide some of the first robust evidence that presidential electoral motives drive public policy and that presidents, not just legislators, engage in pork barrel politics.

Chapter 5 examines a unique period for federal spending: 2009–11. During that period, the American Recovery and Reinvestment Act was being implemented and stimulus funds were being distributed along with non-stimulus funds, creating an administrative environment that mirrored the historic challenges facing the macro economy. I examine stimulus and non-stimulus grant receipts to illustrate that while presidential electoral interests informed the execution of public policy, those interests induced a unique type of presidential influence and response.

In chapters 6 and 7 I continue to identify the mechanisms by which presidents harness administrative power across a vast bureaucracy to induce agencies to respond to their electoral interests. Chapter 6 uses a survey of federal executives from 2007 to examine which actors wield policy influence, how communication within agencies (the communication environment) is politicized, and how officials dealing with the distribution of federal dollars face unique political pressures. Chapter 7 employs original interviews with individuals directly engaged in the federal grants process to shed light on the extent of presidential influence and the ways in which presidential preferences affect even micro-level policy outcomes.

Finally, chapter 8 offers an overview of the results and implications for presidential power and public policy in the United States. The chapter poses the normative question of whether presidential influence on nonmandatory spending is a problem for the system and evaluates the strengths and weaknesses of possible reforms.

2

Spending Power and the Election-Driven President

The president derives little if any spending authority from the U.S. Constitution. In fact, Article I specifically empowers Congress to appropriate funds, and scholars often note that the legislative branch has "the power of the purse." However, each year Congress delegates spending authority to the executive branch. It relies on the president to do what legislators and their staff cannot: allocate hundreds of billions of dollars across hundreds of federal programs and policy areas to help meet citizens' needs and desires.

Congress can limit executive branch discretion by writing restrictions into legislation, developing formulas to determine distribution, creating block grants, and inserting earmarks into legislation. But it must delegate its spending authority because of its own resource constraints. Even if Congress preferred to make every federal distributive decision throughout the nation, lack of time, expertise, and staff requires that the federal bureaucracy take on much of that responsibility. When Congress does delegate spending power to the executive, it expects responsible action. Louis Fisher noted in 1975 that "a customary congressional control has been to delegate broad discretionary authority, confining that discretion by a combination of statutory guidelines and a trust in the integrity and good faith of executive officials."[1] However, because presidents and their appointees are political actors who have their own interests, that good faith can often be strained. The result is a conflict between

---

1. Fisher (1975, p. 259).

Congress's need to delegate authority and desire to reap political and electoral benefits that the executive branch also covets.

The battle for discretionary spending power is not a ceremonial or ideological fight over what is right. It is a political conflict that has serious implications for policy and the electoral benefits reaped from policy. Fisher described those consequences and their magnitude, arguing that "unless Congress strengthens its control over budget execution, it cannot legislate back to reality its vaunted 'power of the purse.'"[2] Moreover, with the power of the purse also comes the power of pork, and presidents seek it out just as aggressively as legislators.

The Federal Grants Process: An Overview

Federal spending is a complex tool of public policy regulated by various formal and informal administrative procedures often developed and implemented in the federal bureaucracy. Lack of uniform procedures makes it difficult to design a single visual representation of the process or to detail the manner in which grant programs are administered. However, the federal grant process generally has four stages. First, grant programs are designed and developed. Second, the programs are made public and prospective applicants are invited to seek funds. Third, applications for funds are evaluated and accepted or rejected. Fourth, grant programs allocate funds to eligible applicants.

Designing a Grant Program

The conception and design of federal grant programs may involve the input of several actors and institutions. Because Congress authorizes spending and appropriates funds, it can play a role. Its influence, though limited, can extend even to federal discretionary grants, particularly at the design stage. A look at the text of federal law demonstrates the variation in discretionary authority. Some legislative language gives the executive branch broad discretion over the distribution of grant money. For example, in the Omnibus Appropriations Act of 2009, Congress authorizes and appropriates to the Department of Justice "$178,000,000 for discretionary grants to improve the functioning of the criminal justice system, to prevent or combat juvenile delinquency, and to assist victims of crime."[3]

Such broad discretion gives the Department of Justice great leeway to design a program as it sees fit. Congress often authorizes distributive programs in this

2. Ibid., p. 260.
3. Omnibus Appropriations Act of 2009, P.L. 111-8, 123 Stat. 524, March 11, 2009, p. 580.

way, delegating substantial authority to the bureaucracy under the heading of broad policy goals. However, Congress can also insert specifics into authorization and appropriations legislation that restricts discretion. In the Consolidated Appropriations Act of 2010, Congress appropriates $600,000,000 to the Department of Transportation but includes a number of conditions for its use:

> That the Secretary of Transportation shall distribute funds provided under this heading as discretionary grants to be awarded to a State, local government, transit agency, or a collaboration among such entities on a competitive basis for projects that will have a significant impact on the Nation, a metropolitan area, or a region: Provided further, That projects eligible for funding provided under this heading shall include, but not be limited to, highway or bridge projects eligible under title 23, United States Code; public transportation projects eligible under chapter 53 of title 49, United States Code; passenger and freight rail transportation projects; and port infrastructure investments: Provided further, That in distributing funds provided under this heading, the Secretary shall take such measures so as to ensure an equitable geographic distribution of funds, an appropriate balance in addressing the needs of urban and rural areas, and the investment in a variety of transportation modes: Provided further, That a grant funded under this heading shall be not less than $10,000,000 and not greater than $200,000,000: Provided further, That not more than 25 percent of the funds made available under this heading may be awarded to projects in a single State: Provided further, That the Federal share of the costs for which an expenditure is made under this heading shall be, at the option of the recipient, up to 80 percent: Provided further, That the Secretary shall give priority to projects that require a contribution of Federal funds in order to complete an overall financing package: Provided further, That not less than $140,000,000 of the funds provided under this heading shall be for projects located in rural areas: Provided further, That for projects located in rural areas, the minimum grant size shall be $1,000,000 and the Secretary may increase the Federal share of costs above 80 percent: Provided further, That of the amount made available under this heading, the Secretary may use an amount not to exceed $150,000,000 for the purpose of paying the subsidy and administrative costs of projects eligible for federal credit assistance under chapter 6 of title 23, United States Code, if the Secretary finds that such use of the funds would advance the purposes of this paragraph: Provided further, That of the

amount made available under this heading, the Secretary may use an amount not to exceed $35,000,000 for the planning, preparation or design of projects eligible for funding under this heading: Provided further, That projects conducted using funds provided under this heading must comply with the requirements of subchapter IV of chapter 31 of title 40, United States Code (pp. 3036-7).[4]

In this case, Congress has exerted significant influence on the design of the grant program. As the quotation suggests, the phrase "Provided Further" becomes the nemesis of discretion and a power-seeking president. Although ultimately the bureaucracy has substantial allocation authority within the bounds imposed, it is clear that Congress seeks to restrict the president's ability to design programs and distribute dollars.

Within the limits of discretionary authority, several executive branch actors influence the nature and structure of grant programs. In many cases political appointees (both within and outside agencies) have formal and final authority over program design or effectively convey their preferences to those who do. Presidential and other White House policy initiatives can give grant programs incentives to reflect specific goals or charge agencies to focus on specific priorities. A recent example is President George W. Bush's White House Office of Faith-Based and Community Initiatives,[5] which worked closely with federal agencies to expand the participation of faith-based organizations in delivering federally funded social services.

Career civil servants with substantial and long-term policy and program experience can also weigh in on program design, offering suggestions about effectiveness and administration. Depending on the program, issue area, agency, and governing administration, different combinations of elite actors affect how requests for proposals are crafted, criteria are developed, eligibility is determined, and programs are structured and managed. These actors include political appointees, White House officials, and the Office of Management and Budget's program associate directors and their liaisons within federal agencies.

Publicizing Grants and Motivating Applicants

After grant programs are designed, agencies give public notice that funding is available. In all cases, grant program announcements are printed in the *Federal Register;* often they are published on the U.S. government's grants

---

4. Consolidated Appropriations Act of 2010, P.L. 111-117, 123 Stat. 3034, December 16, 2009.
5. Now the White House Office of Faith-Based and Neighborhood Partnerships.

clearinghouse website.[6] In addition, federal agencies use informal means of notifying citizens of the availability of funding and the criteria that must be met to receive it. State, local, and regional agency offices often are charged with developing and implementing information campaigns that include conventional advertising but also involve communication with state and local officials and participation in town hall meetings. Agencies also work closely with interest groups and other stakeholders to communicate funding opportunities and identify key groups that may benefit from funding. Because unused appropriations may be returned to the Department of the Treasury or reallocated to other areas of the country, it is in the interest of agencies to increase public knowledge of available grants in order to ensure that they are able to allocate all their program appropriations.

With the advent of improved communications and the Internet, advertising grant opportunities has become an art. National as well as regional, state, and local offices find unique and what they hope are effective methods and media to inform the public and entice prospective applicants. The application process can be time consuming and complicated, though resources often exist to assist applicants in preparing the documents and materials needed to obtain federal funds. The federal grants website provides program-specific and general guidelines and tips on how to prepare applications. Other institutions also help. Federal agencies themselves, particularly those with regional, state, and local offices, frequently have staff liaisons who specialize in assisting applicants—for example, by conducting workshops. Interest groups often specialize in the federal grants process. They may help prepare applications on applicants' behalf or work closely with applicants to answer questions and provide guidance in the application process. Interest groups also are often highly skilled at translating complex grant announcements, eligibility criteria, and guidelines into terms that applicants can more easily understand.[7] The intent of all of these efforts is to make applicants more competitive and to ensure that federal funds are allocated.

Evaluating Grants, Inviting Politics

Once applications are received, a more complex, variable, and often opaque process begins: evaluation. Federal agencies evaluate the quality of grant proposals to determine eligibility and decide which applicants receive funding.

6. See www.grants.gov/.

7. Though it should be noted that federal agencies, including the Office of Management and Budget and the Office of Information and Regulatory Affairs, have taken steps over the past several years to improve accessibility and simplify the language used.

It is important to understand how proposals are judged. In the most basic terms, proposals are evaluated according to formal and informal criteria, both of which can be developed or implemented according to either political or nonpolitical (need-based or technocratic) factors. However, political influence often lies in the informal, discretionary, and often opaque criteria that are applied in considering a proposal but are not detailed in the formal announcement. In that case, the published criteria serve as a minimum standard for consideration and the additional factors may affect the evaluation of applications. Often, applications are scored using a numeric rubric that assigns point values to various criteria; other discretionary point values can be assigned as well.[8] In the latter case, some values often are difficult to understand. This sometimes informal process allows political influence to affect consideration of applications and empowers decisionmakers to manipulate outcomes.

Although a scoring system serves as the standard method in evaluating grant applications, it is important to know who participates in scoring. Both internal and external participants may take part in reviewing grant applications. Within federal agencies, the administrative review process often involves both career program staff and political appointees, who may serve in central agency offices in Washington or in regional, state, and local offices throughout the country. Frequently, political appointees have formal or final authority to approve career staff recommendations for grants. The Office of Management and Budget (OMB) or its liaison offices within agencies and departments frequently play a role in the development of both program details and eligibility criteria in order to ensure that the evaluation process reflects both budgetary (nonpolitical) and administration (political) priorities. OMB thus serves as a powerful player at multiple stages of the federal grants process. Given the political relationship between OMB and the president and OMB's power within and outside the grants process, OMB is one of many paths taken to advance presidential influence.

Another way of evaluating grant applications involves the use of external actors—often policy experts and stakeholders—in a peer review process. This process is used in particular for large grant programs and ones that require specific expertise in the evaluation of applications. In cases in which grant proposals include scientific data and information, for example, the agencies rely on outside experts to provide insight into the quality of applications, likelihood of success, and reflection of agency aims. For example, university faculty

---

8. Discretionary point values can be used for a multitude of reasons, including applicant reputation, urgency of need, or other less transparent and more political reasons.

often are called on to participate in the evaluation process at the National Science Foundation and at the National Institutes of Health. Experts rate proposals and often make recommendations to career or appointed agency leaders who can set thresholds, determine final funding levels, and make allocation decisions.

The grant application evaluation process also varies in terms of the timing of evaluations, and timing can have serious implications for applicants. Essentially, applications are evaluated on either a rolling basis or en masse. When applications are evaluated on a rolling basis, funds often are distributed on a first-come, first-served basis, meaning that those who apply later may have a reduced chance of being funded, regardless of the quality of their application. When all applications are evaluated at the same time, the quality of applications can be more easily compared and decisionmakers can see funding decisions from a broader perspective and get a better grasp of who is benefiting from funding across the nation.

Spreading the Wealth: Allocations

The final stage in the federal grants process involves allocation. After agencies make funding decisions and OMB and other budget offices approve those decisions, applicants receive their money, often with specific guidelines and restrictions on its use. To ensure that funds are being used as the agency intended, grant recipients must comply with sometimes extensive federal reporting requirements. Politics can even influence federal reporting, depending on the type of information that the administration considers politically relevant. For example, early in the Obama administration, reporting requirements emphasized job creation and the manner in which job creation numbers were calculated, an obvious reflection of the political implications of economic policy at the time.

What results is a complex system in which federal spending policy is administered and evaluated. Other factors influence grant programming. This intricate bureaucratic process gives rise to several competing hypotheses about who influences policymaking and how that influence manifests. One of these hypotheses, which may be more of a straw-man hypothesis, represents the ideal in apolitical bureaucratic administration. It stems from the fact that career bureaucrats play key roles in the administration of grants and that they dramatically outnumber political appointees in the executive branch. In this hypothesis, career bureaucrats' commitment to the technocratic missions of agencies, applicant need, and good public administration drive the creation of grant programs and the distribution of funds.

Alternatively, the appropriations and authorization legislation offers Congress the opportunity to play a critical role in the distribution of federal funds, and political science research is flush with illustrations of its impact on distribution. However, the federal grants process also offers executive branch actors the opportunity to affect policy. These actors can range from the president himself, White House and OMB staff, and political appointees within agencies to career civil servants making daily distributive decisions.

A number of rival explanations exist with respect to when influence occurs. Influence can occur at various stages—for example, during the design of programs and the creation and authorization of program criteria. It can also occur while grant applications are being evaluated, when a host of actors can and do participate in the scoring and rating of applications. Finally, because allocation decisions are not automatic upon evaluation, actors can affect outcomes when final decisions are made regarding who gets how much.

Although the federal grants process offers presidents myriad opportunities to influence the allocation of federal grants, surprisingly little public attention is paid to political influence on grant allocation. That lack of attention generally comes from limited awareness. While several stages of the grants process allow for political influence, strategic actors have incentives (political and in many cases legal incentives) to be less than transparent when capitalizing on opportunities to advance their political or other nontechnocratic interests. As a result, politics may quietly and preemptively enter the decisionmaking process. Moreover, only a few select decisionmakers may observe the final stages of the process, so that even some of those involved in the earlier stages may be unaware of the role of politics. A lack of attention among citizens also emerges from a misguided view of presidential interests and behaviors.

Impediments to Observing Presidential Pork

The idea that presidents participate in pork barrel politics is not entirely new, but it has been largely overlooked by media, academics, and citizens; it is more commonly associated with members of Congress. For a variety of reasons, presidents are often seen as unwilling, unable, or uninterested in the strategic allocation of federal funds. This perspective has limited theory-building and empirical assessments of the presidential role.

A Strictly Congressional Pursuit?

A tremendous amount of academic, media, and public attention has been paid to legislative pork. That attention is not misplaced—legislative pork is alive and well, and it is an integral part of congressional behavior. However, that focus often comes at the expense of presidential pork, and it presents a challenge to the comprehensive understanding of distributive politics. The extensive political science literature on the congressional pork barrel examines a variety of ways in which legislators manipulate funding for their interests,[9] focusing on legislators' "almost paranoid concern for reelection."[10] Such behavior is, of course, encouraged and facilitated by Congress's control of the government purse strings. Scholars have noted that Congress strategically allocates funds to districts and states for several reasons, including electoral competitiveness,[11] partisanship,[12] members' institutional power,[13] and legislative coalition building.[14] The benefits are believed to be profound for any group or individual within Congress that is able to engage in pork barrel politics. Members chase committee assignments and leadership posts, participate in logrolling and negotiations, and engage with congressional campaign committees in order to better position themselves to direct funds back home.[15] This is considered a pervasive and an accepted—even expected—practice among members of the legislative branch. It has also served to drive a substantial part of research on Congress over the past forty years.

This practice is not theoretical; it is not even an internal process that is more accurately considered fodder for arcane empirical research than an example of real world behavior. The pursuit of congressional pork happens every day, and its effects are felt in every state and every congressional district across the United States. Evidence of its importance is seen in the fact that legislators publicize—even brag about—their ability to secure federal funding for their constituents. Every day, congressional websites display press releases hailing the efforts of members to bring funds home. In fact, through tacit agreement, many federal agencies notify relevant House and Senate offices in advance of an official fund allocation to allow them to bask in public glory.

9. A whole chapter could be devoted to presenting the research on congressional pork and still cover just a fraction of it. The discussion here is intended to offer only a brief overview citing some of the best research work on the topic.

10. Moe and Wilson (1994, p. 8).

11. Bickers and Stein (2000); Stein and Bickers (1994, 1995)

12. Balla and others (2002); Hurwitz, Moiles, and Rohde (2001); Levitt and Snyder (1995).

13. Carsey and Rundquist (1999); Lee and Oppenheimer (1999); Rundquist and Carsey (2002); Rundquist, Rhee, and Lee (1996).

14. Stein and Bickers (1994); Lee (2000, 2003); Lee and Oppenheimer (1999).

15. When a congressional campaign committee designates a race as a target or determines that an incumbent is vulnerable, it can signal to the party in Congress the need for additional federal funding.

Presidential efforts are far less obvious and receive correspondingly less attention. Every four years there will be a handful of new articles that mention—with an almost scandalous tone—that a president may be announcing funding in an electorally strategic way or at the most opportune time. The difference between the treatment of presidential and congressional pork is enlightening. Behavior that is viewed as wholly routine or even part of the job description for a member of Congress is seen as improper, rare, or scandalous for a president. A legislator who fails to secure federal funding for constituents may be turned out of office. A president who tries to do so risks "pork barrel–gate." With few exceptions, media and academics have avoided examining the presidential pork barrel. These exceptions, however, are instructive.

Research into presidential (or more aptly, executive branch) pork has been sparse, and it has emerged largely over the past 10 years. In examining aggregate federal spending programs, research demonstrates that partisan alignment of governors and members of Congress with the president translates into greater distributive benefits for their constituencies.[16] In fact, Berry and others (2010) suggests that partisan alignment with the president serves as a dominant influence in distribution, trumping even the traditional congressional effects. Similarly, Bertelli and Grose (2009), in an examination of contracts from the departments of defense and of labor, finds that the ideological position of select cabinet secretaries influences federal grant distribution.

Other research considers how presidents use pork to advance their own electoral interests. Shor (2006) tests whether considerations such as number of Electoral College votes and the competitiveness of state presidential elections influence which states receive more grants. More recent work examines the constituent connection more precisely. In an examination of allocation of FEMA disaster grants, Chen (2009) finds that disaster-affected Florida neighborhoods that supported President Bush's 2004 reelection fared better than similarly affected Democratic localities. Mebane and Wawro (2002) explores how different types of funds during Reagan's second term were effectively targeted to important constituencies in order for the president to claim credit for the funding. Additional work argues that timing, not geography, determines presidents' electoral strategies. Presidents strategically time their grant allocation announcements in order to maximize the political benefits of claiming credit.[17]

16. Berry, Burden, and Howell (2010); Gasper and Reeves (2011); Larcinese, Rizzo, and Testa (2006).
17. Anagnoson (1982); Hamman (1993).

Another challenge in observing presidential pork is its magnitude. Much of the research on presidential influence on federal funding (and congressional influence as well) does not find that all federal funding is allocated for political interests. As with most instances of political influence, much of the effect is at the margins. If presidents or legislators abuse their ability to capitalize on their spending power, there can be a serious pushback from the media and the public. Recent examples of perceived abuse include Alaska senator Ted Stevens' proposed "bridge to nowhere," which was lambasted in the press as unnecessary pork. Large-scale effects of influence may induce certain political benefits but may also come at the risk of enormous political costs. As a result, when engaging in pork barrel politics, all political elites—presidents included—must strike a careful balance in order to maximize electoral benefits and minimize external costs.

Research on the pork barrel presents key empirical findings regarding presidential behaviors and interests, challenging the monopoly of Congress on distributive politics. Nonetheless, pork barrel politics is viewed primarily as a legislative technique or tool. Why is presidential pork largely ignored?

The Elusive Electoral Motive and the National President

Despite the media obsession with presidential elections, research often overlooks the presidential electoral interest. Research frequently examines a host of other presidential efforts instead, including executive actions,[18] appointments,[19] administration,[20] legislative endeavors,[21] and rulemaking.[22] Much of this work, which represents some of the best research on the executive branch, looks at the critical inner workings of the presidency. It pays little attention to presidential elections or the implications of presidential behavior for elections.

While substantial research has examined the nuances of presidential elections and campaigns, far less connects presidential power and administrative action with electoral consequences. Even less work develops the idea of presidential electoral interests or engagement in pork barrel politics. Among the exceptions are works on "the permanent campaign"—a term that describes

---

18. Cameron (2000); Cooper (2002); Howell (2003); Moe (1999); Moe and Howell (1999).

19. Clayton (1992); Lewis (2008); Moe (1982, 1985); Randall (1979); Snyder and Weingast (2000); Stewart and Cromartie (1982); Wood (1990); Wood and Waterman (1991, 1994).

20. Heclo (1977); Light (1995); Nathan (1986); Pfiffner (1991); Rourke (1984); Seidman and Gilmour (1986).

21. Baumgartner and Jones (1993); Canes-Wrone (2001); Canes-Wrone and Shotts (2004); Cohen (1995); Kernell (1993); Wayne (1978).

22. Cooper and West (1988); Wiseman (2009).

a campaign that is not simply unending but also all-encompassing. In 2000, Tom Mann and Norm Ornstein traced the term back to a 1992 book by Sidney Blumenthal of the same name, noting that

> for years it was shorthand . . . for the use of governing as an instrument to build and sustain popular support. . . . But this conception of the permanent campaign has proven much too limited to capture the growing importance of campaign strategies, tactics, and resources."[23]

Tenpas and Dickinson (1997) and Tenpas (2000) examine precisely how institutions within the White House have facilitated presidential efforts to campaign by crafting policy and messaging and managing organization, timing, and outreach to critical groups in ways that benefit the president and the president's electoral interests.[24] Other efforts have connected presidential travel and fundraising with presidential campaign interests.[25] Shaw (2006) offers some of the most detailed insight into presidential campaign strategy, gained from the author's role in the 2000 and 2004 presidential campaigns, noting in particular the extensive resources devoted to presidential elections.[26]

The research mentioned above that does focus on presidential pork offers quite a bit of theory and empirical evidence, yet often these studies are limited in a variety of ways. First, much of the research focuses on a small number of grant programs and agencies or examines a narrow time period. Second, systematic studies of presidential influence often fail to consider the effect of a presidential electoral strategy in the distribution of federal funds. Finally, those studies that do consider presidential electoral strategy consider either the geographic or temporal nature of the strategy.

What then is responsible for the limited research into the presidential pork barrel? One major stumbling block is the common perception of the chief executive as the "national" president. A widely held view has developed in which modern presidents have a unique vantage point in the policy process and, as the only nationally elected representative in government, *must* focus on matters of broad public significance and import to be effective. Their national constituency shapes their views of governance and their choices of public policy issues. Kagan (2001) argues that presidents are distinctive in that "they are the only governmental officials elected by a national constituency in votes on general,

23. They also note that "Pat Caddell coined the term in a transition memo to president-elect Jimmy Carter in 1976." See Mann and Ornstein (2000, p. vii).

24. See also Cook (2002).

25. Charnock, McCann, and Tenpas (2009); Doherty (2007, 2010).

26. Shaw (2006).

rather than local, policy issues" and that because of the nature of that constituency, presidential elections are "focused on broad public policy questions."[27] At the service of this constituency, presidents are charged with and held responsible for the creation and execution of public policy that is more universal in nature. Thus, their constituency influences their exercise of power.

Even presidents themselves have noted their distinctive role. Andrew Jackson defended presidential decisions on "a question of transcendent importance" as made "in justice to the responsibility which he owes to the country."[28] Herbert Hoover explained that "the President must represent the nation's ideals,"[29] while Harry Truman explained that presidents try to "accomplish something that will be for the benefit of all the people of the Nation."[30] Thinking on the presidency has always alluded to the president as a unique actor in the American system who is alone in having an electoral connection to a national constituency. This institutional position means that presidential policymaking "is occupied with numerous and important national problems,"[31] while parochialism is left to legislators. In describing presidential interests, Moe (1993) notes of presidents that

> the heterogeneous national constituency leads them to think in grander terms about social problems and the public interest. . . . Reelection, moreover, does not loom so large in their calculations (and in the second term, of course, it is not a factor at all). They are more fundamentally concerned with governance.

In fact, Moe proceeds to explain, "If there is a single driving force that motivates all presidents, it is not popularity . . . it is leadership."[32] Peterson and Greene (1994) explains,

> Because the executive has a national constituency, it is primarily concerned with matters of national policy. Members of Congress, who have smaller, more homogeneous constituencies, are more concerned with the geographically distributive effects of these policies. . . . Similarly, when issues have important distributional impacts but do not seriously affect

27. Kagan (2001, p. 2334).

28. Andrew Jackson, "Message Read to the Cabinet on Removal of the Public Deposits," September 18, 1833.

29. Herbert Hoover, "Radio Address to the Nation from Elko, Nevada," November 7, 1932.

30. Harry S. Truman, "Rear Platform and Other Informal Remarks in Oregon," June 11, 1948.

31. Franklin Delano Roosevelt, "Letter on the Misuse of the President's Name in the Pennsylvania Political Campaign," October 26, 1938.

32. Moe (1993, pp. 363, 364).

the country as a whole, members of Congress will have more at stake than executive officials. To preserve scarce resources, presidents and their advisers will often defer to congressional wishes on these issues.[33]

That the motivations of presidents and legislators are different is regarded almost as a truism and as an obvious implication or consequence of constitutional design and policy design. While legislators focus much attention on electoral efforts,[34] "reelection obviously cannot explain the behavior of (modern) presidents during their second terms, since they cannot run again. And even in their first terms, presidential behavior seems to be driven more centrally by other things."[35] This results in a forced separation, theoretically and empirically, in the way that scholars and observers think about the behavior of presidents vis-à-vis that of legislators.

In fact, compared with the local and varied nature of the legislature, the unitary nature of the American executive suggests that presidents are resource restricted from dealing with policy minutiae.[36] Overseeing the scope of executive and administrative duties in the U.S. government is beyond the reach of one individual; accordingly, the legislative branch and the vast bureaucracy focus on the details of policy while the president focuses on the bigger picture: government functions and public policymaking.

In summary, the view of the "national" president depends on four common assumptions about presidential elections, behavior, and motives. First, presidents are assumed to be responsive to a national constituency. Unlike legislators, who represent small portions of the American electorate, presidents are seen to be elected by the whole, to represent the whole, and to be responsive to the whole. Second, elections are viewed as a secondary presidential concern, outranked by others such as historical legacy, policymaking, and institutional power. Third, if presidents have electoral interests, they are assumed to evaporate during a second term. Light (1999) notes that "we expect the [reelection] goal to dissipate in the second four years. Theoretically, the search for electoral success declines."[37] Fourth, presidents are resource

33. Peterson and Greene (1994, p. 34).

34. Moe and Wilson (1994, p. 8).

35. Moe and Howell (1999, p. 136).

36. Adding to this assumption is a literature on executive branch management and the problems that can ensue for presidents seeking to advance specific policies and to control the bureaucracy (Miller 1992; Rourke 1984; Wilson 1989). In fact, some claim that the president's "ability to direct that bureaucracy toward the achievement of the administration's policy objectives and program goals is actually limited" (Pika and Maltese 2006, p. 219).

37. Light (1999, p. 66) In fact, Light suggests that while "presidents may continue to court the public" (p. 66), they do so mainly out of habit.

constrained from engaging in micro-level policymaking and constituency-centered electoral politics. Legislators with local staffs and smaller constituencies have both the drive and greater freedom to deal with localized politics, a luxury that presidents do not enjoy.

These four assumptions drive much of the theory about presidential goals and behavior. However, when these assumptions are analyzed, it becomes clear that they are flawed. They conflict with much of what is known about presidential preferences and behaviors, generating a view of presidents not as politicians but as strictly policy-driven actors who have little interest in engaging or power to engage in electoral politics on their own behalf and who are disengaged from the election of their successor. This view is inconsistent with reality and requires a reassessment of both the assumptions about presidential motives and the consequences of those motives for presidential behavior.

The Election-Driven President

While presidents have unique powers, status, and obligations, in many other ways they have the same incentives as members of Congress to use the powers of their office to advance their electoral interest through pork barrel politics.

The Fallacy of the President's National Constituency

Although constituency size can surely affect the manner in which an individual candidate campaigns, the claim that the president serves a broad, national constituency fails to reflect the institutional design of presidential elections and the reality of presidential campaigns.[38] The national constituency thesis assumes that presidents consider the interests of the median voter in the nation, much as legislators try to please the median constituent in their district. If that is true, focusing on the national median voter provides a clear incentive for presidents to purse broad policy initiatives or risk electoral defeat. Such an electoral constraint may be true for a president chosen by national plebiscite; however, the president of the United States is not.

The president is elected through the Electoral College system, which provides for individual, state-level, winner-take-all elections for each state's electoral votes. Those votes are subsequently aggregated to determine the winner: whichever candidate compiles 270 electoral votes. As a result, presidential candidates must compete not in a national plebiscite, but in fifty individual elections for each state's electoral votes. The "national" presidential constituency is truly a series of individual state constituencies. During a campaign,

---

38. See Nzelibe (2006).

candidates choose which states they will target, opting not to appear or spend campaign funds in many others.[39] In modern presidential politics, most Democratic candidates can be expected to win Massachusetts, Vermont, and California while the Republicans take Oklahoma, Utah, and Wyoming. However, in a small subset of states, the outcomes are largely uncertain. It is in those states—the swing states—that presidential elections are won and lost. Swing states become not only the focus but the obsession of presidential candidates and their campaigns.

The structure of the Electoral College determines which constituencies presidents target, thereby incentivizing their electoral behaviors. Whereas an executive selected through a national vote must focus on the national median voter, the U.S. president cannot. For example, if the median voter in the United States resides in San Diego, California, it would be useless for a president to work for his or her vote because California is not a competitive state in presidential elections and resources spent in that state are largely wasted. Instead, presidents must win over the median voters in swing states—states that are competitive in presidential elections. If the preferences of the median voter in Pennsylvania or New Hampshire or Colorado differ from those of the national median, appealing to the latter may actually be a self-defeating strategy. In fact, presidential electoral strategy is even more complex. Presidents also are committed to achieving a substantial turnout of their base voters in swing states. Depending on turnout, the characteristics and preferences of a given state's median voter can vary dramatically and depart even further from the national median.

Shaw (2006) notes that presidential candidates "identify those states most at risk and most critical to amassing 270 electoral votes."[40] By doing so, they face a much smaller electoral constituency that generally excludes both the states they are nearly certain to win and the states that they will surely lose. This view of a substantially narrowed presidential constituency affects assumptions about presidential concerns and behavior.[41]

The design of electoral institutions has serious implications for the behavior and pursuits of elected officials. Failure to account for the structure of the

39. Shaw (2006).

40. Shaw (2006, p. 52).

41. Attention to both states and a small subset of states can be observed with regard to presidential travel and fundraising (Charnock, McCann, and Tenpas 2009; Doherty 2007, 2010), use of local media and public events (Shaw and Roberts 2000), and the distribution of campaign resources (Shaw 2006). In some cases such attention can be seen in the distribution of aggregate federal funding (Larcinese, Rizzo, and Testa 2006) and federal contracts (Taylor 2008).

Electoral College—resorting instead to a stylized view of a plebiscitary president—has serious theoretical and empirical consequences. Only by accounting for the effect of the Electoral College system on presidential behavior can
presidential goals, incentives, and preferences be fully explored and how presidents manage to target constituents with federal spending be fully explained.

Presidential Electoral Concerns: Primary or Secondary?

Electoral interests are among a host of forces that influence the behavior of
the chief executive. In fact, this claim finds support in the literature that outlines congressional behavior. Mayhew writes that "a complete explanation (if
one were possible) of a congressman's or anyone else's behavior would require
attention to more than just one goal."[42] He argues that members of Congress
may value good public policy or institutional power but that they are motivated primarily by their electoral interests. In reality, presidents operate in the
same way. Before presidents can achieve any other goals, they first need electoral success. Presidents seek election, reelection, and ultimately the election
of a successor from their own party. Essentially, electoral success "has to be
the *proximate* goal of everyone, the goal that must be achieved over and over
if other ends are to be entertained."[43] Mayhew's reference to legislators' goals
must also extend to presidents.[44]

The idea that the same electoral interests that are primary for legislators are
secondary for presidents clashes with the commonly observable behaviors of
the chief executive. Presidents appear to be raising money, making strategic
campaign visits, and eyeing the electoral and political consequences of official
actions. Presidential campaigns are starting earlier than ever; those campaigns
now cost *billions* of dollars. News coverage of the next presidential campaign
often starts immediately after the conclusion of the previous one. In fact,
during the 2012 presidential campaign, the media discussed positioning and
gamesmanship for the 2016 race for the out party (the Republicans) and with
regard to how President Obama's actions might affect his would-be Democratic successor. Coverage of presidential elections is profound, and discussion
of presidential elections is widespread. Presidential behavior is dramatically
affected by the pervasiveness of electoral coverage.

42. Mayhew (1974, p. 14).
43. Mayhew (1974, p. 16).
44. Although the quotation from Mayhew suggests that reelection must be repeated, an effort
from which presidents are constitutionally barred, I argue that presidents maintain electoral
interests in their second term because doing so is necessary if they hope to pursue other goals.

As mentioned previously, scholars and journalists have come to call this pervasive electoral environment "the permanent campaign." It allows for observation of the primacy of presidential electoral interests in practice. Presidents are highly political and constantly campaigning. Sitting presidents become consumed with electoral considerations as "reelection remains a critical goal through much of the first term. Both the President and the staff have considerable energy invested in returning for a second term."[45] This drive for electoral success is not reserved just for the campaign trail; it also dominates behavior inside the White House.[46] Tenpas and Dickinson (1997) describes a transformation of presidents and staff outside and even inside the White House, as the chief executive enters campaign mode.[47] The changes are profound, affect those working on the campaign and those who are not, and influence decisions made inside of government. Electoral interests are not a secondary proposition; they are the primary force in presidential behavior.

The primacy of presidential electoral interests is critical to understanding presidential pork. Moe and Wilson (1994) explains that legislators' desire for particularistic control stems from their desire to deliver benefits back to their constituents—often in the form of pork. The centrality of electoral motives drives members of Congress to focus on pork barrel politics; the same is true of presidents. If electoral interests dominate presidential interests, incentives, motivations, and behaviors, then presidents should engage in pork barrel politics whenever, wherever, and however possible. Winning elections requires that constituents and voters attribute good works to the official or candidate who is running for office. One path to maintaining constituent satisfaction and claiming credit for good works is through the delivery of government benefits to key constituencies. Presidential electoral motives drive presidential pork.

The Election-Driven President's Term Limits

In any analysis of the president's electoral drive, one key difference between the chief executive and members of Congress must be factored in: term limits. The term limits established by the 22nd Amendment are often used as an argument against a president's interest in electoral politics and micro-level policy. A president can be reelected only once. Scholars and observers often note that second-term presidents focus on a policy agenda, access to and exercise of institutional power, and the solidification of a historical legacy. For

45. Light (1999, p. 64).
46. Tenpas (2000).
47. Tenpas and Dickinson (1997).

example, President Clinton devoted a fair portion of his second term to trying to achieve Mideast peace, hoping resolution of the conflict would bolster the historical account of his presidency. However, that did not prevent Clinton from working to help his vice president, Al Gore, win the presidency (to the extent that Gore would let him help).

The 22nd Amendment certainly creates a unique institutional dynamic that must be accounted for in assessing the president's electoral motives.[48] Scholars argue that term limits *reduce* presidents' electoral motives, which are strong and personal during the first term. However, for both personal and partisan reasons, those motives should persevere into the second term,[49] particularly because electoral success facilitates the achievement of other goals. Having a same-party successor ensures that policy will be made by a president with similar preferences. For example, despite differences between President Reagan and Vice President Bush, Reagan clearly preferred to have Bush succeed him in the 1988 elections rather than the Democrat, Michael Dukakis. Moreover, even during the 2000 presidential election, when Vice President Gore sought to distance himself from President Clinton, Clinton went as far as to give the Gore campaign final approval of his travel schedule in an attempt to enhance Gore's chances.[50] Thus, while self-interest may be a stronger electoral motivation during a president's first term, institutional and ideological forces ensure that the electoral motivation endures throughout a president's tenure and does not dissipate in the second term.

A retiring president seeks to create an electoral environment in which voters will credit his party and its new standard bearer with success. Retiring presidents who facilitate the election of a same-party successor benefit from a continuation of similar policy initiatives; they may also benefit from enhancement of their historical legacy.[51] The assumption that presidents' electoral interests fade because of term limits is unfounded.

The Path to Pork: A Resourceful President

Presidents have not only the desire and the institutional motive to participate in electoral politics but often the resources to engage in electorally strategic,

---

48. See Taylor (2008) for an excellent discussion of the topic.
49. Rottinghaus (2006).
50. Lacey (2000).
51. Generally, electoral success is a necessary but not sufficient condition to achieve secondary goals (except, perhaps, for the exercise of institutional power). Of particular note is historical legacy. While an improved legacy is not ensured by the achievement of a second term, most one-term presidents face a reduced historical legacy.

micro-level policymaking, such as pork barrel politics. For example, a president seeking voter support in Ohio can hold a press conference beneath a bridge in Cleveland that *his* Department of Transportation constructed. Like members of Congress, presidents can ensure that funds are targeted, local needs are addressed, and credit is claimed. In many ways, the capacity and ability of presidents and their subordinates are evidenced by a Congress that delegates such extensive policymaking power.

Beyond simply having discretionary authority over a host of policy areas—including electorally critical spending policy—the president and his subordinates are best positioned and equipped to make such micro-level allocation decisions and ensure outcomes are consistent with his (electoral) preferences. The president oversees a bureaucracy that is large and filled with experts on every policy issue. The expertise and ability of the bureaucracy to handle micro-level policy decisions is one reason that Congress delegates certain powers to the executive branch. These individuals serve under political appointees who serve at the pleasure of the president, and in many institutions those appointees wield final decisionmaking authority over many micro-level policy decisions, including fund distribution, in a variety of policy areas. These actors are more responsive to presidential preferences and help ensure that policy outcomes are as well.

For presidents to have maximum influence, personnel must have knowledge of presidential preferences. For an election-driven president keen on the distribution of pork, appointees and bureaucrats who have final spending authority must be aware of how the president wants money spent; they must be aware of the president's geographic and electoral preferences. The president's geographic preferences are widely known. There is little mystery about which states are considered competitive in presidential elections; that information is nearly universally reported in the media and broadly understood within the electorate. Most important, the political appointees and decisionmakers who hold positions in the Washington establishment know the president's electoral preferences and can employ discretionary spending authority to target specific constituencies. In addition to reliance on political appointees, presidents have many other tools to control the bureaucracy, including presidential directives, executive orders, and signing statements. Further, presidential goals are easily communicated through and pursued under pressure from the White House, the Office of Management and Budget, and political appointees.[52] In fact, Gordon demonstrates that White House staff can effectively convey the

---

52. See Gordon (2010); Lewis (2008); Wood and Waterman (1991).

preferences of the president to political appointees regarding the allocation of federal funds and that such pressure can have an impact on distributive outcomes.[53] Moreover, OMB or its subsidiary offices within federal agencies approve many criteria governing funding policy. Their support allows a president and his staff to be better positioned to affect the minor details of policy; that not only motivates the president to be wholly engaged in electoral politics but allows him to succeed in that endeavor.

Indirect mechanisms can also facilitate presidential control. Agencies understand the value of presidential support in terms of maintenance of funding levels, protection from reorganization or closure, and attention to priorities. Responsiveness to presidential electoral interests can mean continuing, gaining, or rehabilitating presidential support. Further, shared ideological or policy goals can also enhance agency responsiveness to the president. Ideological alignment means that a conservative agency such as the International Trade Administration (ITA) would prefer to work with a Republican rather than a Democratic president. ITA decisionmakers may be more willing to support a friendly president's electoral goals. What results is a process whereby agencies can enhance or limit the president's ability to control the policy coming out of those agencies. As a result, presidential power and the ability to extract electoral benefits from policy can depend on various characteristics of given agencies, including their ideological bent.

For these reasons, presidents are well positioned to engage in micro-level decisions in a host of policy areas including the distribution of federal funds. Moreover, legislative discretion offers presidents the power to influence distributive outcomes in order to pursue their goals. Finally, the electoral pressures that presidents face give them incentives to rely on the powers of their office and access to resources to enhance their electoral prospects.

---

53. Gordon (2010). Gordon argues in the context of the 2006 General Services Administration (GSA) scandal that GSA appointees had not "internalized the administration's political goals" and instead needed them spelled out (p. 3). The political goals involved a puzzlingly patterned set of congressional districts labeled "marginal." The precise reasoning for inclusion/exclusion from this group was not entirely clear, making goal internalization nearly impossible. However, I argue that even an observer with only a mild political interest—no matter the interest of appointees—can easily identify which states are competitive in presidential elections.

3

Pork Barrel Politics at the Presidential Level

Between October 8 and October 14, 2004, presidential appointees in the U.S. Department of Energy, including Secretary of Energy Spencer Abraham, scheduled and attended ceremonies announcing nearly $300 million in alternative energy grants. Much of that money came from the Power Plan Improvement Initiative and the Clean Coal Power Initiative, programs that President George W. Bush promoted or started as a way to meet the nation's growing demand for energy. The Clean Coal Power Initiative sought to support "innovative concepts for reducing mercury, smog-causing nitrogen oxide, and small particulate matter from existing and future power plants."

Distributing large sums of grant money, particularly to support a policy that the president's party favors, likely seems a routine part of the bureaucratic process. However, those grants were not distributed evenly across states. Instead, as Election Day approached, President Bush and his administration announced grants in five of the most competitive states in recent electoral history. The magazine *Inside Energy with Federal Lands* noted that in October 2004, the initiatives delivered funds to Ohio, New Mexico, Florida, Pennsylvania, and Wisconsin.[1] Some awards were relatively small, but many were in the millions, including a $235 million grant to support clean coal technology in central Florida.

Many states benefited from these initiatives, including some that were not swing states, like Kentucky, Alaska, and Mississippi. However, many states critical to President Bush's reelection campaign were targeted with multimillion-dollar grants, large public announcement ceremonies, and visits from the

1. "DOE Swing State Visits Continue in Fla. as Abraham Unveils $235M Coal Grant," *Inside Energy with Federal Lands,* October 15, 2004, p. A3; also see Loveless (2004).

president or his energy secretary in the weeks leading up to Election Day. How critical were the states targeted by these grants? Florida, New Mexico, and Wisconsin—where results were decided by an average of 0.096 percent of the votes—were the three closest states in the previous presidential election. In fact, in that election, those states were decided by a total of only 6,611 votes of the more than 9.1 million cast. All five states—Ohio, New Mexico, Florida, Pennsylvania, and Wisconsin—were among the twelve most competitive in the election, all having been decided by about 4 percent or less. In 2004, these states were once again among the twelve most competitive states, and four of them were among the six closest states. The five states also accounted for 62.4 percent of all campaign spending on television advertising, despite making up only 16.6 percent of the nation's population.

These states—along with other Energy Department grant recipients like Michigan and West Virginia—were critical to President Bush's reelection strategy. They were the key to winning the White House, and the president and his appointees at the Energy Department made sure that in the days leading up to November 2, 2004, residents of those states reaped whatever benefits the administration could offer. As the president criss-crossed the swing states in the pursuit of votes, he made sure to take the time to announce new federal funding for communities in need.

This chapter takes the first empirical step toward assessing whether and to what extent presidents engage in pork barrel politics. The previous chapter developed the idea that the nation's chief executive not only is motivated by elections but also has at his disposal the means and opportunity to target federal funds to advance his electoral interests. While the president's control over federal funding affects a variety of policy areas and types of spending, this chapter—and much of this book—will focus on a large subset of that spending: federal discretionary grants. These grants serve as a vehicle to assess the theory of the election-driven president and to measure presidential pork. Because federal grants draw from a large pool of government revenue (taxpayers' funds), have an impact on numerous areas of public policy, and affect citizens in every town in the United States, evaluating the political forces acting on distribution is critical to understanding the function of government.

Predicting Presidential Pork

The point of pork barrel politics, regardless of the actors engaging in the behavior, is to target government dollars to key constituencies at opportune times in order to gain electoral benefits. The behavior of members of Congress is straightforward: representatives direct funds to their legislative districts and senators to their states. The people whom they represent are considered their key constituency, but some studies suggest that some types of groups, recipients, and subconstituencies benefit more from legislative pork. Often the practice in Congress sees legislators fighting over a fixed sum, delivering money to their own constituencies at the expense of those of their colleagues.

Presidential pork is a bit more complicated. As mentioned in the previous chapter, the presidential constituency is unique. Although it is not as large as observers often claim, it is still large and dynamic. In addition, unlike federal legislators, presidents face term limits. Moreover, the type of funding that presidents can use to gain electoral benefits differs from that of Congress. Congress has substantial authority to distribute particularized (targeted) benefits through various funds, such as formula grant funds in areas like transportation and block grant funds in areas like education and housing. Presidents, on the other hand, must rely on discretionary, competitive grants—targeting them to electorally competitive states.

To capture fully the concept of presidential electoral competitiveness, I divide states into three categories: swing states, core states, and lost cause states.[2] Core states are those that are almost certain to support the incumbent presidential candidate; lost cause states are those that are almost certain to support his opponent. In modern presidential politics, Vermont is a core state and Mississippi is a lost cause state for Democrats. Presidents and presidential candidates largely ignore both core and lost cause states; instead, they focus attention on swing states. An election-driven president directs the campaign to critical states, particularly swing states, at key times. However, that strategy should also extend to other areas of policy that presidents believe will provide electoral benefits, such as distributive policy.

Hypothesis 1: Swing states receive more in grants than core states or lost cause states.

Directing federal grants to particular states and running campaign ads and making campaign stops in those states may have an impact on a sufficient number of voters to allow the president to win those states. In addition, grants allow presidents to connect with and gain support from local officials who publicly support, endorse, and work for them. Presidents, recognizing that

2. Swing states are those decided by 10 percentage points or fewer in the previous presidential election. Core states are those in which the party of the incumbent president receives more than 55 percent of the vote. Lost cause states are those in which the party of the incumbent president receives less than 45 percent of the vote.

elections are won or lost in key states, use whatever resources they can to maximize their chance of winning.

It is important to evaluate presidential strategy in terms of time and location. An electorally strategic distribution of federal grants is not uniform throughout a president's tenure; time also affects grant distribution, in two important ways. First, grants are more appealing as an electoral tool as an election nears. Because voters tend to use more recent events in their judgment of elected officials,[3] effective credit claiming and advertising must occur in the period preceding an election.[4]

In addition, in a study of macroeconomic policy, Alesina and Rosenthal (1989) distinguished between policies that have long- and short-term impacts, arguing that long-term policies should be pursued in the first two years of a presidential term because their effectiveness should coincide with the presidential election. Meanwhile, policies that have short-term impacts should be pursued in the final two years of a term as the immediacy of their impact should boost the president's electoral goals. Presidents engage in a variety of long- and short-term efforts and policy endeavors. By their very nature, federal grants tend to be short term, often addressing discrete needs and providing funding for one, two, or three years.[5]

Although Alesina and Rosenthal rely on a formal model in which completely informed voters reward presidents for observed economic growth and success, Hetherington (1996) demonstrates that the public's mere perception of economic conditions may motivate voters to punish or reward presidential candidates. Because the grants that I analyze in this study are typically short term, they are more likely to be used as a presidential election draws near. These grants may provide either immediate positive impact or at least the perception of positive impact in voters' recent memory.

Hypothesis 2: Swing states receive more in grants in the two years prior to a presidential election than in the two years after.

While presidents are motivated not only by their own reelection but by the electoral success of their potential same-party successor, self-interest should trump partisan interest. The two-term limit does not eliminate the electoral

---

3. Zaller (1992).

4. Fiorina (1981); Shaw (2006); Shaw and Roberts (2000).

5. Funding can occur for longer or shorter periods. Depending on the grant program, grants often are designed to last for yearly periods, with opportunities for renewal or extension for additional years. Regardless, federal grants, particularly discretionary grants, are not intended to be long term or permanent streams of funding to specific recipients.

drive because presidents still maintain electoral preferences regarding the next occupant of the White House. Rottinghaus (2006) argues that presidential electoral interests can extend to the second term because a president seeks a partisan hold on the Oval Office.

Broadly, research finds that a personal electoral motivation influences the behavior of senators;[6] in addition, Canes-Wrone and Shotts (2004) find that while presidents are responsive to the public across presidential terms, the effect is enhanced during the first term, when personal electoral preferences inform their behavior. Although interest in the success of their party's next standard bearer influences the behavior of presidents across terms, it may not influence their behavior as strongly as their own electoral interest. As a result, a president's commitment to the electorally motivated distribution of grants should be stronger in his first term than in his second.

Hypothesis 3: Swing states receive more in grants in a president's first term than in his second.

An allocation strategy that significantly increases funding to swing states, particularly as a presidential election approaches and in a president's first term, suggests that a president's electoral preferences are a consideration in the distribution of funds.

These hypotheses set up a framework for exploring presidential influence in the aggregate distribution of federal grants by examining both the geographic and temporal influences on the distribution of these grants.

Why Federal Grants?

Federal discretionary grants are quite appealing for a number of reasons in evaluating presidential pork. Given the large sums of grants appropriated each year and the level of discretion granted to the executive branch, they serve as an ideal electoral tool. The "discretion" that distinguishes these grants is power delegated from Congress to federal agencies to determine not only the distribution of these funds, but often the nature and structure of the programs that govern them. These grants provide the executive with a clear avenue to influence allocations and a clear context in which to advance his electoral goals.[7]

---

6. Kuklinski (1978).

7. Discretionary grants by no means offer the "hard case" in demonstrating presidential influence. However, because Congress influences distributive politics in so many areas, it is important to focus on a setting that can facilitate executive influence. Discretionary grants provide that setting.

Because different spending programs often have different masters, any effort to examine all federal spending or multiple types of spending (discretionary grants, formula grants, and block grants, for example) would encounter problems in isolating sources of influence and political control. The focus on discretionary grants offers an efficient and reliable way to evaluate presidential power.[8]

Another appeal of these grants (although it is not entirely unique to this type of federal spending) involves recordkeeping. The federal government keeps meticulous records on the allocation of discretionary grants, which have at different times been publicly available for various years.[9] Those records, which allow for valid and reliable measures of the core concept (grant allocations) of this analysis, create confidence in both the data and the results. These grants also offer additional benefits for the purposes of this analysis. Like campaign funds, federal grants can be allocated in strategic ways to target key constituencies. However, while the goal of much campaign spending is to get a candidate's message, qualifications, and accomplishments into the consciousness of voters, pork dispensed through grants works in different ways.

Grants provide advertising opportunities for presidents as local media cover grant announcements and disbursements, offering free publicity. These announcements are always associated with the federal agency from which the funds are flowing. Ribbon-cutting or groundbreaking ceremonies are always attended by a host of elected officials, often including a political appointee representing the president. Besides providing free advertising, grants serve as a direct transfer from the federal largesse to a state's economy. Grants can provide for various improvements, services, or aid. They offer short-term fiscal and labor market support to a community in a way that involves little additional cost to a local constituency. Chubb (1985) describes grants as ideal for localities because they provide a good (or service or both) without raising local taxes, especially grants that come with few conditions or expectations for local

8. Variation in levels of discretion can occur from program to program, even among discretionary grants. The measurement of variation in discretion can be controversial, and it is not the purpose of this analysis, which assumes that there is a given, positive level of discretion for all grants and that discretion empowers presidents in substantial ways. In reality, I assume substantial presidential discretion. Any limitation on presidential discretionary authority simply makes it more difficult to reject the null hypotheses from the previous section. That is, if a set of discretionary grant programs provides limited authority for the president and his appointees, it makes it more difficult to illustrate presidential pork, making the findings more conservative.

9. Records for some of the data are available for a fee and may require a Freedom of Information Act request. However, the data, in whatever context they are available, are maintained in clear, consistent, and reliable datasets.

government matching.[10] Presidents are able to claim credit for these grants among the state's voters. Grants serve as an appealing vehicle for presidents to engage in pork barrel politics and thus become an appealing vehicle for studying the phenomenon.

An Overview of Discretionary Grants

The data used in this chapter and chapter 4 include every discretionary federal grant distributed to the fifty states from 1996 to 2008. During that period, the bureaucracy doled out more than $962,000,000,000 in grants, allocated through 3,692,084 grant disbursements. Data are drawn from the Federal Assistance Award Data System (FAADS), which is compiled by the Office of Management and Budget and maintained by the U.S. Census Bureau. The data found in FAADS are extensive, including information not only on discretionary grants but also on other types of federal funding, including formula and block grants, government insurance, cooperative agreements, and more. The dataset allows for the straightforward isolation of funding by numerous categories, including funding type, and provides for the isolation of discretionary grants.[11]

The data available through FAADS offer a wealth of information about each grant allocation, including location, amount, program, agency, and date of distribution, among other details. Each detail can offer insight into the structure of an allocation or serve as part of a critical set of explanatory variables (and in many cases I capitalize on this additional information in just that way). The data also allow for measuring grant allocations in two substantively different ways. Grants are easily understood in terms of dollars, which are comparable across space and, if adjusted, over time they are an appealing quantitative measure of the basic variable of interest. However, grants can also be understood in terms of number of allocations, independent of dollars.

For example, the state of Rhode Island may receive a single grant worth $3 million to construct several new fire stations in Providence. It improves public safety in the city of Providence and the surrounding communities and provides an economic stimulus to the area. The elected official responsible for the grant may receive media attention and the appreciation of Rhode Island voters for bringing the money to the state for much-needed improvements. On the other hand, the state of Arizona may receive a series of twelve grants,

10. Chubb (1985). In fact, when additional funds flow to a constituency, taxes often remain constant. As a result, it could be argued that this inflow of funding is a zero-cost, high-benefit transfer for states and municipalities. And, unlike formula and block grants, discretionary grants often come with limited conditions or contingencies.

11. FAADS labels discretionary grants "project grants."

Figure 3-1. *Inflation-Adjusted Discretionary Grant Dollars to the States, 1996–2008*

Inflation-adjusted dollars (millions)

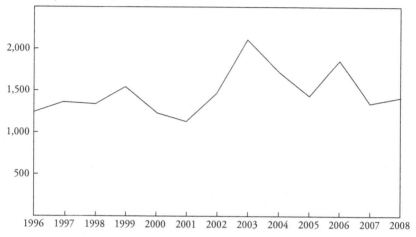

Source: Grants data drawn from the Federal Assistance Award Data System.

each valued at $250,000, to purchase fire equipment for Maricopa County. The area receives a similar $3 million economic stimulus, but the residents of the area may perceive the funds differently. Rather than providing media coverage of a single $3 million grant, the *Arizona Republic* may publish a steady stream of articles about grant allocations, keeping voters constantly aware of the flow of federal funds to the area.

These examples show that it is critical to measure grants in two different ways, as their usefulness in terms of credit claiming could vary depending on the number or the value of the grants. Figures 3-1 and 3-2 present the real dollar value and population-controlled number of federal grant allocations for each year of the 1996–2008 period. The figures demonstrate that there is substantial variation in both the number and value of grants allocated over time.

As the figures illustrate, discretionary grant funding involves significant amounts of federal tax revenue in nearly every policy area that the federal government administers. For example, the grants in the dataset come from all fifteen cabinet departments and dozens of independent agencies and commissions. For perspective, the complete database took approximately 11 months to complete because research was required to find additional data and those data needed to be formatted for entry into the macro-dataset. Because of

Figure 3-2. *The Number of Discretionary Grants Allocated to the States, 1996–2008*

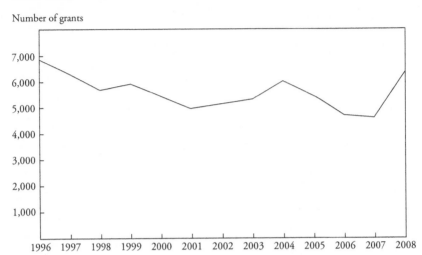

Number of grants

Source: Grants data drawn from the Federal Assistance Award Data System.

the sheer amount of time and effort required to construct the datasets, I had to make some choices regarding the data used. Ideally, the dataset would include grant spending across all available years and federal agencies. Although FAADS makes the spending data itself relatively accessible, the collection of necessary independent variables limited my ability to expand the dataset. I had to choose between collecting additional years of spending data or more comprehensive independent variables across fewer years. The latter became the more appealing option because it allowed for a more rigorous evaluation of whether presidents engage in pork barrel politics and testing of relevant hypotheses. Because limiting the years opens the analysis to criticism, I sought to diversify the data as much as possible. The data in this chapter and chapter 4 include data for two presidents (Clinton and Bush), data from at least one year in both terms of both presidents, and data from periods of divided and unified government.[12] Ultimately, these data provide the most comprehensive

12. Chapter 5 includes data from the first three years of the Obama administration, the only ones for which data were available at the time of the writing of this book. Those data are separated for theoretical reasons. During that time, the federal government was administering the large and all-encompassing American Recovery and Reinvestment Act in concert with standard grant allocations, making data from this period both historically and theoretically unique.

and rigorous evaluation of presidential influence over the distribution of federal funds to date.

Measuring Presidential Pork

Because of the breadth of the data used in this study, it is necessary to provide a discussion of measurement techniques, particularly for the variables of central interest in the analysis.

The State as the Unit of Analysis

Throughout much of this book and particularly this chapter, the geographic unit of analysis is the state. In this chapter, grants are examined by state by year (state-year). In chapter 4, grants are examined by agency by state by year (agency-state-year). The use of the state is important to the research because it is the most accurate and logical level to use in analyzing the data and testing the hypotheses.

Presidents focus their attention on swing states, and much electoral strategy centers on states. However, presidential campaigns also focus on segments (or subpopulations) of swing states. For example, not every corner of Florida is treated the same by a campaign. However, a systematic, government-wide analysis of grant allocations at the sub-state (county, city, and so forth) level presents serious challenges. First, as mentioned, constructing a state-level dataset required a substantial investment of time and resources; construction of a dataset below the state level would require exponentially more resources or a reduction in the scope of the data.

Second, data for key independent variables that measure congressional impact and especially constituent need are either difficult to collect or nonexistent. In addition, in many cases data would have to be collected from multiple state-level sources; however, using multiple sources can lead to issues in data validity because of differences in measurement. Finally, the grant data are valid and reliable at the state level. Because of reporting procedures, efforts to evaluate the allocation of grants to counties and municipalities would be much less accurate and would introduce serious error into the analysis. For example, many grants are allocated to recipients in a state but administered using a state cabinet department as an intermediary. For instance, a farmer in Ottumwa, Iowa, may receive a grant from the U.S. Department of Agriculture (USDA). However, the USDA may send the funding first to the Iowa Department of Agriculture and Land Stewardship in Des Moines, which then sends the funding to the Ottumwa farmer. In many cases, the data indicate the first rather than the final recipient. As a result, efforts to see where funding goes in Iowa are compromised when a grant that went to Ottumwa was registered in the dataset as going to Des Moines. That the funds were distributed to Iowa is correct, but beneath the state level, the tracing of funds becomes complicated. In an ideal setting, this analysis would examine recipient-level grant allocations, daily, over the tenure of all presidents, across every federal grant program. Research environments rarely allow the ideal, and this study errs on the side of balancing data accuracy with comprehensive analysis.

Dependent Variables

Measures of grant disbursements serve as the dependent variables in the analysis in much of this book. However, measures of grant distributions come in two forms: dollar amount of grants and number of grants. In addition, each form has some unique measurement issues that must be accounted for to ensure a more rigorous analysis. To capture the two types of grant allocations accurately, I measure both number of grants and grant dollar value in specific ways. First, I measure grant dollars as the logged real grant dollars per 100,000 people per state-year. This measure is methodologically appealing for several reasons. First, it naturally controls for population, which is a key concern given dramatic population differences across states and their expected effect on the distribution of federal funds. Next, I control for inflation by indexing allocations for price, using 1996 dollars. Because grants can have a direct economic impact and an impact on public perceptions, it is critical to make sure that funds are comparable, not simply across space (as population controls allow) but also over time. Finally, while the population and inflation controls help reduce the impact of outliers (smooth the data), these efforts fail to control sufficiently for outlier effects. I therefore use the logarithmic value of the population-adjusted real grant dollars per state-year to standardize the measure and limit the effect of outliers.

To measure the number of grants, I employ a similar approach to overcome some characteristics in the data that can present analytical challenges. I measure this dependent variable as the logged number of grants per 100,000 people per state-year.[13] Essentially and for the same reasons, I measure this

---

13. To clarify, for both dependent variables in chapter 4, the unit of analysis is the agency-state-year, the grant allocations by an agency to a state in a given year. In this analysis, the measure of the number of grants no longer controls for population because the values become so small that interpretation is difficult. Instead, I include an independent variable that measures population as a means of controlling for such effects.

variable and the grant dollars variable the same way, with the omission of the unneeded inflation adjustment for the number of grants variable.

Characteristics of the Data and Key Independent Variables

As mentioned, presidents' electoral interests are best served when resources are used to target swing states, which are the most competitive in presidential elections. Although debate exists in the literature on pork barrel politics regarding which type of constituency an elected official should target,[14] both empirical findings[15] and theory demonstrate clearly that the nature of the Electoral College motivates presidents to focus on swing states.[16]

To measure state electoral competitiveness, I use a common metric: the incumbent share of the two-party vote in the previous presidential election.[17] This measure is quite appealing for understanding presidential motivations in pork barrel politics. While scholars have used other measures of competitiveness in evaluating campaign behavior, those measures are temporally limited for the purpose of this analysis. For example, Shaw (2006) uses lists of competitive states compiled by campaigns in the months leading up to a presidential election to understand competitiveness and electoral strategy. These lists are very useful and are often updated rapidly in advance of elections using the most recent information available.

For this analysis, such a measure is insufficient. I hypothesize that presidents engage in grant-centered pork barrel politicking throughout their tenure, but the campaign lists are unavailable during much of that time. However, the vote results from the previous election are immediately available and can serve as a useful guide in allocating funds to key states. This measure also

14. See Dixit and Londregan (1996) for a discussion of the debate between swing and core hypotheses.

15. See Shaw (2006).

16. It should be noted that while the campaign focus on swing constituencies is true at the state level, it may not be true at the sub-state level. Because of the winner-take-all and first-past-the-post nature of state electoral vote allocations, presidential candidates focus on winning states and concentrate resources (campaign or pork) on swing states. However, the strategy by which presidential candidates achieve success within swing states does not necessarily reflect the swing hypothesis. In fact, one can imagine that within a swing state, a presidential campaign may target core voters in an effort to win that state. See Chen (2009) for an example of a core constituency strategy being implemented within the swing state Florida.

17. The discussion of these data is by no means exhaustive; it serves instead as an introduction to the core data used in this study. Additional independent variables used as controls and used to assess alternative hypotheses are discussed as relevant in the chapters that follow. An overview of the measurement of the variables discussed in this chapter can be found in appendix table 3A-1.

serves as a stable reflection of competitiveness, not subject to revision based on polling results or media information.

Specifically, I operationalize state competitiveness as a two- and a three-category measure. The two-category (dichotomous) measure indicates whether a state is a swing state. I denote a state as swing if it was decided by 10 percentage points or fewer in the previous presidential election and as a non-swing state otherwise. This measure has been used by other scholars as a standard measure of competitiveness for an upcoming election.[18] The 10-percentage-point measure also maintains a level of face validity. Table 3-1 lists the swing states for each upcoming presidential election year analyzed in this study. Although the measure can be blunt, including a few states that typically are not competitive and excluding a few that are, the table generally represents competitiveness in an accurate way. Furthermore, while 10 percentage points can reflect a large number of votes, political fortunes can be reversed by simply changing the minds of just over 5 percent of a state's population. Moreover, a state decided by a margin of 55-45 or less is commonly viewed as a competitive state.[19]

Although the swing hypothesis is theoretically and empirically consistent with the institutional nature of the Electoral College, the dichotomous measure of state electoral competitiveness does not allow for a straightforward evaluation of the core-state hypothesis—a key alternative explanation in the study of distributive politics that argues that elected officials target funds to constituencies that offer the most electoral support. To overcome this limitation, I also include a three-category measure of state electoral competitiveness. As discussed above, the categories for this variable are swing state, core state, and lost cause state. Table 3-2 demonstrates the manner in which each competitiveness category is measured.

18. See Abramowitz, Alexander, and Gunning (2006); Ansolabehere, Brady, and Fiorina (1992).

19. For much of the analysis, I use a measure of an 8-percentage-point difference or less as an alternative. Some literature considers this measure more conservative because it includes fewer states. However, the conservatism of this measure is up for debate given that it gives greater weight to the most competitive states at the expense of moderately competitive states. In addition, in terms of face validity, the reduction of the competitiveness margin to 8 percentage points excludes in several cases states that are widely considered (publicly and by campaigns) to be swing states. The expansion of the margin to 10 percentage points often captures those states. Another alternative, the use of a continuous (folded) measure of state electoral competitiveness, may be appealing, but it fails to capture the manner in which presidential campaigns view states. While states are seen as more or less competitive, Shaw (2006) clearly demonstrates that presidential campaigns think of states in terms of being swing or non-swing states and less in terms of a continuous measure.

Table 3-1. *Swing States, by Presidential Term, 1996–2008*

Clinton, Term 1 (1996)	Clinton, Term 2 (1997–2000)	Bush, Term 1 (2001–04)	Bush, Term 2 (2005–08)
Alabama	Alabama	Arizona	Arkansas
Arizona	Arizona	Arkansas	Colorado
Colorado	Colorado	Colorado	Delaware
Connecticut	Florida	Florida	Florida
Florida	Georgia	Iowa	Hawaii
Georgia	Indiana	Louisiana	Iowa
Indiana	Kentucky	Maine	Maine
Iowa	Mississippi	Michigan	Michigan
Kansas	Missouri	Minnesota	Minnesota
Kentucky	Montana	Missouri	Missouri
Louisiana	Nevada	Nevada	Nevada
Michigan	New Mexico	New Hampshire	New Hampshire
Mississippi	North Carolina	New Mexico	New Jersey
Montana	North Dakota	Ohio	New Mexico
Nevada	Ohio	Oregon	Ohio
New Hampshire	Oklahoma	Pennsylvania	Oregon
New Jersey	Oregon	Tennessee	Pennsylvania
North Carolina	South Carolina	Virginia	Virginia
Ohio	South Dakota	Washington	Washington
South Carolina	Tennessee	West Virginia	Wisconsin
South Dakota	Texas	Wisconsin	
Tennessee	Virginia		
Virginia			
Wisconsin			
Wyoming			

Sources: McCutcheon and Lyons (2009); Koszcuk and Stern (2005); Stern (2001); Duncan and Lawrence (1997).

Table 3-3a shows the average number of grants and grant dollars allocated to each type of state. The results appear inconsistent with the theoretical predictions of this study. Lost cause and core states receive far more in grants than swing states do. However, a deeper look at the data shows that a few datapoints are driving the results. First, California and New York are extreme outliers, and in every year in the dataset they are coded as either a core state or a lost cause state. These states' grant allocations far exceed those of all other states. In fact, in some years, their grant allocations are more than 6 standard deviations above the mean of all allocations. In addition, during the period under analysis two exogenous shocks affected certain states that would be expected to drive up grant receipts in those areas. The first shock occurred in New York following the September 11, 2001, terrorist attacks. The second occurred in Louisiana and Mississippi following Hurricane Katrina in 2005. The data show

Table 3-2. *Measurement of State Electoral Competitiveness*
Percent

Category	Incumbent share of the two-party vote in previous presidential election
Swing state	$45 \leq$ Vote share ≤ 55
Core state	Vote share > 55
Lost cause state	Vote share < 45

that grant receipts increased dramatically in those years. In fact, grant receipts in California, New York, and these locations during the disaster years drive almost a fifth of the variation in the grant allocation means, despite making up less than 5 percent of the datapoints.[20] While these data are not irrelevant, their exclusion provides a different view of the remaining 95.1 percent of the data.

Table 3-3b shows the means when the California, New York, and disaster state-year data are excluded. These data show greater consistency with the theoretical expectations of this study. In terms of both the number of grants and grant dollars, swing states received more than other states and substantially more than average. In fact, on average, swing states received $240 million more in grants per year than core states and nearly 900 more grants annually. This examination of means suggests that a more comprehensive examination of the relationship between state competitiveness and grant allocations is warranted. On its face, this bivariate relationship offers the first systematic evidence of grants being allocated according to presidential electoral calculations.

In addition to the geographic nature of federal fund allocations, I also include variables that measure the strategic timing involved in the distribution of grants. To measure timing, I rely on two measures. The first reflects the salience of electoral considerations. This measure of electoral proximity is a dichotomy indicating the two years leading up to a presidential election (and after a midterm congressional election). The second dichotomous measure indicates a president's first term, reflecting expectations that term effects may exist in the data.

Table 3-4 captures various characteristics in the data that are important in the evaluation of political behavior and inter-branch relations. The data cover two presidencies and at least one year in each term of the two. The two presidents under analysis—Bill Clinton and George W. Bush—hailed from

---

20. In this description of the data, New York is coded as a disaster state for 2002, 2003, and 2004. In these years, the states are even greater outliers than New York is typically. However, the non-disaster years for New York are outliers in their own right.

Table 3-3a. *Mean Yearly Grant Allocations, by State Competitiveness*

Category	Grant dollars (millions)	Number of grants
All states	148	5,680
Swing states	131	5,486
Core states	135	5,286
Lost cause states	226	7,177

Source: Census Bureau (2011a).

Table 3-3b. *Mean Yearly Grant Allocations, by State Competitiveness, Excluding Outlier States*[a]

Category	Grant dollars (millions)	Number of grants
All states	120	4,994
Swing states	131	5,486
Core states	107	4,618
Lost cause states	121	4,523

Source: Census Bureau (2011a).
a. The data exclude New York and California, as well as Mississippi and Louisiana from 2005 to 2007, as they are extreme outliers.

Table 3-4. *Party Control of the Elected Branches of Government, 1996–2008*

Year	President	House	Senate	Style
1996	Clinton	Republican	Republican	Divided
1997	Clinton	Republican	Republican	Divided
1998	Clinton	Republican	Republican	Divided
1999	Clinton	Republican	Republican	Divided
2000	Clinton	Republican	Republican	Divided
2001	Bush	Republican	Democratic[a]	Semi-divided
2002	Bush	Republican	Democratic	Semi-divided
2003	Bush	Republican	Republican	Unified
2004	Bush	Republican	Republican	Unified
2005	Bush	Republican	Republican	Unified
2006	Bush	Republican	Republican	Unified
2007	Bush	Democratic	Democratic	Divided
2008	Bush	Democratic	Democratic	Divided

Source: U.S. Senate, "Party Division in the Senate 1789–Present" (www.senate.gov/pagelayout/history/one_item_and_teasers/partydiv.htm).
a. During 2001, the Senate changed from Republican control to Democratic control from the swearing in of the 103rd Congress on January 3 until the conclusion of the Clinton presidency on January 20 (as Vice President Gore broke a 50-50 tie). Starting on January 20, Vice President Cheney broke the 50-50 tie, giving party control to Republicans. The Republican party controlled the Senate until June 3, 2001, when Senator Jim Jeffords of Vermont switched his affiliation from Republican to Independent status and caucused with the Democrats. That move gave Democrats a 51-49 majority, which endured through the end of the 103rd Congress. I designate Democratic control in 2001 because Democrats controlled the Senate for a majority of the year (230 days).

different parties and governed during periods of varying partisan relations with Congress, including periods of unified, semi-divided, and divided government. In addition, the data include periods of divided government for both presidents. This variation allows for the evaluation of presidents' behavior in the middle of their own reelection efforts and as lame ducks supporting their party's next standard bearer. Thus, although the data include only 13 years, this period exhibits remarkable variation in terms of national leadership.

State-Level Congressional Controls

In light of a substantial literature that argues that Congress is the solo player in distributive politics, any analysis of the politics of federal spending must account for the role of Congress. Although the aggregate dataset (using data at the state-year level) can complicate the assessment of congressional effects, I include a series of measures that seek to capture the influence of Congress in the distribution of grants. First, I use a measure indicating state representation on the Senate Appropriations Committee.[21] Because all funding bills pass through this committee, this measure serves as one effective proxy for congressional influence. It is likely that membership on this committee allows for direct influence in the allocation of grants.

Moreover, I control for whether it is an election year for a member of the Senate Appropriations Committee, whether it is an election year for an incumbent senator, whether there is a competitive Senate election in a state, and whether the state is represented by a member of the Senate leadership. I also control for the number of majority-party senators representing a state, the House delegation's partisan alignment with the president, and whether a member of the congressional delegation chairs an appropriations subcommittee. To control further for the role of Congress, all models in this chapter are estimated using fixed effects for states to control for the influence that individual senators may have on fund allocations.[22] These variables subject the

21. Different measures of congressional influence were considered. This measure seemed theoretically and empirically sound. Membership on both House and Senate appropriations committees offered almost no variation, as almost every state has a representative or senator on the committee. Even membership on the House Appropriations Committee offers little variation, as most states maintain membership. States with small populations are less likely to have a member on the House committee. In chapter 4, the unit of analysis is agency-level allocations, and I am able to introduce more textured congressional controls in examining the influence of legislative factors in fund distribution.

22. For example, senators Ted Stevens (R-Alaska) and Robert Byrd (D-W.Va.), who were notorious for benefiting from the appropriation of government funds, used their individual influence to secure substantial money for their states.

presidential influence hypothesis to rigorous testing. I do not argue that Congress is powerless to influence the distribution of federal grants but instead that presidents are powerful players in a complex allocation system.

Intergovernmental Controls

Some research suggests that federalism is an alternative explanation for the distribution of federal funds, often arguing that the political environment that state governors face influences how grants are distributed.[23] Accordingly, I include controls for whether it is an election year for a governor and whether there is partisan alignment between the president and a governor; I also include an interaction of gubernatorial election year and partisan alignment with the president. These measures control for gubernatorial electoral concerns and their effects. This is a critical point in the analysis of federal spending. Governors can be crucial allies to sitting presidents, responsible for the execution of much of the policy that reaches constituents. Presidents care about the electoral interests of governors and work to support their fellow partisans in the governor's mansion. Just as presidents assist the political and electoral needs of members of Congress, they may also help their friendly state executives.

State Capacity and Demand

Measures of state capacity and demand also are likely to influence grant distribution. Because some states have larger needs and require more federal assistance than others, I control for yearly real gross state product and the miles of roads within a state, which are stable and comparable measures of the economic capacity of each state. Next, because many federal grants fund research and development, particularly in education and health care, it is important to control for the amount of research conducted in each state. I control for the number of colleges, universities, and hospitals. I further consider a measure of the elderly population as a proxy for demographic demands on government.

Because there is a theoretical reason to believe a priori that a few cases will be profound outliers due to disasters, I use a variable, labeled "disaster," to control for New York in the three years following the September 11, 2001, terrorist attacks and Louisiana and Mississippi after Hurricane Katrina. To put the increased need in these states into perspective, between 2001 and 2003, New York's grant receipts increased by 148 percent, or $9.7 billion. From the year prior to Hurricane Katrina (2004) to the year following the storm (2006), Mississippi's grant receipts increased 395 percent and Louisiana's increased

---

23. Berry, Burden, and Howell (2010); Larcinese, Rizzo, and Testa (2006).

by 658 percent. These states had a profound and unique need for federal assistance from a variety of programs in the wake of those disasters. Failure to account for increased demand following such events would under-specify the model.

Evaluating Influence

I estimate a series of models using ordinary least squares with fixed effects for state and year. The fixed effects serve as part of the larger effort to ensure that the results are robust even when I control for a multitude of alternative hypotheses. The use of fixed effects offers a more conservative estimation by adding layers of controls beyond those described above.[24] The results of this study generally lend support to the hypotheses presented above. Presidents use their discretion over federal grants to institute an electorally strategic process of distribution. This presidential strategy reflects both the electoral significance of states and the significance of the time when an election takes place.

A Significant Electoral Strategy

Table 3-5 shows the estimates of the number of grants regressed on state competitiveness and election timing and a set of controls. In this table, both models are estimated in identical fashion except that model 1 uses a three-part measure of state competitiveness while model 2 employs a dichotomous measure. The analysis indicates that swing states receive between 7.3 percent and 7.6 percent more grants than do other states. When this measure of competitiveness is used, core and lost cause states are statistically indistinguishable, suggesting that when distributing grants the executive branch focuses on electorally competitive states. This swing state benefit translates to substantial gains for a state. For example, in 2007 Tennessee was a core state and received 4,110 federal grants. These results suggest that if Tennessee had been a swing state, it would have received more than 300 additional grants in that year alone.

The proximity of an election also is associated with an increase in grant allocations. The estimates suggest that states will receive 10 percent more grants in the two years prior to an election than in the two years following one. This finding offers additional evidence that the electoral interests of the executive branch influence the federal grant allocation strategy, and it lends support to a theory of presidential influence in another way. If the grant distribution process were dominated by Congress, one would expect to be unable to reject the null hypothesis because of the frequency of congressional elections. More

24. All estimates are reported with robust standard errors.

Table 3-5. *Models of the Number of Federal Discretionary Grants, 1996–2008*[a]

Variable	Model 1	Model 2
State competitiveness		
Swing State (0,1)	0.073**	0.076**
	(0.029)	(0.029)
Lost Cause State (0,1)	−0.024	—
	(0.032)	
Timing		
First Term (0,1)	−0.006	−0.009
	(0.011)	(0.011)
Election Proximity (0,1)	0.100**	0.101**
	(0.008)	(0.008)
State-level congressional controls		
Senate Appropriations Committee (0,1)	0.045	0.046
	(0.031)	(0.032)
Appropriations Committee Election Year (0,1)	0.007	0.006
	(0.018)	(0.018)
Incumbent Senator Election Year (0,1)	−0.007	−0.007
	(0.014)	(0.013)
Competitive Senate Election (0,1)	−0.012	−0.011
	(0.023)	(0.023)
Senate Leadership (0,1)	−0.043	−0.045
	(0.031)	(0.031)
Majority Party Membership (0,1,2)	−0.001	−0.002
	(0.009)	(0.009)
House Delegation with President (0,1)	−0.012	−0.005
	(0.021)	(0.022)
Cardinals (0,1)	0.001	0.004
	(0.030)	(0.030)
Intergovernmental controls		
Governor Election Year (0,1)	0.007	0.007
	(0.017)	(0.017)
Governor-President Party Alignment (0,1)	−0.001	−0.0001
	(0.020)	(0.020)
Governor Election Year × Alignment (0,1)	−0.044*	−0.044*
	(0.022)	(0.022)
Controls and constant		
Real Gross State Product	−0.940**	−0.949**
	(0.115)	(0.115)
Roads (miles)	−0.065	−0.082
	(0.228)	(0.224)
Research Institutions	−0.002	−0.002
	(0.001)	(0.001)
Percent Elderly	−0.131**	−0.126**
	(0.039)	0.039
Disaster (0,1)	0.023	0.019
	(0.037)	(0.037)
Constant	6.783**	7.000**
	(3.089)	(3.052)
R^2	0.44	0.44
Observations	650	650

a. The dependent variable is the logged number of grants per 100,000 people per state-year. Both models are estimated using ordinary least squares with fixed effects for state and year. Robust standard errors are reported. In model 1, the reference case for state competitiveness is Core State. In model 2, the reference case for state competitiveness is Non-Swing State.

**$p < .01$ (one-tailed test); *$p < .05$ (one-tailed test).

specifically, if congressional electoral interests—the cornerstone of the study of legislative pork barrel politics—affected discretionary grant allocations, the electoral proximity variable should not have an effect. If congressional elections exclusively drove the distribution of funds, allocations should be similar across a presidential term, given the frequency of legislative elections. Instead, the two years approaching a presidential election see higher grant allocations than the two years approaching a midterm.

Besides the number of federal grants, I also examine the allocation of federal dollars. Table 3-6 presents the results. In this table, the models are identical to those found in table 3-5, except that they are estimated using grant dollars as the dependent variable.[25] The results of the grant dollars models echo the previous findings. Swing states see a benefit of 5.7 percent more grant dollars than other states—a substantial result given that states received hundreds of millions or billions of grant dollars annually. These findings provide further evidence that presidential electoral preferences affect the geographic distribution of federal grant allocations. To use Tennessee as an example again: in 2007 Tennessee received about $1.06 billion in grants; however, the results suggest that as a swing state, Tennessee would have reaped an additional $60 million in grants in that year. Not only do swing states receive more grant dollars than non–swing states, those differences in benefits can have substantial effects on the citizens of those states.

More to the point, as in the number-of-grants models, states receive about 6.6 percent more grant dollars when a presidential election is approaching than when one is distant. This is consistent with hypothesis 2, further demonstrating a timing element to the strategic allocation of grants. In both the number-of-grants and grant dollars models, the estimates for term are imprecise and preclude rejection of the null hypothesis. This null finding could signal the pervasive nature of presidential electoral interests. The finding suggests that presidential term has little impact on the distribution of federal grants. Specifically, grant allocations are unaffected whether a president is or is not eligible for reelection.

Figure 3-3 charts the substantive effects of these estimates for number of grants and grant dollars. The figure presents the influence of electoral strategy on an average-sized state. The strategic allocation of grants with regard to geography and timing is immediately clear. Not only do state competitiveness and electoral proximity have statistically significant effects for allocations, but those effects translate into important consequences for a state of average size.

---

25. Once again, specifically, the dependent variable is measured as logged real grant dollars per 100,000 people.

Table 3-6. *Models of Federal Discretionary Grant Dollars, by State-Year, 1996–2008*[a]

Variable	Model 1	Model 2
State competitiveness		
Swing State (0,1)	0.057*	0.056*
	(0.033)	(0.033)
Lost Cause State (0,1)	0.01	—
	(0.048)	
Timing		
First Term (0,1)	0.024	0.025
	(0.022)	(0.020)
Election Proximity (0,1)	0.066**	0.066**
	(0.014)	(0.014)
State-level congressional controls		
Senate Appropriations Committee (0,1)	0.076*	0.075*
	(0.038)	(0.038)
Appropriations Committee Election Year (0,1)	0.019	0.019
	(0.027)	(0.027)
Incumbent Senator Election Year (0,1)	−0.043*	−0.043*
	(0.019)	(0.019)
Competitive Senate Election (0,1)	0.013	0.013
	(0.025)	(0.025)
Senate Leadership (0,1)	0.045	0.045
	(0.056)	(0.056)
Majority Party Membership (0,1,2)	0.002	0.002
	(0.017)	(0.017)
House Delegation with President (0,1)	0.029	0.026
	(0.028)	(0.025)
Cardinals (0,1)	−0.007	−0.008
	(0.035)	(0.034)
Intergovernmental controls		
Governor Election Year (0,1)	0.046*	0.046*
	(0.021)	(0.021)
Governor-President Party Alignment (0,1)	−0.031	−0.032
	(0.026)	(0.026)
Governor Election Year × Alignment (0,1)	0.008	0.008
	(0.031)	(0.031)
Controls and constant		
Real Gross State Product	−0.113	0.109
	(0.130)	(0.126)
Roads (miles)	0.164	0.172
	(0.178)	(0.176)
Research Institutions	−0.001	−0.001
	(0.002)	(0.002)
Percent Elderly	−0.092*	−0.094*
	(0.039)	(0.039)
Disaster	0.964**	0.966**
	(0.282)	(0.282)
Constant	17.772**	17.682**
	(2.728)	(2.649)
R^2	0.10	0.10
Observations	650	650

a. The dependent variable is the logged real grant dollars per 100,000 people per state-year. Both models are estimated using ordinary least squares with fixed effects for state and year. Robust standard errors are reported. In model 1, the reference case for state competitiveness is Core State. In model 2, the reference case for state competitiveness is Non-Swing State.

**$p < .01$ (two-tailed test); *$p < .05$ (one-tailed test).

Figure 3-3. *Estimated Effects of State Electoral Competitiveness and Electoral Proximity on Grant Allocations, 1996–2008*

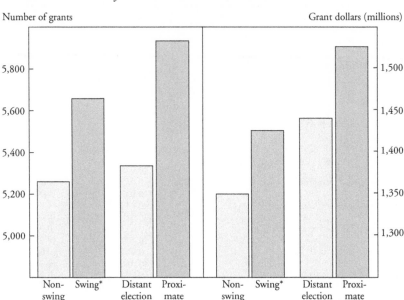

*Indicates statistically significant difference p < .05 (one-tailed test) between swing and non-swing or proximate election and distant election.

For a swing state, particularly in advance of an election, the influx of additional federal funds to the state is huge. The benefits are undeniable, and the motive—the president's electoral interest—appears quite obvious.

Legislative Effects

In the grant dollars models, the results show that a senator's membership on the Senate Appropriations Committee is associated with about a 7.6 percent increase in grant dollar allocations to his or her state. This finding is generally consistent with previous research that indicates a legislative influence in the distribution of federal dollars. However, the result is not robust across the number-of-grants models. That is, membership on the Senate Appropriations Committee appears to have no effect on the number of grants that a state receives, although the finding approaches statistical significance. In due deference to the impact of Congress, this distinction may not signify a diminished

benefit for key legislators; instead, it may reflect the type of benefits that legislators prefer.[26] Taken as a whole, the results suggest that there exist both executive and legislative pressures on the allocation of federal grants.

However, these results cannot detail whether the source of the congressional
effect is driven by Congress itself or by the president. The distinction is an
important one. The benefits that Senate appropriators enjoy are likely indirect,
given the discretionary authority of the president. Grants may—and likely do
in many cases—get allocated because of legislative requests. Yet presidents and
political appointees have the authority to deny such requests. It could also be
some combination of legislative pressure and presidential acquiescence.

Beyond the effect of membership on the Senate Appropriations Committee, there is very little support for partisan, institutional, or electoral influences
of Congress. In general, the estimates for legislative effects are not robust, are
null, or are inconsistent with regard to positive legislative effects. As mentioned
previously, employing measures of legislative influence is difficult, given the
unit of analysis used with these data. However, the myriad variables used
generate little support for congressional effects. While the results demonstrate
that a presidential electoral effect is at play, they do not categorically indicate
that Congress is unable to influence federal grant distribution. It can only be
argued that the results presented here offer limited support for congressional
effects. This distinction may appear minor but is critical to understanding the
scope of the findings.

An Extended Look at Presidential Electoral Strategy

The models presented in tables 3-5 and 3-6 offer evidence that presidential electoral interests influence the geographic distribution of federal grants.
Swing states receive more grants and grant dollars than do core states and non-
swing states. Furthermore, the proximity of a presidential election changes the
way in which grants are allocated, increasing both the number of grants and
grant dollars allocated to the states.

However, the timing variables specified in both models describe only the
effect of time on allocations to *all* states. While the evidence suggests that
federal grant allocations are strategically timed, it does not provide a comprehensive explanation of that strategy. To understand allocation strategy
more completely, it is important to examine the intersection of timing and
geographic distribution. To do that, I re-estimate the number-of-grants and

---

26. As mentioned previously, Congress uses block grants and formula grants as more direct
mechanisms to influence outcomes.

grant dollars models using variables that interact the timing and swing state variables. Table 3-7 presents the results of the estimation. In all four models, state electoral competitiveness is a dichotomous measure of whether a state is a swing state. The first and third models are specified with variables that interact "swing state" with "first term." The second and fourth models interact "swing state" with "election proximity." The addition of these variables and the extended analyses are critical. Specifically, they offer a disentangling of sorts, providing insight into whether the proximity of an election affects swing and non-swing states differently. One would suspect that if the presidential electoral strategy is pervasive, electoral competitiveness would not just affect the distribution of grants but also the timing of distribution. This analysis offers a more nuanced evaluation of both strategic timing and geographic allocation.

The results presented in table 3-7 show that the proximity of a presidential election continues to play an important role in the distribution of funds. Although the interaction terms fail to reach statistical significance, the parameter estimates suggest that swing states receive more grants and grant dollars when an election is proximate than when it is distant.[27] The results from the interaction of proximity and competitiveness and the implications of the variable for the fit of the model offer additional support for the expectations from hypothesis 2. They suggest that presidents act strategically with regard to both where and when grants are allocated.

Moreover, the estimates suggest that swing states receive more grants and grant dollars in a president's *second* term than in the first. Hypothesis 3 suggests that presidential self-interest should lead to increased grant allocations in the first term. A contrary finding could be attributable to presidential, executive branch, and appointee learning curves and acclimation periods. Influence during the first term may be artificially low as new members of the executive branch face a type of on-the-job training.[28] Such factors may conform with a liberal interpretation of the estimates reported in table 3-7. In reality, the findings offer very limited, non-robust statistical and substantive support for the claim that more grants are allocated in the second term than in the first

27. Further, F tests on the impact of the interaction variables for each model show that the interaction variables have a significant impact on model fit for both models analyzing grant dollars. For the election proximity interaction, $F = 79.95$, $p < .0001$; for the term interaction, $F = 54.99$, $p < .0001$.

28. The ideal test of this proposition would require a three-term presidency in which acclimation effects would exist during the first term, the president would develop electoral self-interest during the second term, and the president could not succeed himself after the third term. However, the 22nd Amendment to the U.S. Constitution bars this test.

Table 3-7. *Models of Federal Discretionary Grants, Including Timing Variables*[a]

	Number of grants		Grant dollars	
Variable	Model 1	Model 2	Model 3	Model 4
State competitiveness				
Swing State (0,1)	0.083*	0.062*	0.067	0.040
	(0.035)	(0.031)	(0.041)	(0.033)
Timing				
First Term (0,1)	−0.001	−0.009	0.038	0.025
	(0.015)	(0.011)	(0.027)	(0.020)
Election Proximity (0,1)	0.101**	0.090**	0.066**	0.054**
	(0.008)	(0.010)	(0.014)	(0.017)
Swing × Term	−0.018	—	-0.030	—
	(0.026)		(0.044)	
Swing × Proximity	—	0.025	—	0.028
		(0.020)		(0.030)
State-level congressional controls				
Senate Appropriations Committee (0,1)	0.046	0.048	0.076	0.077
	(0.032)	(0.032)	(0.038)	(0.038)
Appropriations Committee Election Year (0,1)	0.006	0.006	0.018	0.019
	(0.018)	(0.018)	(0.027)	(0.027)
Incumbent Senator Election Year (0,1)	−0.006	−0.006	−0.043*	−0.043*
	(0.014)	(0.013)	(0.019)	(0.019)
Competitive Senate Election (0,1)	−0.011	-0.011	0.013	0.013
	(0.023)	(0.023)	(0.025)	(0.025)
Senate Leadership (0,1)	−0.045	−0.044	0.045	0.046
	(0.031)	(0.031)	(0.055)	(0.056)
Majority Party Membership (0,1)	−0.003	−0.003	0.002	0.001
	(0.009)	(0.009)	(0.017)	(0.017)
House Delegation with President (0,1)	−0.005	−0.005	0.027	0.026
	(0.022)	(0.022)	(0.026)	(0.025)
Cardinals (0,1)	0.003	0.005	−0.010	−0.008
	(0.030)	(0.030)	(0.033)	(0.034)
Intergovernmental controls				
Governor Election Year (0,1)	0.006	0.007	0.046*	0.047*
	(0.017)	(0.017)	(0.021)	(0.021)
Governor-President Party Alignment (0,1)	0.0004	0.001	−0.031	−0.031
	(0.020)	(0.020)	(0.026)	(0.026)
Governor Election Year × Alignment (0,1)	−0.044*	−0.045*	0.008	0.007
	(0.022)	(0.022)	(0.031)	(0.030)
Controls and constant				
Real Gross State Product	−0.951**	−0.948**	−0.112	−0.108
	(0.114)	(0.114)	(0.127)	(0.127)
Roads (miles)	−0.080	−0.076	−0.175	−0.179
	(0.225)	(0.225)	(0.176)	(0.179)
Research Institutions	−0.002	−0.002	−0.001	−0.001
	(0.001)	(0.001)	(0.002)	(0.002)
Percent Elderly	−0.125**	−0.126**	−0.093*	−0.094*
	(0.038)	(0.039)	(0.039)	(0.040)
Disaster	0.017	0.018	0.963**	0.964**
	(0.038)	(0.036)	(0.283)	(0.281)
Constant	6.981*	6.924*	17.656**	17.602**
	(3.049)	(3.054)	(2.637)	(2.706)
R^2	0.44	0.44	0.10	0.10
Observations	650	650	650	650

a. The dependent variable in models 1 and 2 is the logged number of grants per 100,000 people per state-year. The dependent variable in models 3 and 4 is the logged real grant dollars per 100,000 people per state-year. All models are estimated using ordinary least squares with fixed effects for state and year. Robust standard errors are reported. In all models, the reference case for state competitiveness is Non-Swing State.

**p < .01 (one-tailed test); *p < .05 (one-tailed test).

Given that those findings are also inconsistent with the expectations from the third hypothesis, one can be comfortable that the relationship between grant allocations and presidential term is spurious.

In sum, the results from table 3-7 are mixed and limited in their support of hypotheses 2 and 3. They suggest that a relationship may be present, but the interaction variables may be over-specifying the model and limiting the ability of the estimation technique to sort out a clear relationship. As an additional test of hypotheses 2 and 3, I divide the data according to state competitiveness and re-estimate them. The results of this analysis, reported in table 3-8, add context to the interactions reported in table 3-7. These results show that the failure of the interaction of competitiveness and election proximity is driven by the robustness of the election proximity effect. More clearly, when an election is proximate, presidents generally allocate more grants and grant dollars overall than when an election is distant. Although there is suggestive evidence that presidents allocate more funds to swing states when an election is proximate, the general flood of money to the states overall in advance of presidential elections blurs the statistical significance of this distinction. Such results could reflect some of the efforts that presidents make to strengthen their party, particularly as elections draw near.[29] The president's effort to serve his own electoral interest may occur simultaneously with his effort to party-build—both of which affect distribution as elections near. Table 3-8 offers support for the robust electoral effects in the distribution of funds, both with regard to targeting allocations to key states and a party-building effect.

Table 3-8 also reports mixed results for presidential term effects. Hypothesis 3 predicts that while presidential electoral preferences should be salient across a president's tenure, the personal nature of the electoral interest in the first term should increase that salience. This analysis challenges that claim, showing little empirical ability to tease out robust term effects, particularly with regard to state electoral competitiveness. The estimates reported in the preceding tables offer evidence of a more continuous electoral interest— one unaffected by the institutional and electoral implications of the 22nd Amendment.

These findings demonstrate that the proximity of a presidential election motivates a change in executive branch allocations of federal grants. During the two years prior to a presidential election, the executive branch allocates a significantly higher percentage of grants, and grant dollars are concentrated in swing states. The evidence indicates not only that presidents think about

29. See Galvin (2010).

Table 3-8. *Models of Federal Discretionary Grants, Isolated for Competitiveness*[a]

	Number of grants		Grant dollars	
Variable	Swing state	Non-swing state	Swing state	Non-swing state
Timing				
First Term (0,1)	0.029*	0.017	0.047	0.050*
	(0.017)	(0.017)	(0.032)	(0.029)
Election Proximity (0,1)	0.101**	0.078**	0.080**	0.056**
	(0.019)	(0.012)	(0.030)	(0.022)
State-level congressional controls				
Senate Appropriations Committee (0,1)	0.028	0.058	0.034	0.178**
	(0.044)	(0.039)	(0.047)	(0.061)
Appropriations Committee Election Year (0,1)	−0.029	0.023	0.020	0.025
	(0.028)	(0.026)	(0.043)	(0.042)
Incumbent Senator Election Year (0,1)	−0.002	0.011	−0.033	−0.043
	(0.018)	(0.019)	(0.031)	(0.032)
Competitive Senate Election (0,1)	−0.031	−0.032	0.025	−0.009
	(0.023)	(0.030)	(0.029)	(0.034)
Senate Leadership (0,1)	−0.044	−0.015	0.084*	0.063
	(0.050)	(0.039)	(0.049)	(0.064)
Majority Party Membership (0,1)	−0.004	0.001	0.001	0.027
	(0.013)	(0.009)	(0.029)	(0.022)
House Delegation with President (0,1)	0.003	0.020	−0.023	0.039
	(0.022)	(0.029)	(0.051)	(0.034)
Cardinals (0,1)	−0.016	0.030	−0.033	0.015
	(0.045)	(0.050)	(0.058)	(0.049)
Intergovernmental controls				
Governor Election Year (0,1)	0.004	0.012	0.042	0.050
	(0.029)	(0.024)	(0.038)	(0.031)
Governor-President Party Alignment (0,1)	−0.046*	−0.014	−0.040	0.021
	(0.027)	(0.027)	(0.045)	(0.026)
Governor Election Year × Alignment (0,1)	−0.035	−0.073*	0.031	−0.009
	(0.036)	(0.028)	(0.046)	(0.045)
Controls and constant				
Real Gross State Product	−0.653**	−0.831**	0.207	−0.256
	(0.158)	(0.126)	(0.190)	(0.169)
Roads (miles)	0.765*	−0.037	0.845*	0.383*
	(0.324)	0.169	(0.388)	(0.200)
Research Institutions	−0.003	−0.002	−0.003	−0.001
	(0.001)	(0.002)	(0.003)	(0.002)
Percent Elderly	−0.111	−0.116**	−0.203**	−0.036
	0.064	(0.043)	(0.071)	(0.040)
Disaster	—	−0.018	—	0.795**
		(0.030)		(0.239)
Constant	−5.770	4.973*	8.086	16.434**
	(3.830)	(2.852)	(5.880)	(3.510)
R^2	0.50	0.42	0.004	0.02
Observations	278	372	278	372

a. The dependent variable in the number of grants models is the logged number of grants per 100,000 people per state-year. The dependent variable in the grant dollars models is the logged real grant dollars per 100,000 people per state-year. All models are estimated using ordinary least squares with fixed effects for state and year. Robust standard errors are reported. In all models, the reference case for state competitiveness is Non-Swing State.

**p < .01 (one-tailed test); *p < .05 (one-tailed test).

states in terms of electoral competitiveness but that the urgency of electoral demands motivates increasingly strategic grant allocations.[30]

Analyzing Influence

Research into executive branch politics seeks to understand changes in the presidency over time. Researchers consider, among the changes, whether and how the president has become more responsive to political or electoral considerations. The dawning of the politicization (or perhaps hyper-politicization) of the U.S. presidency has been pegged at numerous points in time, including Nixon's second term, the period following Carter-era bureaucratic reforms, the Reagan presidency, and the Clinton years. What is clear is that the Office of the President is now more politically and electorally motivated than in previous periods (see Ragsdale 1997).

Because of this institutional transformation, the findings presented here may not extend to earlier eras of the presidency, and it is unclear from previous research what would be an acceptable historical starting point. However, it is quite likely that the findings of this project will inform understanding of the presidency into the future. The politicization of the presidency and the strategic use of appointees that were seen in the Reagan era and that accelerated during the Clinton and George W. Bush administrations will, at the very least, ensure that the presidency remains a highly political institution. It is therefore important to evaluate how politics influences presidential behavior.

Several implications emerge from the results presented in this chapter. In a very straightforward way, presidents care about their own electoral interests and use their influence over the federal largesse to further their goals. This finding adds to a growing literature that argues that presidents, like members of Congress, are motivated by elections and behave in a manner that reflects electoral concerns.[31] Specifically, presidents engage in a targeted and electorally strategic allocation of government funds to crucial constituencies (states). This finding echoes recent work that suggests that electoral considerations motivate and inform presidential influence over the distribution of funds.[32]

---

30. As a final test on the robustness of the findings regarding the interaction terms, I reestimated the data by splitting the sample according to the elements of the interactions. Appendix table 3A-2 separately examines proximate and distant elections data, testing the effect of the swing state variable on both dependent variables. This analysis offers additional support for the theoretical claims in the central analysis in this study.

31. Shaw (2006); Shaw and Roberts (2000); Canes-Wrone and Shotts (2004).

32. Berry, Burden, and Howell (2010); Berry and Gersen (2010).

However, rather than showing that presidents use funds to aid co-partisans in their bids for reelection, this analysis shows that presidents are concerned with their own electoral interests.

In short, this chapter demonstrates that the often overlooked executive branch plays an important and influential role in the distribution of federal funds. The literature in this area often and accurately argues that Congress plays an important role in distributive politics, and this analysis also offers support for that claim. The power to allocate federal dollars is not dominated by a single branch of government; it is shared.

An important distinction in research evaluating presidential power emerges from the type of spending being analyzed. This study uses federal discretionary grants for an important reason: the executive branch has authority over the distribution of those funds. Unlike some other types of funds (or federal outlays generally), federal grants—which compose a nontrivial portion of annual spending—offer presidents a clear path to participate in pork barrel politics. In any study of the strategic distribution of government funds by elites, it is important to consider both the motive and opportunity to influence allocations. Discretionary authority offers presidents the opportunity to influence the process. Because the executive branch also maintains authority over the allocation of spending in other areas, such as contracts and procurement, the findings presented here have broader implications, extending into any of the areas of spending in which the president and the executive branch have the opportunity to influence outcomes directly.

Given the institutional design of the Electoral College and the nature of competition in presidential elections, swing states serve as the key constituencies in the race for the White House. By delivering funds to these states, presidents seek to perform a basic and strategic task in distributive politics: to target constituencies with a "relatively high willingness to abandon their ideological preferences in exchange for particularistic benefits."[33] In this way, federal grants function as an incumbent-controlled pool of campaign funds that presidents and their subordinates are able to allocate strategically.

This research also engages the distributive politics literature that focuses on the recipient constituency. Studies debate whether core constituencies (see, for example, Levitt and Snyder 1995) or swing constituencies (see, for example, Dixit and Londregan 1996) benefit most in the allocation of funds. The core-state hypothesis is often posed in the context of legislative elections and reflects a strategy that is particularly effective in popular elections. This study

---

33. Dixit and Londregan (1996, p. 1133).

lends support to the theory that there is a positive bias toward swing constituencies in the presidentially influenced allocation of federal government funds.

However, I also suggest that presidents may make more nuanced calculations regarding the distribution of grants within states. While this chapter suggests an interstate swing state bias in distribution, it does not preclude a differently motivated distribution bias at the intrastate level. For example, Chen (2009) argues that within the swing state of Florida, FEMA grants are delivered to core constituencies in the state's eastern counties. Such a finding may be entirely consistent with the results of this analysis, which simply suggests which states receive more grants. Research that examines intrastate grant funding may well find that presidents target core constituencies within swing states in an attempt to enhance their electoral prospects. Conversely, research may demonstrate that the swing state bias is true at both the inter- and intrastate levels. The analysis presented in this chapter offers support for the swing hypothesis in presidential elections specifically at the interstate level, as is consistent with the institutional design of the Electoral College.

Finally, the analysis presented here pertains strictly to presidential influence and behavior and offers evidence that the distribution of federal grants reflects a strategy consistent with presidential electoral preferences. It does not necessarily speak to the effectiveness of this strategy on voting behavior. A presidential administration has an annual duty to distribute federal grants. Because the bureaucracy is charged by Congress to perform that duty with discretion, the executive branch's allocation of grants is relatively low cost. Because grants offer an annual pork barrel opportunity for presidents, serve as an opportunity for media advertising, and can be targeted in strategic ways, grants are allocated to states that are electorally important to a president. Presidential elections can be decided by a few hundred popular votes in a single state or set of states. The allocation of grants, therefore, is a nearly costless action that may have the ultimate payoff.

Conclusion

Just as members of Congress indulge in earmarking and fiddle with funding formulas, presidents use executive branch discretion over federal grants to advance their own electoral interests. Federal grants provide presidents credit-claiming opportunities in key constituencies, such as swing states, and they direct federal grants to those states, particularly in advance of a presidential election. It appears that all else being equal, applying for a grant from a swing state may be a more fruitful endeavor than applying for one from a non–swing state. Moreover, the bureaucracy's generosity is greatest in advance of a presidential election.

While this analysis offers support for research that posits that swing constituencies receive more government funds, it offers a more nuanced interpretation of that research. For example, this work suggests that interstate fund distribution is consistent with the swing hypothesis, but intrastate distribution may not be. The institutional structure of the Electoral College can allow (and may encourage) different distribution strategies at the inter- and intrastate levels.

Moreover, this study suggests the importance of incorporating presidential power and executive branch influence into studies of distributive politics. However, the extent of presidential influence in the realm of federal spending may depend in large part on the type of spending. As the literature on delegation suggests, presidential power is most effective in areas with the greatest executive discretion. Future research must shift away from an examination of aggregate federal outlays and focus more clearly on the independent effects associated with specific types of spending.

Finally, this analysis suggests that students of the U.S. presidency should consider the possibility that executive behavior may be less exceptional than is often argued in the literature. Although presidential and congressional powers and duties are certainly different, presidential behavior is likely to be driven by the same basic forces that motivate members of Congress and other elected officials. In a fundamental way, presidents are election-minded individuals who depend on electoral success to influence outcomes, accomplish secondary goals, and advance their political agenda.

Appendix 3A-1. *Description of Variables*

Variable	Coding	Source
Dependent variable		
Number of Grants	Logged number of grants per 100,000 people per state-year	Census Bureau (2011a)
Grant Dollars	Logged real grant dollars per 100,000 people per state-year	Census Bureau (2011a)
Electoral competitiveness		
Swing State	Dichotomous, based on incumbent two-party presidential vote from previous election if share is between 45 and 55 percent	*CQ's Politics in America*[a]
Core State	Dichotomous, based on incumbent two-party presidential vote from previous election if share is greater than 55 percent	*CQ's Politics in America*[a]
Lost Cause State	Dichotomous, based on incumbent two-party presidential vote from previous election if share is less than 45 percent	*CQ's Politics in America*[a]
Timing		
First Term	Dichotomous, 1 = First presidential term	
Election Proximity	Dichotomous, 1 = Presidential election year and prior year	
State-level congressional controls		
Senate Appropriations Committee	Dichotomous, 1 = State is represented on the Senate Appropriations Committee	*CQ's Politics in America*[a]
Appropriations Committee Election Year	Dichotomous, 1 = State has a senator on the Appropriations Committee who is up for reelection in a given year	*CQ's Politics in America*[a]
Incumbent Senator Election Year	Dichotomous, 1 = State has a senator seeking reelection in a given year	*CQ's Politics in America*[a]
Competitive Senate Election	Dichotomous, 1 = State has a competitive Senate election in a given year as defined by *CQ Weekly* ranking "leans" or "no clear favorite"	*CQ's Politics in America*[a]
Senate Leadership	Dichotomous, 1 = State is represented by a senator who is a floor leader, whip, or caucus chair	*CQ's Politics in America*[a]
Majority Party Membership	Number of senators from a state from the majority party in the Senate (0,1,2)	*CQ's Politics in America*[a]
House Delegation with President	Dichotomous, 1 = State has a majority of the House delegation from the president's party	*CQ's Politics in America*[a]
Cardinals	Dichotomous, 1 = State has a representative who serves as chair of a House Appropriations Subcommittee	*CQ's Politics in America*[a]

Variable	Coding	Source
Intergovernmental controls		
Governor Election Year	Dichotomous, 1 = Governor is up for reelection in a given year	*CQ's Politics in America*[a]
Governor-President Party Alignment	Dichotomous, 1 = Governor and president come from the same party	*CQ's Politics in America*[a]
Governor Election Year × Alignment	Dichotomous, interaction of Governor Election Year and Governor-President Party Alignment	
State controls		
Real Gross State Product	Logged real gross state product	Bureau of Economic Analysis (2012)
Roads	Logged miles of roads	Federal Highway Administration (2008)
Research Institutions	Number of hospitals and universities	National Center for Education Statistics (2012)
Percent Elderly	Percentage of population aged 65 and over	Census Bureau, (2001, 2011b, 2012)
Disaster	1 = New York in 2001, 2002, 2003; Louisiana and Mississippi in 2005, 2006, 2007	

a. Includes McCutcheon and Lyons (2009); Koszcuk and Stern (2005); Stern (2001); Duncan and Lawrence (1997).

Appendix 3A-2. *Model of Federal Discretionary Grants,
Isolated for Election Proximity*[a]

	Number of grants		Grant dollars	
Variable	Proximate	Distant	Proximate	Distant
State competitiveness				
Swing State (0,1)	0.091**	0.057*	0.045	0.050
	(0.033)	(0.031)	(0.039)	(0.034)
Timing				
First Term (0,1)	0.090**	−0.115**	0.178**	−0.144**
	(0.016)	(0.016)	(0.024)	(0.029)
State-level congressional controls				
Senate Appropriations Committee (0,1)	0.047	0.053	0.069	0.113*
	(0.030)	(0.054)	(0.044)	(0.057)
Appropriations Committee Election Year (0,1)	−0.055	0.031	−0.019	0.010
	(0.028)	(0.026)	(0.051)	(0.054)
Incumbent Senator Election Year (0,1)	0.025	−0.029	−0.120**	0.034
	(0.019)	(0.023)	(0.024)	(0.043)
Competitive Senate Election (0,1)	−0.002	−0.011	0.037	−0.017
	(0.027)	(0.019)	(0.027)	(0.023)
Senate Leadership (0,1)	−0.036	−0.046	−0.059	0.044
	(0.031)	(0.047)	(0.048)	(0.078)
Majority Party Membership (0,1)	0.004	−0.015	0.016	−0.020
	(0.013)	(0.010)	(0.021)	(0.014)
House Delegation with President (0,1)	−0.019	−0.005	0.011	0.035
	(0.024)	(0.026)	(0.030)	(0.030)
Cardinals (0,1)	−0.023	0.048	−0.063	0.056
	(0.034)	(0.049)	(0.039)	(0.071)
Intergovernmental controls				
Governor Election Year (0,1)	0.061*	−0.045*	−0.002	0.057
	(0.028)	(0.021)	(0.047)	(0.035)
Governor-President Party Alignment (0,1)	−0.021	−0.032	−0.015	−0.052
	(0.027)	(0.019)	(0.046)	(0.036)
Governor Election Year × Alignment (0,1)	−0.064**	−0.005	−0.093	0.078*
	(0.042)	(0.024)	(0.051)	(0.043)
Controls and constant				
Real Gross State Product	−0.715**	−1.127**	0.038	−0.178
	(0.124)	(0.119)	(0.144)	(0.155)
Roads (miles)	−0.262	−0.216	−0.464	0.516*
	(0.286)	(0.207)	(0.269)	(0.287)
Research Institutions	−0.001	0.000	0.001	−0.001
	(0.002)	(0.001)	(0.002)	(0.002)

Variable	Number of grants		Grant dollars	
	Proximate	Distant	Proximate	Distant
Percent Elderly	−0.122**	−0.128**	−0.153**	−0.041
	(0.045)	(0.036)	(0.053)	(0.054)
Disaster	−0.048	0.051	0.835**	1.088**
	(0.051)	(0.033)	(0.106)	(0.379)
Constant	6.046	10.425**	23.448**	13.852**
	(3.517)	(2.931)	(3.512)	(4.055)
R^2	0.43	0.48	0.17	0.003
Observations	350	300	350	300

a. The dependent variable in the number of grants models is the logged number of grants per 100,000 people per state-year. The dependent variable in the grant dollars models is the logged real grant dollars per 100,000 people per state-year. All models are estimated using ordinary least squares with fixed effects for state and year. Robust standard errors are reported. In all models, the reference case for state competitiveness is Non-Swing State.

**$p < .01$ (one-tailed test); *$p < .05$ (one-tailed test).

4

Aiding and Abetting the President: The Role of Federal Agencies

> Article I Section 9 says, clearly, we are the ones who are supposed to make these spending determinations in Congress. Now there are a lot of spending determinations that are made that I bitterly oppose. But if you say that you end all—they call them "earmarks". . . . then that means all that is going to be done by Barack Obama in the White House. It will go to the Executive.
>
> —Senator James Inhofe, March 14, 2010[1]

In the quotation that opens this chapter, Senator James Inhofe (R-Okla.) refers explicitly to a battle that is constantly being waged between the executive and legislative branches of government regarding which one controls public policy. Inhofe defends the power of Congress to direct federal agencies in the allocation of funds. Failure to provide direction amounts to what Senator Richard Lugar (R-Ind.) calls a "surrendering of Constitutional authority to Washington bureaucrats and the Obama Administration."[2] Two issues drive this debate and underlie the senators' concerns: To whom are agencies responsive? Whose preferences do agency outcomes reflect?

Agency responsiveness to political elites has long been a topic of interest to scholars. Research usually characterizes agency responsiveness in terms of a uniform relationship between the bureaucracy and particular political actors. However, not all agencies function in such a way that Congress (or the president or the agencies themselves) is singularly empowered to affect all policy outputs. Instead, because the system of separated powers drives compromises regarding the creation, reauthorization, existence, and behavior of agencies, a

1. Jeffrey (2010).
2. Lugar (2010).

diversity of interests influences policymaking. The responsiveness of agencies to those interests is a function of interbranch relations and agency design, which itself is a product of interbranch relations.

The debate in which Senators Lugar and Inhofe engage—about the proper exercise of power and the responsiveness of policy to politicians—is not just a pet cause of theirs. Nor is the debate restricted to a particular year or Congress or to the Obama presidency. Questions over power sharing between the legislative and executive branches have been raised since the earliest days of the republic and permeate every facet of federal policy. Addressing these questions is central to understanding how the U.S. government functions and the effects that it has on the lives of citizens.

The previous chapter made it clear that more federal grants flow to swing states than non–swing states—an outcome consistent with the president's electoral interests. Understanding *that* presidents engage in pork barrel politicking is interesting and informative, but it fails to illustrate exactly *how* politicking occurs. Much of the remainder of this book sheds light on the "how."

One way to examine how presidents inject electoral politics into grant making is to look at the details of the administrative process and at how presidential power and influence vary across a burgeoning bureaucracy. Most work examining federal fund distribution fails to account for a simple fact: not all agencies are created equal. The Department of Commerce and the Environmental Protection Agency are likely to distribute funds differently. This chapter takes on that task, offering deeper detail about the presidential pork barrel.

The Myth of Agency Homogeneity

The executive branch is a large, diverse, and unique macro institution with component parts that operate in dramatically different ways. Bureaucratic institutions are often not the product of efficient design but of political compromise, and their structural features have important implications for their function. In fact, agencies often are designed for the purpose of facilitating or hindering political and policy influence from specific elected officials.

As a result of the varied nature of bureaucratic organization, any theory of presidential policymaking must incorporate institutional effects on political influence and policy outcomes. In simple terms, to know how presidents get agencies to work for them, it is important to know how agencies themselves work. However, research on distributive policy assumes homogeneous responsiveness across agencies, and that assumption manifests in a multitude of ways. One approach examines federal spending at the aggregate level. Often annual fund allocations to states or congressional districts serve as the unit of analysis;[3] in fact, that is the approach that I use in chapter 2 of this book. Such research offers insight into how government operates at the macro level, but texture and context about individual agencies and structures are lost.

Another approach entails a detailed examination of the allocation process of one or a few federal agencies that serves as a basis for drawing conclusions about broad government outlays.[4] These approaches either assume that distributive federal agencies operate similarly or treat them as wholly unique entities. As research in this area advances, a natural next step that has received less attention[5] is to focus on how institutional variation and trends influence agency operation and responsiveness to principal political actors.[6] Because specific agency characteristics are intended to affect political control over policy, an analysis that focuses on agency-level variation is critical to a comprehensive understanding of presidential control over distributive policy specifically and bureaucratic behavior generally.

Research into the presidential pork barrel must acknowledge, as Moe notes, that "structural choices have important consequences for the content and direction of policy."[7] In other areas of policy research, scholars have discussed myriad agency structures and characteristics that affect agency responsiveness and outcomes. Generally, those characteristics fall into one of two categories: external (design) traits and internal (behavior) traits—the latter of which can, of course, be a product of agency design. External traits, which are numerous, include politicization, centralization, insulation and independence, and discretion, among others. Internal behavioral traits can include agency ideology, professionalization and expertise, and the personality of bureaucrats.[8]

3. Berry, Burden, and Howell (2011); Hoover and Pecorino (2005); Larcinese, Rizzo, and Testa (2006); Shor (2006).

4. Bertelli and Grose (2009); Chen (2009); Gasper and Reeves (2011). To be clear, the authors cited here are clear to frame their findings with a sensitivity to the limitations of their generalizability.

5. But see Berry and Gersen (2010).

6. Of course, there may be many reasons for overlooking the importance of agency structure, including availability of data. I do not suggest that previous approaches represent a lack of thoughtful research design, only that the presidential pork barrel is an emerging area of research.

7. Moe (1989, p. 268).

8. For external traits, see Clayton (1992), Lewis (2008), Moe (1982), Nathan (1986), Randall (1979), Stewart and Cromartie (1982), Wood (1990), Hammond (1986), Moe (1985); Krause (1999), Lewis (2003), Moe and Wilson (1994), Seidman (1998), Seidman and Gilmour (1986), Wood and Waterman (1994). For internal traits, see Altfield and Miller (1984), Bertelli and Grose (2009), Bendor, Taylor, and van Gaalen (1985), Carpenter (2001), Clinton and Lewis (2008), Gailmard and Patty (2007), Heclo (1977), Huber and McCarty (2004), Rourke (1984), Wilson (1989), and Wood and Waterman (2004).

From a theoretical perspective, agency characteristics are critical to evaluating the presidential pork barrel. Distributive decisionmaking occurs within some agency (sub-presidential) hierarchy, so any theory of presidential intervention in policymaking must consider both presidential preferences in outcomes and the structural features of agencies that may affect their responsiveness to those preferences.

Agency Responsiveness to Presidential Preferences

To address the question of which agency characteristics influence agencies' responsiveness to presidential electoral preferences, it is important to consider the tools that presidents use to motivate agencies to respond. I argue that four specific institutional features condition agency responsiveness to presidential electoral interests: presidential discretion; agency proximity to White House control (insulation); the saturation of political appointees (politicization); and agency ideology. All four features affect the personnel and processes within agencies as well as agency outcomes. These features have been found to have substantial effects on policy and political control, and I provide a theoretical foundation for evaluating their effect on the president's ability to engage in pork barrel politics.

Moe and Wilson (1994) hold that four attributes of agencies condition the elected branches' power over the bureaucracy. "The design, location, staffing, and empowerment of administrative agencies," the authors write, all influence the ability to control the institutions of the executive branch.[9] Such attributes are key components of agency operations and can dictate not just the level of political control but which branch of government exercises control. A fuller understanding and accounting of each allows insight into the means by which presidents control agencies and how that control translates into presidential pork.

Discretion: The Gateway to Presidential Pork

Presidents rely on institutional mechanisms to control bureaucratic institutions. The first means by which presidents obtain greater responsiveness is through the discretionary powers delegated to them by Congress. Discretion is the lifeblood of executive power and offers presidents their primary opportunity to affect policymaking. In some statutes Congress meticulously outlines not only public policy processes but also expected outcomes. On the other hand, when the locus of decisionmaking is the executive branch, presidential influence is greatest. Discretion can be obtained when Congress relies directly

9. Moe and Wilson (1994, p. 4).

on agencies (delegates its authority) to make policy decisions; when congressional inaction allows executive interpretation of vague statutes; and from unilateral action by the president.[10]

Congress delegates to presidents discretionary spending authority over tens of billions of government dollars annually. I control for discretion by examining federal discretionary grants. For the grants under analysis, I view discretion as present; in other areas of spending, however, discretion (and thus presidential power) is limited or nonexistent. The analysis in this chapter focuses more closely on variation in the other institutional features described below.

Insulated Independence: Keeping Your Friends Close

In addition to discretion, an agency's internal structure and location (its proximity to political influence) can affect responsiveness. The intersection of structure and location can lead to *insulated independence*. Insulated independence occurs when an agency is designed in such a way that presidential control over the agency is dramatically limited. In the political science literature, the definition of "independence" ranges from an agency's being located outside of a cabinet department[11] to an agency's having "no layers of bureaucratic organization above it."[12] According to those definitions both the Executive Office of the President and the Nuclear Regulatory Commission are independent, but the level of presidential control is quite different in each. Therefore, while institutional independence vis-à-vis location is important, it alone does not explain political control.

Instead, it is important to understand both internal structures (independence) and location (insulation). The internal structures of agencies can insulate them from direct presidential control and thus allow them to be less responsive to presidential preferences. Here, certain agency rules and obligations can serve as a buffer to political control. Lewis (2003) explains that if an agency is governed by a commission structure, it tends to be insulated "from presidential control by increasing the number of actors who must be

---

10. Epstein and O'Halloran (1999); Huber and Shipan (2002); Moe (1999); Cooper (2002); Howell (2003); Lewis (2003). If discretion empowers a president, even motivating him to enhance his electoral prospects, why would Congress delegate? Eisner argues that in a basic way, "delegation is the child of necessity" (Eisner 1991, p. 6) because lack of time and information are key congressional resource constraints (Epstein 1997; Epstein and O'Halloran 1999; Gilligan and Krehbiel 1987; Kiewiet and McCubbins 1991; Ripley and Franklin 1984). In addition, some describe delegation as a means of shifting blame (Fiorina 1977) or as a necessary part of coalition building in the legislative process (Arnold 1990; Epstein and O'Halloran 1999; McCubbins 1985).

11. Seidman and Gilmour (1986).

12. Lewis (2003, p. 46).

influenced to change the direction of an agency."[13] What Lewis called "specific qualifications for administrators,"[14] such as fixed or staggered terms of office and party balancing requirements, limit not only presidential influence but the effectiveness of appointees as presidential agents. In this way, insulated independence closely reflects what Krause (1999) calls "the institutional proximity of bureaucratic and political institutions."[15] The location of an agency and the president's access to the policymaking mechanisms within that agency influence the president's control and ability to extract policy benefits for political or electoral gain.[16] Therefore the Nuclear Regulatory Commission would rightly be treated as among the most independent of agencies, while the Executive Office of the President would be viewed as the least independent.

The term "insulated independence" is a piece of jargon and surely not a catchy one, but the concept that it represents is far from esoteric. The term is meant to convey how the design of an agency facilitates (or hinders) the ability of the president to reach into that agency and pull out the policy outcomes that he desires—and that ability has huge consequences for the functioning of government. In the context of federal spending, this concept is easy to identify. For example, budgets (both proposals and spending decisions) in cabinet agencies like those in the Department of Commerce almost always are subject to internal executive branch oversight from the White House's very powerful and equally political Office of Management and Budget. That ensures that agencies, offices, and programs within the department are bureaucratically and institutionally linked to the president. However, an independent commission like the Securities and Exchange Commission does not face the same internal checks from the White House. It has a level of independence not shared by agencies of the Department of Commerce and fosters a serious limitation on presidential power. Insulated independence therefore affects not only how different institutions allocate federal funds but how capable the president is of influencing allocations.

Politicization: The President's Handpicked Helpers

When institutional features such as insulated independence limit presidential influence, the chief executive can rely on other institutional processes. For example, the appointed leaders of individual agencies can have an important impact on responsiveness. The number of appointees within bureaucratic institutions, which varies dramatically across agencies, affects responsiveness, as

13. Ibid., p. 46.
14. Ibid., p. 27.
15. Krause (1999, p. 37).
16. Seidman and Gilmour (1986); Seidman (1998); Wood and Waterman (1994).

does the saturation of political appointees within an agency (politicization).[17] Presidents staff the upper echelons of federal agencies with individuals who are sympathetic to their interests (including electoral interests) and who, because they occupy key leadership and decisionmaking positions, have a dramatic effect on policy outcomes.[18]

The appointment power can have profound effects on how closely policy outcomes mirror presidential preferences. Agencies that are organized with few if any presidential appointees are likely to be more responsive to other forces (Congress, interest groups, or their own preferences). However, more politicized agencies are likely to respond to presidential will. Nathan (1986) explains that presidents use signals to convey their satisfaction with outcomes—or lack of it—and says that if signals are "used skillfully . . . [they] can reinforce the idea that presidential appointees should pursue presidential purposes and should devote time and attention to administrative process."[19]

Appointees generally affect policy in three distinct ways. They serve as core decisionmakers or gatekeepers of outcomes, adjusting policy recommendations from career staff in ways that affect policy results for a variety of political and nonpolitical reasons (essentially an ex post appointee effect). Appointees also convey to career staff information about leadership and presidential preferences and make clear their expectations about policy outcomes (an ex ante appointee effect).[20] Finally, appointees can design or redesign internal agency processes to ensure that outcomes reflect their and the president's interests (a deterministic appointee effect). In the context of the presidential pork barrel, appointees can directly control the targeting of funds or create an environment that produces a similar responsiveness among bureaucratic actors.

In an agency with a relatively high proportion of political appointees in leadership positions, such as the Rural Housing Service or the Federal Aviation Administration, politics can be more pervasive. By virtue of their numbers, appointees have more time and resources to affect and monitor behaviors

---

17. Clayton (1992); Lewis (2008); Moe (1982); Randall (1979); Stewart and Cromartie (1982); Wood (1990). Politicization is not entirely separable from insulated independence, but each concept describes unique aspects of the administrative process and affects responsiveness differently. Politicization focuses on the saturation of appointees within an administrative agency. Although insulated independence incorporates aspects of the appointment power (particularly limitations), it also involves the location of the agency vis-à-vis White House staff, budgetary proposal power, regulatory requirements, and rules governing the president's appointment power.

18. Lewis (2008); Moe (1982, 1985); Nathan (1986); Snyder and Weingast (2000); Stewart and Cromartie (1982); Wood and Waterman (1991, 1994).

19. Nathan (1986, p. 91).

20. That information can be conveyed in a multitude of ways, including through staff meetings, memorandums, mission statements, and administrative directives.

within agencies and to coordinate communication environments within agencies in order to help ensure that their interests and those of the president are enacted into policy. In agencies with more political appointees, the task of politicizing spending decisions—targeting key recipients in key areas at key times—is easier than it is in a less politicized agency. That is not to say that less politicized agencies are incapable of such behavior. However, more political staff can surely facilitate more political decisionmaking.

Agencies, Ideology, and Politics

Ideological congruence between an agency and the president, which is influenced by agency staffing and design, is another important condition for bureaucratic responsiveness. Congruence—a result motivated by shared preferences and overlapping interests—facilitates the production of policy that is consistent with presidential goals. The ideology of bureaucrats and appointees has been shown to influence the type of policy produced[21] as well as its responsiveness to presidential preferences.[22] Beyond shared interests, ideologically proximate agencies also see external benefits to having an ideologically congruent president (or successor) elected or reelected. For example, the Department of Health and Human Services administers the Temporary Assistance for Needy Families (TANF) program. During the Clinton administration, this program replaced the Aid to Families with Dependent Children (AFDC) program as part of the welfare reform legislation signed into law in 1996.[23] The TANF program, as the name implies, assists needy families, and it does so through a policy solution generally supported by liberals and opposed by conservatives. Accordingly, the mission and the agency tend to be supported by Democratic presidents. TANF, then, is a program that would be ideologically congruent with the preferences of a Democratic president and ideologically divergent from those of a Republican president.

The ideology of a bureaucratic institution is influenced by three key factors. First, the mission of an agency naturally lends itself to a specific range of outcomes. Second, individuals may self-select into agencies that pursue friendly policy goals, leading to staff-level homogeneity within an institution. Finally, burrowing—a practice whereby appointees take career positions in agencies with which they align ideologically—can entrench agency ideology.[24]

---

21. Clinton and Lewis (2008).

22. Bertelli and Grose (2009).

23. The legislation was formally titled the Personal Responsibility and Work Opportunity Reconciliation Act of 1996 (P.L. 104-193).

24. Burrowing also can occur when individuals take positions in agencies whose mission they oppose in order to change policy and processes. However, such efforts are limited in number and their effectiveness remains unclear.

Agency responsiveness thus depends on the unique relationship between an agency and presidential preferences and powers. By design, certain agencies are likely to be more responsive to presidential (electoral and policy) preferences because of their institutional proximity to the White House. However, in situations in which agencies are more insulated (or an agency is subject to drift[25]), factors such as politicization and ideological congruence influence presidential power and affect responsiveness.

From this theoretical discussion, I present a few basic hypotheses to test agency responsiveness to presidential electoral interests. These hypotheses predict the manner in which agency structure affects presidential influence over agencies and ultimately how responsive agencies are to presidential electoral preferences.

—*Hypothesis 1 (insulated independence hypothesis)*: Insulated agencies will be less responsive to presidents' electoral interests.

—*Hypothesis 2 (politicization hypothesis)*: More politicized agencies will be more responsive to presidential electoral interests.

—*Hypothesis 3 (ideological congruence hypothesis)*: Liberal agencies will be more responsive to a Democratic president's electoral interests and conservative agencies to a Republican president's electoral interests.

Data

To analyze the questions presented in this chapter and to test my hypotheses, I examine agency-level discretionary grant allocations to the states during the 1996–2008 period. Drawn from the same datasets presented in the previous chapter, these data have been organized so that the unit of analysis is the agency-state-year. More specifically, each datapoint measures an agency's annual allocation in grant dollars to a given state. This step refines the grants data from chapter 3 by allowing for the examination of variation in agency characteristics. The result is a database of 59,650 agency-state-year allocations.[26] Table 4-1a presents an overview of the average annual allocations

25. Agency or bureaucratic drift occurs when the behaviors or outputs of an agency depart (or drift away) from the preferences of appointees or the president.

26. Between 1996 and 2008, 152 agencies allocated grants to the states. However, not every agency allocated funds in every year. Agencies that failed to allocate any funds in a given year do not appear in the dataset for that year. Also excluded was a set of data that were allocated not under an agency heading but under a departmental heading. For example, the allocation label "Department of Agriculture" was too broad to be considered consistent with other agency-specific data; allocations so labeled therefore were excluded.

Table 4-1a. *Average State-Year Grant Allocation by Source, 1996–2008*[a]
Dollars, millions

Institution	Average allocation	Institution	Average allocation
Cabinet departments		*Independent agencies*	
Defense	3.5	Agency for International Development	2.1
Agriculture	2.0	NASA	9.1
Commerce	2.3		
Justice	45.2	*Independent commissions*	
Labor	0.4	Appalachian Regional Committee	1.1
Energy	14.3	National Endowment for the Humanities	1.7
Education	15.1		
HHS	59.0		
Homeland Security	99.6		
HUD	14.4		
Interior	1.3		
State	0.2		
Transportation	33.1		
Treasury	0.1		
Veterans Administration	0.002		

Source: Census Bureau (2011a).
a. Allocations are the mean state-year allocations in millions of real dollars. For both independent agencies and commissions, two examples of each type are provided.

Table 4-1b. *Examples of Agencies and Levels of Politicization*[a]

Agency (Department)	Politicization ratio
Centers for Disease Control (HHS)	0.1
Fish and Wildlife Service (Interior)	0.1
Agricultural Marketing Service (USDA)	0.1
Occupational Safety and Health Administration (Labor)	0.5
Office of Bilingual Education and Minority Language Affairs (Education)	0.5
National Historical Publications and Records Commission (IND)[b]	0.5
Office of Community Planning and Development (HUD)	1.0
Office of Justice Programs (Justice)	1.0
Federal Aviation Administration (Transportation)	1.0
Office of the Secretary (HUD)	5.0
Minority Business Development Agency (Commerce)	5.0
Rural Business-Cooperative Service (USDA)	5.0

a. The politicization ratio represents the ratio of appointees to career Senior Executive Service managers (Lewis 2008).
b. IND indicates that an agency is independent.

by agencies in each cabinet department and independent institution. The table shows that while some departments typically distribute large sums of money, grant making occurs across the bureaucracy. For this analysis, like that in chapter 3, I employ two related dependent variables[27] that measure grant distribution: grant dollars and the number of grants.[28]

Independent Variables of Interest

Many of the core ideas examined in this chapter reflect those in chapter 3, with one key exception. The analysis in this chapter deals with several of the key agency-level features hypothesized to influence political control and the distribution of federal funds. Because there are many general similarities between the data, many of the independent variables used in this chapter are also used in chapter 3. To avoid a redundant description of those variables and their measurement, in this chapter I focus on the differences. Variables such as state electoral competitiveness ("swing state"), election proximity, presidential term, gubernatorial variables, control variables (miles of roads, percent elderly, gross state product, and so forth), and many of the congressional variables are measured identically. However, differences do exist. The new variables can be divided into two categories: agency characteristics and additional congressional controls.[29]

Agency Characteristics

As mentioned, there are four features that should affect a president's ability to extract electoral benefits from federal agency funding decisions: discretion, insulated independence, politicization, and ideological congruence. Because discretion is held constant due to the type of spending used in this analysis (federal discretionary grants), the three other features are used to understand presidential power in this context.

To capture an agency's insulated independence, I use a multipart measure that accounts for both the location and structure of agencies, which may insulate them from (or make them susceptible to) political control. Theoretically, there is a continuum of insulated independence, ranging from the most

27. Specifically, I examine the logged number of grants allocated by an agency per state-year. In all models using this measure, I also include a control variable measuring state population in millions. Next, I measure logged real grant dollars per 100,000 people as a dependent variable. This dependent variable naturally controls for the effects of population differences among states and for inflation over time.

28. All models are separately estimated for each dependent variable. This approach offers key insights into allocations at the agency level and serves as a robustness check on the general findings.

29. See appendix table 4A-1 for a complete description of the variables.

political control to the most independence. I formalize this continuum by designating institutions within the Executive Office of the President as the most political and independent commissions as the most insulated; in between are cabinet institutions and independent agencies.[30] I use four indicator variables that denote a bureaucratic institution as being a cabinet secretary's office, a cabinet bureau,[31] an independent agency, or an independent commission.[32]

Next, I include a measure of agency politicization, using the standard measure from Lewis (2008). Specifically, politicization is the ratio of the number of presidential appointees to the number of career-level Senior Executive Service (SES) managers within an agency. (A sample of agencies and politicization scores can be found in table 4-1b.) When one thinks of political appointees, cabinet secretaries who endure challenging confirmation hearings often jump to mind. In reality, there are thousands more appointees who do not appear on television and are not quoted in newspapers. Political appointees fill over 3,000 positions in the executive branch. Besides those confirmed by the Senate, there are Schedule C appointees and non-career SES appointees. My measure of political appointees includes all of those positions. This measure notes the number of political appointees in the decisionmaking structure of agencies relative to the number of senior civil servants. The term "politicization"—and the method of measurement here—simply considers how plentiful political appointees are in the leadership of a federal agency relative to non-appointed leaders (managers). This technique is both straightforward in terms of evaluating the power or potential power of political actors in the bureaucracy and is widely accepted among political scientists as a measure of their power.

Agencies have an almost innate ideology, based on a variety of factors, that can facilitate or hinder presidential power. To measure agency ideological congruence, I compare agency "ideal points" to those of the party of the president, creating a dichotomous measure. Ideal points, developed by Clinton and Lewis, estimate an ideological score for an agency on a liberal-conservative scale.[33] As noted above, the missions of some agencies have natural similarities to ideological causes, and many people believe that federal agencies and the policies that

30. An independent agency is an agency without the structure of a commission, located outside the cabinet or Executive Office of the President. The true measure would be a five-part metric or a series of five dummy variables, wherein the least independent entity is one located within the Executive Office. None of those entities is included in this dataset.

31. A "cabinet bureau" for the purposes of this analysis refers to any grant-making cabinet institution that is not a secretary's office.

32. Data on agency structure and location are drawn from David Lewis's *Administrative Agency Insulation Data Set* (https://my.vanderbilt.edu/davidlewis/data/).

33. Clinton and Lewis (2008).

they produce often are ideological. Comparing the innate ideology of an agency to that of the party of the president provides an important metric for analyzing agency responsiveness. The measure takes the value of 1 for a liberal agency under a Democratic president or a conservative agency under a Republican.

Additional Congressional Controls

Congressional effects are a central alternative explanation for the politicized or electorally sensitive distribution of federal funds. In chapter 3, the modeling goes to great lengths to control for congressional influence. The modeling presented in this chapter allows for an even more refined analysis, incorporating additional measures of congressional influence, particularly at the agency level. These measures include variables measuring a state's representation on House and Senate appropriations subcommittees that have oversight of the agency allocating grants. Because of the tremendous and clear oversight role that the appropriations committees—and their subcommittees—play in monitoring the behavior of federal agencies, these measures offer a direct evaluation of Congress's distributive power and the influence of key members. It is safe to assume that if congressional influence occurs, it will translate into clear benefits for politically interested individuals.

Analyzing Agency Responsiveness to Presidential Electoral Interests

To answer the questions and test the hypotheses presented above, I offer systematic analysis of the grants data in the context of presidential influence over agencies. For all models and both dependent variables, I first estimate the data using ordinary least squares with fixed effects for state and year. Second, I estimate the data using Tobit,[34] given the left censoring of data at zero.[35] The

34. The ordinary least squares method offers insight into this variation in an important, conservative way. However, the abundance of "zero allocations" (left censoring of the data) presents a methodological challenge. In the data, as much as 30 percent of the observations are zero, as many federal grant programs do not allocate universally to all states in all years. Estimating censored data with ordinary least squares can bias estimates downward (Amemiya 1984; Greene 1993; Tobin 1958). Employing Tobit accounts for this characteristic of data. Tobit therefore serves as an appealing alternative while further demonstrating that ordinary least squares with fixed effects is a more conservative estimation technique.

35. Appendix tables 4A-2, 4A-3, and 4A-4 provide estimates of all models employing Tobit to estimate the data. Generally, the findings are robust across estimation techniques; at the very least, the Tobit estimates are imprecise but in the expected direction. For each table in this section of this chapter, there is an appendix table with a corresponding number. For example, appendix table 4A-2 uses Tobit to estimate the same data presented in table 4-2.

empirical effort proceeds as follows. First, I conduct a direct test of hypothesis 1, estimating the effect of insulated independence on agency responsiveness. Second, to evaluate clearly the effects of other institutional characteristics at each level of agency insulation, I divide the data by agency type. I next test hypotheses 2 and 3, estimating the data that include politicization and ideological congruence for each level of insulated independence. In each model, I interact the independent variables of interest with the swing state variable to evaluate responsiveness to presidential electoral interests.

In clearer terms, I first test whether the location of an agency (in terms of proximity to White House power) influences presidential control over the distribution of funds. Then I examine each type of agency (based on location) separately and test whether the saturation of political appointees or the ideology of an agency relates to responsiveness to the president in the distribution of funds.

An Overview of Presidential Influence

Table 4-2 reports the results of the analysis that evaluates the effect of insulated independence on responsiveness to presidential electoral interests. In the first two models, I use a four-part measure of insulated independence that divides cabinet institutions into secretaries' offices and bureaus and divides independent institutions into agencies and commissions. In the next two models, all cabinet institutions fall under the same heading, creating a three-part measure with independent agencies and independent commissions. Broadly speaking, the results support the idea that insulation influences agency responsiveness to presidential electoral interests. More specifically, in an agency in which presidential influence is expected to be stronger, the president is able to reap the most electoral benefits. Cabinet institutions allocate approximately 28 percent more grants to swing states than to non–swing states, which translates into a substantial increase in resources for states that are competitive in presidential elections. For a state of average population, like Tennessee, the results suggest that if it were a swing state, it could expect to see agency-level grant allocations increase by over $4 million a year. In addition to grant dollars, swing states can expect to receive a 10 percent increase in the number of grants allocated.

Conversely—and consistent with the expectations of hypothesis 1—the most insulated type of institution, independent commissions, are less responsive to presidential electoral interests. Because "independent commissions" is the reference category for insulated independence, the estimate for "swing state" suggests that in independent commissions, swing states receive significantly fewer federal grants than do non–swing states. This finding indicates

Table 4-2. *The Effect of Insulated Independence on Discretionary Grant Allocations, 1996–2008*[a]

Variable	Cabinet Secretary Office/ Cabinet Bureau		Cabinet Agency	
	Grant dollars	Number of grants	Grant dollars	Number of grants
State competitiveness				
Swing State	−0.218*	−0.080	−0.218*	−0.080
	(0.121)	(0.055)	(0.121)	(0.055)
Agency characteristics				
Cabinet Secretary Office	−0.455**	−0.609**		
	(0.132)	(0.052)		
Cabinet Secretary Office × Swing State	0.292	0.081		
	(0.199)	(0.079)		
Cabinet Bureau	−0.137	−0.562**		
	(0.084)	(0.038)		
Bureau × Swing State	0.274*	0.100*		
	(0.123)	(0.056)		
Cabinet Agency			−0.159*	−0.566**
			(0.084)	(0.038)
Cabinet Agency × Swing State			0.275*	0.099*
			(0.123)	(0.055)
Independent Agency	−1.347**	−1.025**	−1.355**	−1.027**
	(0.124)	(0.052)	(0.123)	(0.052)
Independent Agency × Swing	0.377*	0.165*	0.377*	0.165*
	(0.181)	(0.078)	(0.181)	(0.078)
Liberal Agency	2.131**	1.005**	2.129**	1.004**
	(0.042)	(0.017)	(0.042)	(0.017)
Staff (logged)	0.317**	0.192**	0.319**	0.193**
	(0.010)	(0.004)	(0.010)	(0.004)
Congressional controls				
Senate Appropriations Committee	0.007	0.030	0.007	0.030
	(0.074)	(0.031)	(0.074)	(0.031)
Senate Majority Party	0.010	0.003	0.010	0.003
	(0.023)	(0.009)	(0.023)	(0.009)
Incumbent Senator Election Year	−0.006	0.003	−0.006	0.003
	(0.050)	(0.020)	(0.050)	(0.020)
Senate Leader	0.021	0.010	0.021	0.010
	(0.085)	(0.037)	(0.085)	(0.037)
Senator with Oversight	0.107*	−0.028	0.107*	−0.028
	(0.049)	(0.020)	(0.049)	(0.020)
House Member with Oversight	0.042	−0.023	0.042	−0.023
	(0.039)	(0.018)	(0.039)	(0.018)

Variable	Cabinet Secretary Office/ Cabinet Bureau		Cabinet Agency	
	Grant dollars	Number of grants	Grant dollars	Number of grants
Intergovernmental controls				
Governor Election Year	−0.017	−0.003	−0.017	−0.003
	(0.066)	(0.026)	(0.066)	(0.026)
Governor-President Party Alignment	−0.043	−0.003	−0.043	−0.003
	(0.050)	(0.020)	(0.050)	(0.020)
Governor Elect × Alignment	0.015	0.000	0.015	0.000
	(0.087)	(0.034)	(0.087)	(0.034)
Controls and constant				
Real Gross State Product (logged)	−0.327	−0.185	−0.327	−0.185
	(0.465)	(0.225)	(0.466)	(0.225)
Miles of Roads (logged)	−0.341	−0.061	−0.341	−0.061
	(0.535)	(0.195)	(0.536)	(0.195)
Research Institutions (logged)	−0.288	−0.122	−0.289	−0.122
	(0.514)	(0.211)	(0.514)	(0.211)
Percent Elderly	0.055	−0.019	0.055	−0.019
	(0.072)	(0.027)	(0.072)	(0.027)
Disaster	0.243	0.057	0.243	0.057
	(0.163)	(0.074)	(0.163)	(0.074)
Population (logged)		0.355		0.355
		(0.326)		(0.326)
Intercept	10.409	−1.316	10.404	−1.312
	(9.606)	(4.987)	(9.608)	(4.988)
Observations	5,9050	59,050	59,050	59,050
Adjusted R^2	0.06	0.12	0.06	0.12

a. All data are estimated using ordinary least squares with fixed effects for state and year. Agency clustered standard errors are reported. In the first two models, the cabinet-level institutions are divided into Cabinet Secretary Office and Cabinet Bureau. In the second two models, all cabinet-level institutions are grouped under the same variable, Cabinet Agency.

**$p < .01$ (one-tailed test); *$p < .05$ (one-tailed test).

that independent commissions allocate funds based on considerations other than the president's electoral interests and offers further evidence of the effectiveness of insulation in limiting presidential power. It is consistent with the broader theoretical claim about the effect of agency design on presidential control. Where the president's appointment power is limited and when the White House's Office of Management and Budget has little if any influence, agencies are less responsive to the president.

The estimates for the interaction between "independent agency" and "swing state" prove interesting as well. Despite efforts to insulate independent agencies from political control—through, for example, limits on budgetary proposal power and regulatory review and their removal from cabinet influence—these agencies are responsive to presidential electoral interests. Specifically, independent agencies allocate over 37 percent more grant dollars and 17 percent more grants to swing states than to non–swing states. This finding suggests that despite efforts to insulate independent agencies, presidential influence still motivates responsiveness to electoral interests.[36]

The estimates reported in table 4-2 offer clear statistical evidence of this relationship, but the substantive effects are even more forceful. Figure 4-1 translates table 4-2 into real effects for states. It demonstrates that less insulated agencies are responsive to presidential influence while the most insulated commissions resist it. Moreover, this figure offers insight into the substantive impact of agency responsiveness to presidential electoral interests. In agencies in which presidents wield greater political control—cabinet institutions and independent agencies—annual agency-level grant funding to swing states is hundreds of thousands of dollars greater than funding to non–swing states. These effects have a serious impact on the daily lives of residents of these states. For those living in swing states, there are real financial benefits; in other states, the political and electoral environment leads to substantial shortfalls in federal funding that can have serious consequences for policy and society.

To evaluate more clearly how differences in insulation across bureaucratic institutions affect responsiveness, I divide the data according to each type of agency; I am thus able to control for agency insulation and determine whether other institutional characteristics influence responsiveness in similar ways. In doing so, I re-estimate the divided data and include measures of politicization and ideological congruence (as well as the interaction of each with the swing state variable). This analysis offers insight into how bureaucratic politics affects distributive public policy. Dividing the data controls for agency type (level of insulation) and allows for clearer analysis of not only the effect of state electoral competitiveness but also of politicization and agency ideology.[37] In the process it offers a direct evaluation of hypotheses 2 and 3 while providing additional detail on the effects of presidential power within federal agencies.

36. While the dollar estimates for the interaction of "independent agency" and "swing state" are substantively more significant than the interaction estimates for cabinet and swing, the two are statistically indistinguishable.

37. This analysis also avoids the messiness of interpreting three-way interactions, offering more digestible findings to the reader.

Figure 4-1. *The Effect of State Electoral Competitiveness on Grant Dollar Allocations by Agency Insulation*[a]

Thousands of dollars

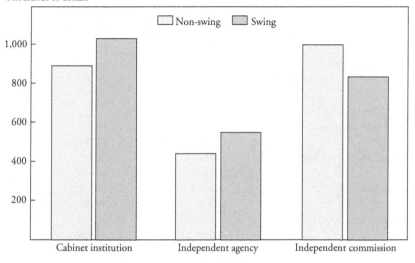

a. For each institution the difference between funding to swing and non-swing states is statistically significant at the p < .05 level (one-tailed test).

Pervasive Presidential Power: The Cabinet

Table 4-3 reports the estimates for cabinet-level data. There is robust support for responsiveness to presidential electoral interests across the models. Cabinet secretaries' offices allocate 46 percent more and cabinet bureaus allocate over 12 percent more grants to swing states than to non–swing states. These findings clearly show the extent of presidential power within the cabinet. There is responsiveness to presidential electoral interests across cabinet institutions; however, variation exists within the cabinet, and that variation is consistent with expectations about presidential power. Where loyalty to the president should be strongest, in the offices of cabinet secretaries, electoral responsiveness is greatest. More than any other entity, secretaries' offices deliver more grant money to swing states than to non–swing states. Cabinet secretaries are often key presidential loyalists who have some of the greatest White House access, and presidents are more likely to have direct contact with cabinet heads than with other members of the bureaucracy. Loyalty and access generate a scenario in which it comes as no surprise that grants flowing directly from the offices of cabinet secretaries reflect presidential interests most clearly.

Table 4-3. *Effects of Politicization and Ideological Congruence on Discretionary Grant Allocations for Cabinet Secretary Offices and Cabinet Bureaus, 1996–2008*[a]

Variable	Cabinet Secretary Office		Cabinet Bureau	
	Grant dollars	Number of grants	Grant dollars	Number of grants
State competitiveness				
Swing State	0.460*	0.124*	0.122*	0.036
	(0.199)	(0.050)	(0.063)	(0.027)
Agency characteristics				
Ideological Congruence	–0.058	–0.077	–0.355	–0.137
	(1.245)	(0.382)	(0.281)	(0.131)
Congruence × Swing State	–0.338	–0.101	–0.033	–0.016
	(0.250)	(0.079)	(0.068)	(0.024)
Politicization (logged)	–1.109	–1.211*	0.176	0.212
	(1.265)	(0.426)	(0.667)	(0.349)
Politicization × Swing State	–0.226*	–0.065*	–0.068	–0.002
	(0.080)	(0.025)	(0.054)	(0.029)
Liberal Agency	8.577**	3.796**	1.624*	0.791*
	(1.313)	(0.442)	(0.894)	(0.403)
Staff (logged)	0.625	–0.024	0.243	0.173*
	(0.666)	(0.219)	(0.212)	(0.088)
Congressional controls				
Senate Appropriations Committee	–0.140	–0.018	–0.053	0.005
	(0.165)	(0.036)	(0.063)	(0.025)
Senate Majority Party	–0.056	–0.017	0.017	0.004
	(0.030)	(0.009)	(0.013)	(0.004)
Incumbent Senator Election Year	–0.117	–0.036	0.005	0.007
	(0.119)	(0.019)	(0.024)	(0.006)
Senate Leader	–0.076	0.050	0.014	0.001
	(0.259)	(0.077)	(0.058)	(0.017)
Senator with Oversight	0.281	0.055	0.239*	0.029
	(0.218)	(0.053)	(0.102)	(0.048)
House Member with Oversight	0.357**	0.104	0.120*	0.016
	(0.065)	(0.069)	(0.065)	(0.035)
Intergovernmental controls				
Governor Election Year	–0.053	–0.009	–0.023	–0.003
	(0.107)	(0.028)	(0.026)	(0.008)
Governor-President Party Alignment	0.097	–0.001	–0.058*	–0.009
	(0.136)	(0.031)	(0.028)	(0.009)
Governor Elect × Alignment	0.067	0.003	0.013	–0.002
	(0.122)	(0.031)	(0.035)	(0.011)

Variable	Cabinet Secretary Office		Cabinet Bureau	
	Grant dollars	Number of grants	Grant dollars	Number of grants
Controls and constant				
Real Gross State Product (logged)	−3.285	−1.586*	−0.098	−0.070
	(2.326)	(0.622)	(0.395)	(0.139)
Miles of Roads (logged)	−4.029*	−0.129	−0.104	−0.054
	(1.781)	(0.294)	(0.365)	(0.113)
Research Institutions (logged)	−4.274	−0.476	−0.107	−0.089
	(2.448)	(0.565)	(0.286)	(0.086)
Percent Elderly	−0.062	−0.136	0.069	−0.017
	(0.285)	(0.120)	(0.076)	(0.028)
Disaster	0.018	0.002	0.239*	0.064*
	(0.401)	(0.123)	(0.117)	(0.031)
Population (logged)		1.327		0.252
		(0.801)		(0.183)
Intercept	103.605*	4.909	4.666	−1.762
	(39.598)	(15.807)	(7.622)	(3.264)
Observations	2,650	2,650	47,900	47,900
Adjusted R^2	0.66	0.78	0.04	0.10

a. All data are estimated using ordinary least squares with fixed effects for state and year. Agency clustered standard errors are reported.

**p < .01 (one-tailed test); *p < .05 (one-tailed test).

Next, I consider whether the ideological congruence of a cabinet institution weakens or enhances responsiveness to the president. The results in table 4-3 fail to find a relationship between agency-president ideological alignment and agency responsiveness. While this finding is inconsistent with the expectations of hypothesis 3, it actually fits neatly with the broader view of presidential power presented in this chapter. This finding suggests that cabinet institutions are responsive to the president regardless of their ideological relationship to him, likely for one of two reasons. The institutions may operate under an expectation of responsiveness, viewing the president, as the head of the executive branch, essentially as a bureaucratic CEO whose interests must be promoted. Alternatively, presidential power is likely its strongest within the cabinet because the chief executive is able to wield myriad powers free of the types of restrictions that exist in independent institutions. Regardless of the reasoning, presidential power within the cabinet is pervasive and allows presidents to engage effectively in pork barrel politics.

Interestingly, in cabinet secretaries' offices, the interaction of "politicization" and "swing state" produces a significant and negative estimate, suggesting that in more politicized secretaries' offices, swing states receive fewer grant dollars than non–swing states. This finding is contrary to the expectations of hypothesis 2. There may be a few explanations for this outcome. First, politicization is not an entirely exogenous concept. Presidents have the power to manipulate agency politicization by increasing or decreasing the number of appointees in a given institution. The theoretical expectation is that in agencies with a greater saturation of political appointees, responsiveness is stronger. However, presidents may politicize cabinet secretaries' offices that are less responsive in an effort to recapture control. In the same vein, if a small cadre of political appointees is ensuring responsiveness in another secretary's office, the president may effectively and strategically de-politicize an office without reducing his influence or the office's responsiveness while freeing up appointees to serve elsewhere.

A methodological reason may explain this result as well. Because of the limited number of cabinet secretaries' offices (fourteen or fifteen) generally[38] and in this dataset specifically (seven), a small number of offices in highly politicized agencies could drive such results, especially because politicization in a given entity is relatively stable over time.

The estimates for the relationship between politicization and responsiveness for cabinet bureaus—cabinet institutions other than secretaries' offices—speak more clearly to this effect. In bureaus, there is no relationship between politicization and responsiveness. This finding once again suggests that the influence of a president over his cabinet is substantial and pervasive and that cabinet bureaus are broadly responsive to his electoral interests regardless of ideology or the saturation of appointees. Once again, a null finding for the interaction of "swing state" and "politicization" is inconsistent with the expectations of hypothesis 2. However, one explanation is that in the bureaus, sub-agencies, and offices captured in the "bureau" variable, grant decisionmaking may not be done by a complex network of appointees; instead, a small number of appointees may make grant decisions. By having a small core of

38. The Department of Homeland Security was created in 2003, during the period analyzed in this study. From 1996 to 2002, there were fourteen cabinet secretaries' offices; from 2003 to 2008, there were fifteen.

decisionmakers, the White House can target its influence more easily and an agency can be responsive without the need for a profound saturation of appointees. The result is that presidents can extract responsiveness from cabinet bureaus whether there are several or few appointees as long as decision-making is structured effectively.[39]

Influence in Independent Institutions

I also estimate the effects of politicization and ideological congruence on responsiveness for independent institutions (see table 4-4). The analysis presented here is similar to that in the previous section; the only difference is that table 4-4 applies that modeling to independent institutions, generally, and this section focuses on independent agencies, specifically. In general terms and as noted above, independent institutions function quite differently from cabinet institutions.

Table 4-4 presents divided data—grant funding only for independent agencies and independent commissions. The division of data allows for a more nuanced understanding of the function of these independent institutions and helps clarify the findings. At first glance, it appears that the findings in table 4-4 are inconsistent with those reported in table 4-2. Table 4-2 suggests that independent agencies respond to presidential electoral interests, funneling money to swing states. Table 4-4 suggests no such direct relationship.

However, table 4-4 does not refute the idea that presidential power over federal funding extends into independent agencies. Instead, it illustrates the means by which that power manifests—a critical element in understanding the relationship between an agency's function and presidential influence. In independent agencies, the saturation of political appointees (politicization) greatly affects an agency's responsiveness to the president's electoral interests. In more *politicized* independent agencies, swing states receive over 83 percent more grant dollars than non–swing states. The estimate for the interaction between "politicization" and "swing state" suggests the critical role that appointees play, particularly in agencies structured in part to be independent of White House influence. Unlike in cabinet agencies, where presidential influence is more pervasive, independent agencies' responsiveness to presidential electoral interests depends on political appointees.

---

39. It should be noted that in cases in which few appointees are required to approve grants, the risk of drift increases because the capability for intra-institutional monitoring is reduced. That said, it appears that despite such risks (and perhaps because of the ability of presidents to move or remove political appointees), agencies remain broadly responsive to presidential electoral interests.

Table 4-4. *Effects of Politicization and Ideological Congruence on Discretionary Grant Allocations for Independent Agencies and Commissions, 1996–2008*[a]

Variable	Independent Agencies		Independent Commissions	
	Grant dollars	Number of grants	Grant dollars	Number of grants
State competitiveness				
Swing State	−0.234*	−0.067	−0.265	−0.064
	(0.126)	(0.062)	(0.206)	(0.088)
Agency characteristics				
Ideological Congruence	−0.058	−0.082	−0.579	−0.310
	(0.423)	(0.162)	(0.494)	(0.255)
Congruence × Swing State	−0.046	0.058	0.214	−0.006
	(0.155)	(0.045)	(0.220)	(0.089)
Politicization (logged)	−2.321	−1.696	1.183	0.009
	(4.032)	(1.906)	(0.726)	(0.396)
Politicization × Swing State	0.838**	0.129	0.052	0.032
	(0.198)	(0.172)	(0.080)	(0.036)
Liberal Agency	−2.614	−1.058	8.922**	4.363*
	(3.174)	(1.465)	(2.727)	(1.516)
Staff (logged)	0.904	0.330	1.384**	0.573*
	(1.041)	(0.451)	(0.446)	(0.228)
Congressional controls				
Senate Appropriations Committee	0.379*	0.148*	−0.159	−0.049
	(0.171)	(0.063)	(0.101)	(0.032)
Senate Majority Party	−0.005	0.015	−0.019	−0.004
	(0.060)	(0.015)	(0.016)	(0.009)
Incumbent Senator Election Year	0.020	0.003	−0.066	−0.012
	(0.043)	(0.014)	(0.060)	(0.018)
Senate Leader	0.158	0.089	0.030	0.028
	(0.184)	(0.067)	(0.084)	(0.062)
Senator with Oversight	−0.496	−0.258	0.271	0.082
	(0.375)	(0.177)	(0.169)	(0.066)
House Member with Oversight	−0.350	−0.317*	−0.211	−0.026
	(0.269)	(0.160)	(0.231)	(0.102)
Intergovernmental controls				
Governor Election Year	0.041	0.001	0.032	-0.012
	(0.090)	(0.016)	(0.040)	(0.016)
Governor-President Party Alignment	−0.087	0.001	0.021	0.026
	(0.071)	(0.027)	(0.035)	(0.018)
Governor Elect × Alignment	0.078	0.032	−0.069	−0.018
	(0.103)	(0.029)	(0.045)	(0.017)

Variable	Independent Agencies		Independent Commissions	
	Grant dollars	Number of grants	Grant dollars	Number of grants
Controls and Constant				
Real Gross State Product (logged)	−0.301	−0.001	−1.294**	−0.876**
	(1.337)	(0.327)	(0.333)	(0.215)
Miles of Roads (logged)	−1.912*	−0.112	0.793	0.089
	(0.972)	(0.314)	(1.522)	(0.444)
Research Institutions (logged)	−0.301	−0.089	0.225	−0.158
	(0.678)	(0.197)	(0.593)	(0.194)
Percent Elderly	−0.020	−0.005	0.023	−0.008
	(0.164)	(0.047)	(0.075)	(0.062)
Disaster	0.654	0.004	0.011	0.082
	(0.501)	(0.059)	(0.190)	(0.101)
Population (logged)		0.574		0.815
		(0.493)		(0.514)
Intercept	26.140	−6.871	−5.914	−6.887
	(23.278)	(12.166)	(12.272)	(4.906)
Observations	4,350	4,350	4,150	4,150
Adjusted R^2	0.19	0.23	0.53	0.53

a. All data are estimated using ordinary least squares with fixed effects for state and year. Agency clustered standard errors are reported.

**$p < .01$ (one-tailed test); *$p < .05$ (one-tailed test).

Given the limits placed on regulatory review and White House budgetary influence and review, independent agencies are designed to be somewhat insulated from presidential control; political appointees therefore serve as the most important means for presidents to influence policymaking. The president relies on his handpicked executives to convey his preferences and work to overcome insulating structures and ensure that policy outcomes are consistent with his interests.

Figure 4-2 presents the estimates reported in the first two models of table 4-4. The effect of an increase in politicization on independent agency responsiveness to presidential electoral interests is clear. In agencies with low levels of politicization, state electoral competitiveness has no effect on grant allocations. However, in agencies with higher levels of politicization,[40] swing states

40. The difference in politicization used in this figure is a one-unit change.

Figure 4-2. *The Effect of Politicization, Ideological Congruence, and State Electoral Competitiveness on Grant Dollar Allocations for Independent Agencies*[a]

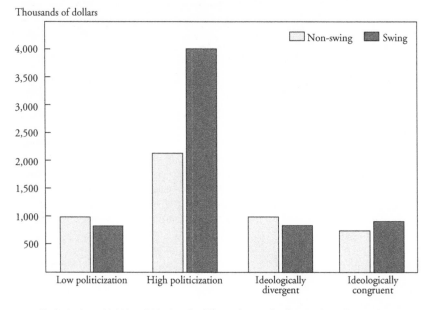

Thousands of dollars

a. For institutions with high politicization, the difference between funding to swing and non-swing states is statistically significant at the $p < .05$ level (one-tailed test). The differences for all other types are statistically indistinguishable.

benefit substantially in the receipt of grant dollars. This finding illustrates that when presidential surrogates saturate independent agencies, presidents are able to extract electoral benefits from them.

Figure 4-2 also demonstrates another significant consequence of politicization for federal spending. It shows that average baseline levels of grant funding in politicized agencies are markedly (and statistically significantly) higher than in less politicized agencies. In agencies with a higher percentage of political appointees, discretionary spending authority is greater, regardless of where funds are allocated.

This result begs the question: why do more politicized agencies have substantially more grant dollars to allocate? For the president, the preference for this scenario is easy to explain. If he is able to extract electoral benefits in highly politicized independent agencies, he will prefer that those agencies have more funding, as funding equals benefits. How, then, do presidents achieve such a scenario? It may come as a result of a president's negotiations with Congress for greater discretionary authority in agencies in which he has greater political control. As with the findings reported in chapter 2, which suggest that presidents bargain for greater discretionary authority when elections are proximate, the effect of politicization suggests that presidents also act strategically with respect to how they use that authority.[41]

The results reported here demonstrate that politicization facilitates presidential influence and motivates responsiveness, particularly where presidential power is institutionally limited. Taken together, the findings demonstrate the importance of understanding the role of institutional characteristics in limiting or enhancing presidential power. The characteristics that insulate independent agencies are effective in limiting responsiveness. However, despite those characteristics, presidents are still able to capitalize on specific tools in order to extract desired policy outcomes from the bureaucracy.

Resisting Influence: Independent Commissions

The estimates for independent commissions further emphasize the role of institutional characteristics in affecting the president's ability to reap electoral benefits from agencies. The findings generally support the idea that independent commissions are insulated from political control. There is no relationship between state electoral competitiveness and grant allocations. Similarly, the interactions also fail to reach statistical significance. These results show that independent commissions do not allocate grants in a way that benefits swing states at the expense of non–swing states.

Unlike in independent agencies, politicization does not facilitate greater responsiveness in independent commissions. This result reflects the limitations on the president's appointment power in commissions and other characteristics that buffer White House influence. Because of specific rules governing appointments—such as party balancing and fixed and staggered terms—appointees are not an effective means of achieving presidents' preferred outcomes. Often such restrictions mean that political appointees in independent commissions have been appointed by presidents other than the incumbent. In the end, commissions are effectively insulated against the desire of a president to extract outcomes consistent with his electoral interests.

The Influence of Congress

Thus far, the reach and limits of presidential power have been illustrated. However, previous research also shows that Congress or at least congressional

41. Also, presidents can add appointees unilaterally, though there are statutory restrictions on their ability to do so in some agencies.

interests influence federal funding decisions. To assess this alternative (or complementary) explanation, I include a host of traditional measures of congressional influence and also introduce some unique means of assessing it.

Across all models presented in this analysis, I test whether members of the Senate leadership or senators facing competitive reelection races reap added benefits in the form of additional grants. It would be expected that the institution's most powerful or vulnerable members would seek such perks. A Congress with influence, of course, is a Congress that helps itself. In general, the results presented in tables 4–2 to 4–4 show that Congress benefits little in the distribution of federal discretionary grants. This result is generally true for the traditional measures of political and institutional power and electoral need.

In addition to traditional measures of congressional influence, I test the power and influence of oversight. The House and Senate appropriations committees play fundamental roles in overseeing the executive branch with respect to federal funding. The data presented in this chapter allow a test of the influence of the whole Senate Appropriations Committee. I also assess the role of the House and Senate appropriations subcommittees overseeing specific agencies.

These members, given their critical oversight role of federal agency spending, may be positioned to reap substantial benefits. For example, in 2013 the House Appropriations Subcommittee for Agriculture[42] had twelve members, charged with developing funding bills for the agencies under their jurisdiction;[43] they also play a role in overseeing how those agencies spend their money. One would therefore expect that the states represented by those twelve members—often between nine and twelve different states—would see added funding from agriculture agencies. Keeping subcommittee members happy is critical for agriculture agencies because members have the power to make life in the Department of Agriculture quite difficult.

Membership on the broader Senate Appropriations Committee offers mixed results. Some models suggest a benefit, while others show no statistical relationship between a state's representation on the committee and grant funding. The one exception is that in independent agencies, Senate appropriators tend to receive about 38 percent more grant dollars and 15 percent more grants than states not represented (see table 4-4).

---

42. The formal name of the subcommittee is the House Appropriations Subcommittee on Agriculture, Rural Development, Food and Drug Administration, and Related Agencies.

43. For this subcommittee, jurisdiction includes the entire Department of Agriculture (except for the U.S. Forest Service), the Food and Drug Administration, and a few agriculture-related independent agencies and commissions.

When the focus is on the subcommittees with more specific oversight authority, identifiable trends exist. The results in tables 4-2 and 4-3 show that agencies direct funds to states represented by their overseers on the House and Senate appropriations subcommittees. These results either achieve statistical significance or approach significance. They are also robust across almost all models estimating grant dollars, and the substantive benefits of the subcommittee variables are reasonably consistent. This relationship is true for cabinet agencies in particular. The results suggest that states represented on the House and Senate subcommittees receive 28 percent and 36 percent more grant dollars respectively from cabinet secretaries' offices and 24 percent and 12 percent more grant dollars respectively from cabinet bureaus. These results mean that substantial funding flows into these states in ways that keep appropriations overseers happy.

In independent agencies and especially in independent commissions, congressional benefits are difficult to find. The results show no statistically significant or robust relationship between a state's representation on an appropriations subcommittee and increases in funding from relevant agencies. Although these subcommittees do exercise oversight and design funding bills for the agencies, there is little responsiveness in terms of grant funding. The one exception, mentioned above, is a single result indicating that independent agencies direct more funds (and grants) to states represented on the broader Senate Appropriations Committee than to states not represented. For independent commissions, there is no relationship between congressional power (electoral, political, institutional, or oversight) and the distribution of federal discretionary grants.

Taken together, these results indicate that insulated independence affects congressional influence as well as presidential influence. More specifically, in agencies in which presidents exercise more influence, there is greater responsiveness to congressional needs than in agencies insulated from presidential power.

Why might that be the case? At first, the relationship seems odd or counterintuitive. Yet a different perspective offers a clearer picture and additional insight into the source of the congressional benefits discussed in chapter 2. Funneling grant money to the states represented by congressional appropriators is not just in the interest of legislators; agencies, appointees, and presidents also profit. Less oversight, fewer reports, fewer conditions, and fewer threats of funding reductions offer presidents the opportunity to reap benefits: in this way, presidents help themselves by helping others (in Congress). The results presented here suggest that that is precisely what is happening. Members of Congress are not exercising proactive influence within agencies by directing discretionary funds to their districts and states. Instead, presidents and other actors in the executive branch are preemptively keeping key legislators satisfied in order to maintain the status quo. If Congress were somehow exercising its own power over discretionary grants through its oversight role (direct action or indirect pressure), it would do so across federal agencies. Instead, the results show that agencies with greater presidential influence are also more responsive to Congress. Agencies in which a president struggles to help himself are also unlikely to help provide benefits to legislative actors.

The result, of course, presents a second question in need of an answer: why would Congress—with oversight authority—not reap benefits from independent agencies and commissions? The answer rests in the type of funding analyzed. Specifically, the funds analyzed are ones in which executive branch institutions make allocation decisions. Although Congress may apply indirect pressure, the distribution of funds occurs elsewhere. In addition, there may be resistance among legislators from applying political pressure within institutions intended to be insulated from political forces. Finally, because independent agencies and commissions allocate funds in sums that pale in comparison to the bounty distributed by cabinet agencies, applying pressure may ultimately be seen as a high cost–low benefit enterprise.

In chapter 3, I note that in the context of Congress, these results cannot detail whether this effect is driven by Congress itself or by presidents seeking to placate Senate appropriators. However, the results presented in this chapter give greater weight to the latter. It appears that such a relationship exists not because of direct congressional action but because a strategic president uses his influence to provide benefits to appropriators in order to continue providing benefits to himself.

Implications for Future Work and Policymaking

This chapter provides additional support for the salience of electoral considerations among presidential incentives. An empirical approach to the study of executive branch politics that incorporates such interests is critical; the scope of the office and the powers and network of people available to the president mean that the administrative presidency has a more micro-level focus. Certainly, this analysis does not support the idea that the president makes a decision on every grant processed in the executive branch. Instead, through a transparent set of electoral preferences, institutional powers, and an army of appointed bureaucratic executives, agencies drive micro-level policy outcomes to be consistent with presidential electoral interests. Executive branch actors may be motivated to respond for a host of reasons including loyalty, political alignment, or the creation of a highly politicized administrative environment in which such behavior is expected.

The findings presented here show the importance of understanding the structure of bureaucratic institutions for the study of agency responsiveness to the president. The insulated independence of an agency, which determines its proximity to the political power and influence of the White House, is a critical first step in evaluating agency responsiveness. Cabinet institutions are broadly responsive to the president's electoral interests. However, independent institutions function differently; the mechanisms and institutional designs that structure independent agencies and commissions limit responsiveness. Rather than rendering a president powerless in all circumstances, agency insulation channels presidential influence into avenues that allow presidents to use key institutional powers to extract policy benefits to support their electoral interests. In independent agencies, presidents rely on political appointees to ensure that policy outcomes are consistent with presidential interests.

Politicization as a means of exerting influence and power within independent agencies is critical to understanding how the bureaucracy functions. Even within independent agencies that are designed to resist political influence, political appointees allow presidents to wield power and affect policy outcomes. That finding has substantial implications for the design of federal agencies, particularly at the legislative level. When designing an agency to be independent as a means of limiting presidential power, Congress should limit the number of political appointees—the president's central means of wielding political control and using policy outcomes as campaign tools—within the agency.

The findings for independent commissions further demonstrate the relationship between institutional design and bureaucratic responsiveness. In independent commissions, unlike in independent agencies, specific rules govern and limit the president's appointment power in order to insulate independent commissions even further. The results suggest that institutional traits such as fixed and staggered terms and party balancing requirements for commissioners do limit the president's ability to elicit responsiveness through politicization or other means.

The design of independent commissions has important consequences for presidential control; however, it does not offer legislators an effective means of corralling presidential power. While it is true that the commission structure limits presidential power, it also restricts legislative influence. Congress therefore should resist creating independent commissions because it impedes their own ability to reap the policy and political benefits of federal spending.

The findings presented here illustrate ideal scenarios for political elites who want to use federal agencies for political gain. Presidents should prefer agencies to be located in the cabinet because their ability to extract pork from cabinet institutions is quite pervasive and does not depend on politicization or ideology. Congress, on the other hand, should seek to create independent agencies and restrict the saturation of appointees in order to enjoy policy benefits and to limit presidential impact.

Conclusion

Understanding agency responsiveness to democratically elected officials is crucial to understanding how the machine of government functions and what forces generate public policy. Often, bureaucratic responsiveness is conceptualized as policy outcomes that reflect the ideological or partisan interests of political actors. I argue that this behavior occurs most often when a federal agency directs federal funds to key states in presidential elections. The National Park Service (NPS), which administers hundreds of nationally protected areas, is one such agency. Chief among those areas, of course, are America's national parks. Eight of the nation's fifty-eight national parks are found in California, the most populous state, where the total protected area is roughly the size of Massachusetts; in fact, thirty sites protected by NPS can be found in California. By comparison, Pennsylvania is the home to no national parks and only eighteen federally protected areas. Between 1996 and 2008, NPS allocated more than 200 percent more grants to Pennsylvania than to California. Despite California's population (300 percent larger), geographic size (400 percent larger), and number of areas protected by NPS (67 percent more), Pennsylvania, one of the most politically important states in presidential elections, saw dramatically more federal grants. In a federal agency situated in the president's cabinet (the Department of the Interior), such behavior should come as no surprise. This analysis suggests that agencies like the National Park Service, while not driven by presidential electoral incentives, are likely to be partly responsive to them.

Bureaucratic structures and design affect agency responsiveness to presidential electoral interests. In key ways, the level of independence and insulation has a significant effect on presidential control of the bureaucracy. However, insulated independence does not wholly stifle presidential control and agency responsiveness. Instead, institutional characteristics of bureaucracies that are intended to limit political (or electoral) influence simply redirect it through different avenues.

The unique behaviors and motivations behind agency responsiveness mark important structural features that lead to variable agency outcomes. The results reinforce the idea that structure matters both for outcomes and the incentives of the individuals operating within an institution. The proximity of institutions to direct political and administrative control, the presence of appointees, and the rules governing the selection of appointees all affect power, influence, and ultimately, responsiveness.

Similarly, the political responsiveness of agencies extends both to presidents and to key congressional constituencies. The findings presented here offer a more integrated view of responsiveness in the context of distributive politics, finding robust support for presidential influence in conjunction with that of Congress. I further suggest that benefits associated with congressional constituencies may come not from direct legislative intervention but from a president strategically seeking to maintain discretionary authority.

Future work must evaluate federal fund distribution and agency responsiveness in more nuanced ways. Institutional and electoral incentives must be considered for both the legislative and the executive branch; a simple focus on one ignores important variations associated with the other. An understanding of institutional differences within the executive branch is central to evaluating the avenues and extent of political control as well as the incentives that presidents face. In the same way that political elites' interests and motivations are multifaceted, so too are the institutional structures in which the component parts of the executive branch operate. These factors call for a more comprehensive and integrated theoretical and methodological approach to these important areas of public policy.

Appendix 4A-1. *Description of Variables*

Variable	Coding	Source
Dependent variables		
Number of Grants	Number of grants per agency-state-year	Census Bureau (2011a)
Grant Dollars	Logged grant dollars per 100,000 people per agency-state-year	Census Bureau (2011a)
Electoral competitiveness		
Swing State	Dichotomous, based on incumbent share of two-party presidential vote in previous election if share is between 45 and 55 percent	CQ's *Politics in America*[a]
Timing		
First Term	Dichotomous, 1 = First presidential term	
Election Proximity	Dichotomous, 1 = Presidential election year and prior year	
Agency Characteristics		
Ideological Congruence	Dichotomous, 1 = Liberal (conservative) agency under a Democratic (Republican) president	Clinton and Lewis (2008)
Politicization	Ratio of political appointees (Senate-confirmed, Schedule C, or non-career SES) to managers (career-SES)	Office of Personnel Management (2012)
Department Appointed Leadership	Count of number of appointees in offices of department leadership (that is, office of the secretary, office of policy)	
Cabinet	Dichotomous, 1 = Cabinet-level agency	Administrative Agency Insulation Data Set (Lewis 2003)
Independent Agency	Dichotomous, 1 = Independent agency	
Independent Commission	Dichotomous, 1 = Independent commission	

Congressional controls

Senate Appropriations Committee Member	Dichotomous, 1 = State is represented on Senate Appropriations Committee	*CQ's Politics in America*[a]
Senate Majority Party Member	Dichotomous, 1 = State is represented by a majority party senator	*CQ's Politics in America*[a]
Incumbent Senator Election Year	Dichotomous, 1 = Senator is facing reelection	*CQ's Politics in America*[a]
Senate Leadership	Dichotomous, 1 = State is represented by a senator who is a floor leader, whip, or caucus chair	*CQ's Politics in America*[a]
House Appropriations Oversight	Dichotomous, 1 = State is represented on a House Appropriations Subcommittee with oversight over a given agency	
Senate Appropriations Oversight	Dichotomous, 1 = State is represented on a Senate Appropriations Subcommittee with oversight over a given agency	
Divided Government	Dichotomous, 1 = Divided government	*CQ's Politics in America*[a]

Intergovernmental controls

Governor Election Year	Dichotomous, 1 = Governor is up for reelection in a given year	*CQ's Politics in America*[a]
Governor-President Party Alignment	Dichotomous, 1 = Governor and president come from the same party	*CQ's Politics in America*[a]
Governor Election Year × Alignment	Dichotomous, interaction of previous two variables	

State controls

Gross State Product	Logged real gross state product	Bureau of Economic Analysis (2012)
Roads	Logged miles of roads per state	Federal Highway Administration (2008)
Research Institutions	Logged number of hospitals and universities	National Center for Education Statistics (2012)
Percent Elderly	Percentage of population aged 65+	Census Bureau (2001; 2011b; 2012)
Disaster	1 = New York in 2001–03; Louisiana and Mississippi in 2005–07	
Population	Logged state population	Census Bureau (2001; 2011b; 2012)

a. Includes McCutcheon and Lyons (2009); Koszcuk and Stern (2005); Stern (2001); Duncan and Lawrence (1997).

Appendix 4A-2. *Effect of Insulated Independence on Discretionary Grant Allocations, Estimated with Tobit, 1996–2008*[a]

Variable	Cabinet Secretary Office/ Cabinet Bureau		Cabinet Agency	
	Grant dollars	Number of grants	Grant dollars	Number of grants
State competitiveness				
Swing State	−0.309	−0.116	−0.309	−0.116
	(0.197)	(0.078)	(0.197)	(0.078)
Agency characteristics				
Cabinet Secretary Office	−0.951**	−0.876**		
	(0.206)	(0.082)		
Cabinet Secretary × Swing State	0.387	0.121		
	(0.314)	(0.125)		
Cabinet Bureau	−0.175	−0.621**		
	(0.135)	(0.053)		
Bureau × Swing State	0.375*	0.140*		
	(0.200)	(0.079)		
Cabinet Agency			−0.230*	−0.639**
			(0.134)	(0.053)
Cabinet Agency × Swing State			0.376*	0.139*
			(0.199)	(0.079)
Independent Agency	−1.786**	−1.263**	−1.807**	−1.270**
	(0.182)	(0.072)	(0.182)	(0.072)
Independent Agency × Swing	0.546*	0.235*	0.545*	0.235*
	(0.268)	(0.106)	(0.268)	(0.106)
Liberal Agency	2.896**	1.355**	2.883**	1.350**
	(0.058)	(0.023)	(0.058)	(0.023)
Staff (logged)	0.417**	0.243**	0.422**	0.245**
	(0.014)	(0.006)	(0.014)	(0.006)
Congressional controls				
Senate Appropriations Committee	0.022	0.039	0.023	0.040
	(0.108)	(0.044)	(0.108)	(0.044)
Senate Majority Party	0.013	0.005	0.013	0.005
	(0.034)	(0.014)	(0.034)	(0.014)
Incumbent Senator Election Year	−0.006	0.004	−0.006	0.004
	(0.073)	(0.029)	(0.073)	(0.029)
Senate Leader	0.035	0.014	0.035	0.014
	(0.126)	(0.051)	(0.126)	(0.051)
Senator with Oversight	0.119*	−0.028	0.118*	−0.029
	(0.070)	(0.028)	(0.070)	(0.028)
House Member with Oversight	0.041	−0.026	0.040	−0.026
	(0.059)	(0.024)	(0.059)	(0.024)

Variable	Cabinet Secretary Office/ Cabinet Bureau		Cabinet Agency	
	Grant dollars	Number of grants	Grant dollars	Number of grants
Intergovernmental controls				
Governor Election Year	−0.026	−0.010	−0.026	−0.010
	(0.095)	(0.038)	(0.095)	(0.038)
Governor-President Party Alignment	−0.072	−0.014	−0.072	−0.014
	(0.072)	(0.029)	(0.072)	(0.029)
Governor Elect × Alignment	0.029	0.005	0.029	0.005
	(0.125)	(0.050)	(0.125)	(0.050)
Controls and constant				
Real Gross State Product (logged)	−0.370	−0.267	−0.366	−0.265
	(0.672)	(0.332)	(0.672)	(0.332)
Miles of Roads (logged)	−0.375	−0.103	−0.371	−0.101
	(0.759)	(0.304)	(0.759)	(0.304)
Research Institutions (logged)	−0.391	−0.168	−0.387	−0.166
	(0.736)	(0.307)	(0.736)	(0.307)
Percent Elderly	0.079	−0.007	0.080	−0.007
	(0.101)	(0.040)	(0.101)	(0.040)
Disaster	0.346	0.097	0.346	0.097
	(0.245)	(0.098)	(0.245)	(0.098)
Population (logged)		0.492		0.490
		(0.494)		(0.494)
Intercept	9.108	−2.956	8.986	−2.985
	(13.738)	(7.337)	(13.739)	(7.337)
Observations	59,050	59,050	59,050	59,050
Pseudo R^2	0.01	0.03	0.01	0.03

a. All data are estimated using Tobit with fixed effects for state and year. In the first two models, the cabinet-level institutions are divided into Cabinet Secretary Office and Cabinet Bureau. In the second two models, all Cabinet-level institutions are grouped under the same variable, Cabinet Agency.

**p < .01 (one-tailed test); *p < .05 (one-tailed test).

Appendix 4A-3. *Effects of Politicization and Ideological Congruence on Discretionary Grant Allocations for Cabinet Secretary Offices and Cabinet Bureaus, Estimated with Tobit, 1996–2008*[a]

Variable	Cabinet Secretary Office		Cabinet Bureau	
	Grant dollars	Number of grants	Grant dollars	Number of grants
State competitiveness				
Swing State	0.919*	0.276*	0.165	0.053
	(0.463)	(0.132)	(0.116)	(0.046)
Agency characteristics				
Ideological Congruence	0.776**	0.134	−0.457**	−0.185**
	(0.292)	(0.085)	(0.078)	(0.031)
Congruence × Swing State	−0.792*	−0.237*	−0.046	−0.020
	(0.382)	(0.110)	(0.116)	(0.046)
Politicization (logged)	−1.328**	−1.339**	0.309**	0.287**
	(0.203)	(0.057)	(0.074)	(0.029)
Politicization × Swing State	−0.355*	−0.112*	−0.103	−0.017
	(0.192)	(0.054)	(0.107)	(0.042)
Liberal Agency	12.288**	5.078**	2.194**	1.054**
	(0.287)	(0.083)	(0.065)	(0.026)
Staff (logged)	0.613**	−0.053*	0.334**	0.221**
	(0.093)	(0.026)	(0.016)	(0.006)
Congressional controls				
Senate Appropriations Committee	−0.241	−0.035	−0.061	0.004
	(0.392)	(0.114)	(0.120)	(0.049)
Senate Majority Party	−0.082	−0.024	0.024	0.007
	(0.114)	(0.033)	(0.037)	(0.015)
Incumbent Senator Election Year	−0.267	−0.082	0.010	0.010
	(0.250)	(0.071)	(0.081)	(0.032)
Senate Leader	−0.184	−0.010	0.024	0.005
	(0.439)	(0.125)	(0.140)	(0.056)
Senator with Oversight	0.543*	0.168*	0.299**	0.049
	(0.274)	(0.079)	(0.079)	(0.031)
House Member with Oversight	0.656**	0.207**	0.145*	0.024
	(0.211)	(0.059)	(0.066)	(0.026)
Intergovernmental controls				
Governor Election Year	−0.073	−0.002	−0.037	−0.011
	(0.325)	(0.092)	(0.106)	(0.042)
Governor-President Party Alignment	0.089	−0.029	−0.091	−0.021
	(0.258)	(0.073)	(0.080)	(0.032)
Governor Elect × Alignment	0.127	0.013	0.029	0.003
	(0.427)	(0.122)	(0.139)	(0.055)

Variable	Cabinet Secretary Office		Cabinet Bureau	
	Grant dollars	Number of grants	Grant dollars	Number of grants
Controls and constant				
Real Gross State Product (logged)	−5.846**	−2.925**	0.015	−0.048
	(2.450)	(0.870)	(0.747)	(0.366)
Miles of Roads (logged)	−7.735**	−1.108	0.037	−0.015
	(2.943)	(0.857)	(0.843)	(0.335)
Research Institutions (logged)	−7.833**	−1.831*	−0.081	−0.070
	(2.720)	(0.815)	(0.818)	(0.339)
Percent Elderly	−0.150	−0.188*	0.101	−0.001
	(0.368)	(0.107)	(0.112)	(0.045)
Disaster	0.151	0.010	0.332	0.100
	(0.796)	(0.224)	(0.273)	(0.108)
Population (logged)		2.654*		0.302
		(1.294)		(0.544)
Intercept	190.331**	17.690	−1.106	−4.561
	(51.372)	(19.107)	(15.261)	(8.091)
Observations	2,650	2,650	47,900	47,900
Adjusted R^2	0.19	0.37	0.01	0.03

a. All data are estimated using Tobit with fixed effects for state and year.
**p <.01 (one-tailed test); *p < .05 (one-tailed test).

Appendix 4A-4. *Effects of Politicization and Ideological Congruence on Discretionary Grant Allocations for Independent Agencies and Commissions, Estimated with Tobit, 1996–2008*[a]

Variable	Independent Agencies		Independent Commissions	
	Grant dollars	Number of grants	Grant dollars	Number of grants
State competitiveness				
Swing State	−0.363	−0.135	−0.449	−0.107
	(0.345)	(0.141)	(0.288)	(0.136)
Agency characteristics				
Ideological Congruence	0.094	−0.009	−0.911**	−0.501**
	(0.273)	(0.112)	(0.253)	(0.127)
Congruence × Swing State	−0.199	0.005	0.261	0.020
	(0.390)	(0.159)	(0.299)	(0.143)
Politicization (logged)	−3.545**	−2.470**	1.759**	0.321**
	(0.677)	(0.280)	(0.105)	(0.049)
Politicization × Swing State	1.500**	0.435*	0.129	0.041
	(0.634)	(0.260)	(0.128)	(0.060)
Liberal Agency	−4.172**	−1.865**	12.863**	6.572**
	(0.356)	(0.147)	(0.259)	(0.128)
Staff (logged)	1.384**	0.551**	1.829**	0.809**
	(0.074)	(0.030)	(0.050)	(0.024)
Congressional controls				
Senate Appropriations Committee	0.585	0.244	−0.205	−0.077
	(0.369)	(0.155)	(0.258)	(0.124)
Senate Majority Party	−0.037	0.006	−0.033	−0.014
	(0.118)	(0.049)	(0.081)	(0.038)
Incumbent Senator Election Year	0.071	0.030	−0.097	−0.026
	(0.248)	(0.101)	(0.171)	(0.080)
Senate Leader	0.204	0.102	0.046	0.027
	(0.441)	(0.182)	(0.299)	(0.141)
Senator with Oversight	−0.752**	−0.378**	0.353*	0.131
	(0.253)	(0.104)	(0.180)	(0.085)
House Member with Oversight	−0.323	−0.310**	−0.412**	−0.130*
	(0.220)	(0.090)	(0.145)	(0.068)
Intergovernmental controls				
Governor Election Year	0.035	−0.009	0.073	0.000
	(0.326)	(0.134)	(0.222)	(0.104)
Governor-President Party Alignment	−0.162	−0.031	0.027	0.020
	(0.251)	(0.103)	(0.172)	(0.080)
Governor Elect × Alignment	0.118	0.056	−0.111	−0.031
	(0.429)	(0.176)	(0.293)	(0.137)

Variable	Independent Agencies		Independent Commissions	
	Grant dollars	Number of grants	Grant dollars	Number of grants
Controls and constant				
Real Gross State Product (logged)	–0.162	–0.246	–1.737	–1.197
	(2.299)	(1.173)	(1.591)	(0.927)
Miles of Roads (logged)	–3.147	–0.696	1.626	0.390
	(2.581)	(1.065)	(1.761)	(0.837)
Research Institutions (logged)	–0.901	–0.381	0.558	–0.055
	(2.521)	(1.080)	(1.736)	(0.851)
Percent Elderly	0.064	0.039	0.035	–0.010
	(0.344)	(0.142)	(0.237)	(0.112)
Disaster	1.036	0.127	–0.018	0.092
	(0.873)	(0.358)	(0.591)	(0.275)
Population (logged)		1.178		1.192
		(1.759)		(1.399)
Intercept	35.750	–7.734	–19.045	–16.612
	(46.833)	(26.050)	(32.275)	(20.691)
Observations	4,350	4,350	4,150	4,150
Pseudo R^2	0.05	0.08	0.16	0.21

a. All data are estimated using Tobit with fixed effects for state and year. Agency clustered standard errors are reported.

**$p < .01$ (one-tailed test); *$p < .05$ (one-tailed test).

5

Presidential Motives in the Shadow of Crisis

The media often focus on federal spending, producing numerous articles on deficits, debt ceilings, and annual budgets. However, early in 2009, a single federal spending bill dominated media, politics, and everyday conversation as President Barack Obama called on Congress to pass his economic stimulus package. Economists, members of Congress, White House officials, pundits, and journalists floated various opinions about the size of the stimulus. Conservatives wanted the stimulus to range in the low twelve digits—a few hundred billion dollars. Others wanted more than $1 trillion injected into the economy. In fact, Noam Schieber reported that economist Christina Romer, chair of the president's Council of Economic Advisers, proposed a $1.8 trillion stimulus.[1]

Like most legislative proposals in Washington, the stimulus package was a compromise. Formally titled the American Recovery and Reinvestment Act of 2009 (ARRA),[2] it totaled over $790 billion in tax cuts, entitlement benefits, and direct federal spending.[3] The legislation, which sent additional federal funding to every cabinet department and most federal programs, was intended to boost a struggling economy. Federal agencies became flush with money intended to help meet the exponentially increasing citizen demands

1. Noam Scheiber, "The Memo That Larry Summers Didn't Want Obama to See," *New Republic*, February 22, 2012 (www.newrepublic.com/article/politics/100961/memo-Larry-Summers-Obama).

2. P.L. 111-5. For the full text, see www.gpo.gov/fdsys/pkg/PLAW-111publ5/pdf/PLAW-111publ5.pdf.

3. Figures available at www.recovery.gov/. That figure was calculated as of December 31, 2012.

for assistance. Was ARRA able to meet every demand placed on the federal government? No. Was the additional quarter trillion dollars in direct federal spending helpful? Absolutely.

Although there has been debate over the success or depth of success of the legislation in promoting recovery, this book does not engage in that debate. Michael Grunwald's *The New New Deal,* which offers a comprehensive assessment of both the debate and the effect of the law on recovery, is the best assessment to date of the construction and implementation of the stimulus package and its impact on the U.S. economy.

For the purposes of this book, ARRA offers both an opportunity and a challenge. The legislation led to a huge injection of federal funding in the fifty states, thereby creating additional data to test the claims in this book. Moreover, this funding flowed largely into *existing* agencies and programs in ways that boosted bottom lines rather than creating new and/or unique institutional structures. In fact, as Grunwald notes in his book,

> [The stimulus] didn't create giant armies of new government workers in alphabet agencies like the WPA, CCC, and TVA; ARPA-E is its only new federal agency, with a staff smaller than a Major League Baseball roster. . . . It didn't set up workfare programs like the Federal Theatre Project, Federal Music Project, or Federal Art Project.[4]

In this way, ARRA fits neatly into the government's network of pre-2009 federal spending. Essentially, ARRA is an extra helping of food rather than a menu change.

Additional data are useful to a researcher, particularly when they fit into an existing analytical framework. However, the ARRA data present a few analytical challenges that must be considered and overcome. First, ARRA is a unique, crisis-centered piece of legislation that departs dramatically from the routine processes of federal spending. While ARRA deals with the same programs, with the same type of funding that were analyzed in earlier chapters, the purpose of ARRA's funding is not identical to that of those programs. It is difficult to treat ARRA as simply an extension of standard practice because its sole purpose is to overcome the deficiencies of standard practice. Second, because the stimulus funds flowed into existing programs that were already allocating federal funds, it is unlikely that stimulus and non-stimulus funds were allocated wholly independently of each other. There is likely a relationship

---

4. Grunwald (2012, p. 16) . ARPA-E is the Advanced Research Projects Agency–Energy, an agency of the Department of Energy.

between the distribution of stimulus and non-stimulus funds. It is therefore important to treat non-stimulus federal spending in stimulus years separately because unique and influential forces are acting on the distribution of non-stimulus dollars.

How the Stimulus Works

The American Recovery and Reinvestment Act was signed into law on February 17, 2009. In many ways it looks and functions like a basic piece of omnibus appropriations legislation. It authorizes and appropriates funds, cabinet department by cabinet department, agency by agency, program by program. The legislation is crafted like a ledger book translated into text, assigning additional values (spending) to line items or accounts in the budget. Its goals and purposes are made clear:

> An Act [m]aking supplemental appropriations for job preservation and creation, infrastructure investment, energy efficiency and science, assistance to the unemployed, and State and local fiscal stabilization, for the fiscal year ending September 20, 2009, and for other purposes.

The legislation continues with a slightly more detailed section, "Purposes and Principles."[5] Section 3 reads:

> (a) STATEMENT OF PURPOSES.—The purposes of this Act include the following:
>   (1) To preserve and create jobs and promote economic recovery.
>   (2) To assist those most impacted by the recession.
>   (3) To provide investments needed to increase economic efficiency by spurring technological advances in science and health.
>   (4) To invest in transportation, environmental protection, and other infrastructure that will provide long-term economic benefits.
>   (5) To stabilize State and local government budgets, in order to minimize and avoid reductions in essential services and counterproductive state and local tax increases.

Each of ARRA's goals, which clearly seek to overcome many of the large-scale challenges that the recession presented for the U.S. economy, is admirable from social and economic perspectives. In addition, the act was designed

5. P.L. 111-5 § 3.

to couple short-term stabilization with long-term growth, a basic goal for a government-provided economic stimulus.

As noted above, despite the rhetoric surrounding the legislation, ARRA was not simply a massive bill laden with direct spending. Instead, the law divided funding, almost equally, into amounts for entitlement programs, across-the-board tax cuts, and direct spending. Specifically, the law provided $290.7 billion in tax benefits, $251.3 billion in entitlement funding, and $255.6 billion in direct spending in the form of contracts, grants, and loans.[6] Essentially, each type of funding satisfied different contingents in the policy community and the electorate. Many Republicans argued that the path to growth was through economic liberation, freeing the public from a tax burden. Democrats generally wanted to take a traditional Keynesian approach to recovery, utilizing massive flows of direct spending in areas such as infrastructure and education. Other concerns emerged about the most vulnerable members of society, such as seniors, the poor, and the newly poor. As a result, entitlement programs delivered funding to Medicare and Medicaid, unemployment insurance, energy assistance, and low-income housing programs.

Presidential Power and ARRA

The manner in which ARRA was implemented provides interesting context for political power over spending. One major debate regarding ARRA and its companion legislation, the Omnibus Appropriations Act of 2009 (passed shortly thereafter), focused on earmarks. Candidate Obama—and later, President Obama—vilified the use of earmarks. For years, Republican legislators also had denounced earmarks as fiscally unsound, unethical, deficit-increasing, and unnecessary,[7] and few legislators opposed efforts to ban congressional earmarking. Among those who did were individuals like Senator James Inhofe (R-Okla.), who argued that the elimination of earmarks simply gives presidents, White House staff, and other political actors in the executive branch greater spending authority. In the end, earmarks were at least ostensibly banned from ARRA.

This debate begs the question of how much power the president retained over the administration and distribution of stimulus funds. Even in the face of the reduction or elimination of earmarks, Congress can still set up barriers to or restrictions on the president's ability to influence federal spending. One of

---

6. Figures available at www.recovery.gov/. Of the $255.6 billion in direct spending, nearly $50 billion was used for the type of discretionary grants analyzed in previous chapters.

7. The denunciations often occurred as the same legislators slipped earmarks into legislation.

the most direct means of reining in executive power is through the specificity of statutes. By detailing quite clearly the ways in which Congress wants federal funds to be allocated, statutes are better able to direct funds to specific targets and retain congressional spending power. However, ARRA presented Congress with a clear challenge in that respect. The legislation was comprehensive, written quickly in response to an emergency, and so broad in scope that such detail was likely out of reach.[8] In addition, under "General Principles Concerning Use of Funds," Congress notes that "the President and heads of Federal departments and agencies shall manage and expend the funds . . . as quickly as possible consistent with prudent management."[9] Detail and specificity fell victim to presidential management and speed in the face of crisis.

A variety of provisions in ARRA enable or enhance presidential spending power, and they differ dramatically in character. In some cases, money is simply appropriated with only one requirement—that an agency notify Congress of its plans. For example, the Veterans Health Administration funds projects related to Department of Veterans Affairs (VA) medical facilities. The provision in ARRA related to those projects reads:

> For an additional amount for "Medical Facilities" for non-recurring maintenance, including energy projects, $1,000,000,000, to remain available until September 30, 2010: *Provided,* That not later than 30 days after the date of enactment of this Act, the Secretary of Veterans Affairs shall submit to the Committees on Appropriations of both Houses of Congress an expenditure plan for funds provided under this heading.[10]

This provision authorizes the Veterans Health Administration to spend an additional $1 billion for medical facilities without any restrictions except those stated in the authorizing legislation for that fiscal year.

In other areas, Congress attaches restrictions on the appropriation of stimulus funds. For example, ARRA provides an additional $100,000,000, to be used before September 30, 2011, for the Office of Lead Hazard Control and Healthy Homes, in the Department of Housing and Urban Development (HUD). Yet Congress includes conditions:

> That funds shall be awarded first to applicants which had applied . . . for fiscal year 2008, and were found in the application review to be qualified for award, but were not awarded because of funding limitations,

8. The final bill was over 400 pages in length.
9. P.L. 111-5 § 3b.
10. P.L.111-5 Title X.; 123 Stat. 199.

and that any funds which remain after reservation of funds for such grants shall be added to the amount of funds to be awarded . . . for fiscal year 2009.[11]

Congress wants to restrict the agency from using new funds in a new fashion, opting for the money to be used simply to fill in funding gaps. However, Congress also includes exceptionally broad waiver authority that empowers the president and the secretary of HUD to eliminate the requirements that it has imposed. This authority essentially neuters the restrictions noted above:

> That in administering funds appropriated or otherwise made available under this heading, the Secretary may waive or specify alternative requirements for any provision of any statute or regulation in connection with the obligation by the Secretary or use of these funds (except for requirements related to fair housing, nondiscrimination, labor standards, and the environment) upon a finding that such a waiver is necessary to expedite or facilitate the use of such funds.[12]

Waiver authority of this sort broadens the discretion of the president and executive branch actors to spend funds in a manner other than Congress originally specified.[13] Presidents and secretaries may well use funds to boost the prior year's funding. However, the waiver language here illustrates a broader point about presidential power: it offers political actors in the executive branch greater authority in the administration of government. Legal scholars call this "Big Waiver," arguing that it "offers a salutary means of managing the practical governance concerns that make traditional delegation unavoidable."[14] However, Big Waiver can also allow presidents and their surrogates to advance their political and electoral goals through the legal authority to ignore or waive congressional attempts to restrict executive spending power.

The legislative language in the Lead Hazard Control and Healthy Homes provision offers a key insight into presidential power. At the same time, it illustrates the connection between stimulus and non-stimulus dollars, further demonstrating the theoretical and methodological necessity of analyzing stimulus data separately from those for other years and from non-stimulus data. In the above provision, Congress intends for HUD to allocate Healthy Homes

11. 123 Stat. 224.

12. Ibid.

13. Waiver authority increases executive branch spending authority, but it can apply to any area of administration.

14. Barron and Rakoff (2013, p. 270).

stimulus grants according to allocation decisions made within the existing program, not independently of existing funding streams.

Other provisions within ARRA offered truly blanket discretionary authority for the executive branch. For example, many of the programs within the Department of Agriculture were provided tens or hundreds of millions of stimulus dollars with only a simple requirement from Congress: to ensure that "funds shall be allocated to projects that can be fully funded and completed with the funds appropriated in this Act, and to activities that can commence promptly following enactment of this Act."[15] This provision put no demands or restrictions on the executive branch's power to determine who received funding. It simply required that projects be funded fully. This is an ideal arrangement for a president who has electoral interests: he gets to choose who receives funding, and Congress requires that the recipients' requests must be met fully.

Although ARRA did not transfer all spending power from the legislative branch to the executive branch, it did much to tip the balance toward the president. The legislation offered few restrictions, often requiring the president, appointees, and bureaucrats to adhere to the existing allocation guidelines in determining eligibility and ultimately funding projects, but as chapters 3 and 4 illustrate, presidents have substantial power to politicize the administration of government and influence the allocation of funds in electorally expedient ways. As a result, when Congress defaults to existing allocation schemes, presidents can resort to politics as usual in the distribution of federal funds. The most stringent legislative restrictions in ARRA placed few restrictions on presidential power.

Opportunities for Congressional Influence

Although the legislative language in ARRA gave the president tremendous discretionary authority, it did not render Congress powerless or without influence. Congress retained its formal oversight role, as well as informal means of having an effect.

ARRA became a highly partisan and politically contentious issue. It became law not because of a broad legislative outcry for policy change. It passed because of skillful congressional negotiations and sizable Democratic majorities in the House and Senate. Despite passage, Republicans were incensed by the law, labeling it fiscally irresponsible during a period

---

15. Identical language appears frequently in the legislation. A few such instances are seen in 123 Stat. 117.

of economic recession. John Boehner (R-Ohio), then the House minority leader, claimed, "This bill is supposed to be about jobs, jobs, jobs, and it's turned into nothing more than spend, spend, spend."[16] Regarding Republican opposition, the *New York Times* noted:

> Republicans argued futilely that the Senate stimulus measure was almost a misnomer. "We're taking an enormous risk—an enormous risk—with other people's money," Senator Mitch McConnell of Kentucky, the minority leader, said in urging his Republican colleagues to vote against the measure. McConnell said the package was "full of waste" and could only be counted on to increase the nation's debt.[17]

Rather than working through bipartisan means, congressional leaders, particularly in the Senate, worked hard to hammer out a bill that would comply with Senate procedural rules and reach the president's desk. In any such setting, legislators can logroll and bargain, making concessions in exchange for votes—just enough votes for passage. Even if earmarks or provisions are not formally written into legislation, deal making is often necessary for final passage. Such was the case with ARRA. The Senate passed the initial version with sixty-one votes and the conference report with sixty, as the legislation barely overcame Senate procedural hurdles to pass. As a result, Congress likely had numerous opportunities to reap benefits from the legislation.

Partisan rancor expands legislative influence because it creates the need for bargaining and deal making. It also enhances the president's interest in quieting criticism from Congress. Because ARRA was controversial, opponents were interested in repudiating it whenever possible. One means of quieting congressional opposition is to make sure that every congressional district is flush with funds and that members' constituents benefit from the law in question. The size of ARRA meant that the executive branch had the capability and the flexibility to respond to legislators' requests and could placate them.

Beyond Politics: The Stimulus and Economic Need

While executive and legislative interests politicize federal fund distribution in general, nonpolitical factors likely played a role in allocating stimulus dollars. In early 2009, the United States was in the midst of one of most serious

16. Shailagh Murray and Paul Kane, "Congress Passes Stimulus Package," *Washington Post,* February 14, 2009 (http://articles.washingtonpost.com/2009-02-14/politics/36848907_1_stimulus-package-president-obama-legislation).

17. David M. Herszenhorn, "Senate Passes Stimulus Plan," *New York Times,* February 10, 2009 (www.nytimes.com/2009/02/10/world/americas/10iht-11webstim.20082806.html).

economic recessions in eight decades. Job losses were accelerating, growth was negative, stock market losses were profound, and state and local governments were facing dramatic deficits. Standard streams of federal funding often cannot meet all of the national needs that exist, and the recession exaggerated the shortfall. Even with the stimulus, need outpaced the assistance available, and the U.S. economy faced a watershed moment. Even if ARRA ultimately proved to be a political and electoral tool for presidents and Congress, its creation and implementation were intended to bring economic relief to an increasingly struggling population. Americans needed help, and President Obama and Democrats in Congress touted ARRA as part of the solution. Nancy Pelosi (D-Calif.), then the Speaker of the House, noted:

> The American people are feeling a great deal of pain, they have uncertainty about their jobs, about health care, about the ability to pay for the education of their children, and sad to say—in our great country—even the ability to put food on the table. And so, today, we have passed legislation that does take that "swift, bold action" on their behalf.[18]

Elected officials had a vested electoral interest in the ability of the stimulus package to improve economic conditions throughout the United States. However, in the context of the economic crisis, those incentives translated into nontraditional behaviors. Traditional means of securing (re)election may still have been appealing, but Democrats in Congress and the president would be held to account if the economy continued to fail. Their electoral interests demanded economic recovery, and that recovery required purposeful use of stimulus funds.

While partisan rancor could lead the executive branch to try to placate the congressional opposition by allocating funds to opponents' districts, that rancor also could have another effect. It could result in a policy-motivated, technocratic, need-centered distribution of funds for fear of backlash from the opposition. If the White House politicized the distribution of funds and Congress—particularly Republicans in Congress—identified such behaviors, the president could pay a substantial political and electoral cost. The U.S. economy was in a delicate and increasingly precarious position. The politicization of the distribution of stimulus dollars intended to save the economy would become a huge liability that any election-minded president (or official)

---

18. Nancy Pelosi, "Today, We Have Passed Legislation That Takes 'Swift, Bold Action' on Behalf of the American People," press release, Office of the Speaker of the House, February 13, 2009.

would want to avoid. As a result, in an ironic twist, it is easy to imagine a scenario in which a strong electoral motive results in *less* political influence.

Non-Stimulus Dollars in an Era of Stimulus Funding

In many ways, non-stimulus grant programs should have continued operating as usual, even after passage of ARRA. Program appropriations and authorizations remained largely intact. Any effort to increase or decrease non-stimulus spending would have been met with stiff opposition, and it did not shift dramatically in either direction. For Republicans and even moderate Democrats, the $800 billion ARRA was already far too expensive and fiscally irresponsible, and any substantial increases in annual appropriations would have been completely unacceptable. Similarly, mainstream Democrats would have opposed any decrease in non-stimulus appropriations because such a move would undercut the stimulus effort.

In addition, because ARRA did not create a New Deal–style alphabet soup of new agencies, there was little need to change authorizing legislation to accommodate new institutions or bureaucratic infrastructure. In fact, many agencies simply created separate grant funding accounts for stimulus dollars that mirrored non-stimulus accounts. In some ways, appropriations and authorization legislation remained a relatively stable force amid a rapidly changing political and economic environment. As a result, many of the same or traditional forces acting on the distribution of funds—presidential influence, placation of Congress, and responsiveness to need—should have persevered, helping to answer the question of "who gets what, when, and why?"

However, despite the many reasons why traditional funding programs should have been administered in traditional ways, the economic crisis of 2008–10 likely affected all areas of federal spending. Most federal grant programs are designed to assist individuals, groups, cities, counties, and states by meeting or helping to meet their needs. The stimulus was intended to assist federal programs in addressing the effects of the recession, and in many programs, need rose to unprecedented levels. As a result, grant-making agencies saw changes not only in who and how many people were in need or struggling but also in the depth and extent of their needs. Grant programs had to respond to the rapidly increasing demands on government, not just with stimulus funds but with non-stimulus funds as well.

The controversies arising from the passage and implementation of ARRA left critics of both the legislation and the president seeking any opportunity to demonstrate failures in federal spending—either through poor administration, failed grant projects, or politicization. As a result, all federal programs likely felt the risks entailed in additional scrutiny, pressure, and oversight as federal spending—stimulus or otherwise—increasingly became ammunition for political attacks.

An Examination of Stimulus Spending 2009–11

The stimulus data that I analyze here include 64,099 discretionary grant allocations throughout the fifty states that total $45.9 billion.[19] As before, I control the data for population and inflation as well as data outliers such that the dependent variable is annual real grant dollars per 100,000 state residents. The data are logged to control for outliers. The data cover three years—2009, 2010, and 2011—because those are the three years in which the bulk of stimulus funds were allocated.[20] Each observation in the data represents federal discretionary grant allocations to a state in a given year. As a result, there are 150 observed "state-years." The separate data were collected for non-stimulus funds for the relevant years.

The analytical approach used in this chapter is similar to that used in chapter 3.[21] I estimate all of the data using ordinary least squares.[22] I employ many of the same control variables as well as identical dependent variables. While the precise magnitude of the results presented below cannot be compared with those in chapter 3, the conclusions drawn from the findings are comparable. However, it is important to note briefly the differences between the models.

---

19. The analysis presented here uses real 2009 dollars to control for inflation. It may come as a surprise that only $46 billion was allocated in grant funding given the size of ARRA. It is important to note that only $250 billion was authorized for direct spending. Portions of those funds were set aside for internal administrative matters. In addition, while discretionary grant funding was a substantial portion of the direct spending, other areas of direct spending such as contracts, cooperative agreements, among other forms of direct funding, were not captured in the "discretionary federal grants" category.

20. At the completion of the manuscript leading to this book, the last year in which data were fully available for all quarters was 2011.

21. This analysis is based on the states that were swing states in 2008: Arkansas, Colorado, Florida, Georgia, Iowa, Indiana, Missouri, Montana, New Hampshire, North Carolina, North Dakota, Ohio, South Carolina, South Dakota, and Virginia.

22. In previous analyses, I estimated the data using ordinary least squares with state fixed effects. Here, state fixed effects are not useful because several of the state-level independent variables do not vary sufficiently over this short period, particularly the Senate Appropriations Committee membership and the state competitiveness variables. As a result, the state fixed effects become highly collinear. The specification of the model without state fixed effects still controls sufficiently for—and offers substantive insight into—that critical variation. State fixed effects provide only blunt measures.

In this chapter, I exclude the first term variable, as all data are drawn from a presidential first term. I also exclude "election proximity" because it would be an incomplete measure given that the data do not extend to 2012.[23]

I also include two new variables. First, I measure the state's unemployment rate, a figure that would likely impact funding specifically intended to relieve the effects of the recession. Vice President Joe Biden noted in a speech about ARRA at the Brookings Institution in September 2009 that "the first part is [to] bring relief to those who were falling into the abyss." The unemployment rate offers an efficient proxy for state economic challenges. Second, because stimulus and non-stimulus funds were related, as I measure the influences on stimulus funding, I control for non-stimulus funding and vice versa. Both types of funding were administered by the same agencies, offices, and programs, and at times, stimulus fund allocations depended in large part on the level of regular funding that localities received.

Table 5-1 presents the results of the analysis of the effects of state electoral competitiveness, congressional influence, gubernatorial politics, and state need/demand on the allocation of discretionary stimulus grants. Model 1 uses a three-part measure of state electoral competitiveness that includes the swing state, lost cause state, and core state variables, with "core state" serving as the reference category. Model 2 uses a two-part measure of competitiveness that includes the swing state and non–swing state variables, with "non–swing state" serving as the reference category.

The results for state electoral competitiveness presented in table 5-1 are mixed. They indicate that there is a positive relationship between being a swing state and receiving stimulus dollars. Model 2 shows that relationship to be positive but the estimate is imprecise (it fails to reach statistical significance). In model 1, the data show that a swing state receives significantly more grant dollars than a core state does (about 181 percent more). However, the results suggest that lost cause states also receive more than core states, which is inconsistent with expectations. In further testing, stimulus grant funding to swing states is also statistically indistinguishable from stimulus funding to lost cause states. Taken together, the results are quite mixed and offer only limited support for the idea that the president systematically targeted stimulus dollars to swing states at the expense of all other states. An examination of some of the other findings of this analysis points to a few explanations for why that may be the case.

---

23. The election proximity variable used in previous chapters is specified as the two years immediately preceding the presidential election; using that specification would leave the concept inappropriately measured in the context of these data.

Table 5-1. *Political Influences and Stimulus Grant Dollars, 2009–11*[a]

Variable	Model 1	Model 2
State competitiveness		
Swing State (0,1)	1.814^	0.356
	(1.162)	(0.826)
Lost Cause State (0,1)	2.886*	
	(1.689)	
State-level congressional controls		
Senate Appropriations Committee (0,1)	−0.383	−0.468
	(0.723)	(0.722)
Appropriations Committee Election Year (0,1)	2.212*	2.105*
	(1.114)	(1.084)
Incumbent Senator Election Year (0,1)	1.141	0.907
	(0.955)	(0.945)
Competitive Senate Election (0,1)	0.470	0.813
	(0.763)	(0.778)
Senate Leadership (0, 1)	−1.081	−1.003
	(1.238)	(1.270)
Senate Majority Party Membership (0,1,2)	0.185	−0.450
	(0.752)	(0.675)
House Delegation with President (0,1)	2.148*	1.641^
	(1.120)	(1.096)
House Cardinal (0,1)	−0.151	0.206
	(0.834)	(0.794)
Intergovernmental controls		
Governor Election Year (0,1)	0.367	0.544
	(1.737)	(1.727)
Governor-President Party Alignment (0,1)	1.053	1.075
	(0.989)	(1.014)
Governor Election Year × Alignment (0,1)	0.364	0.377
	(1.626)	(1.602)
Controls and constant		
Real Gross State Product (logged)	1.452	0.489
	(1.777)	(1.613)
Roads (miles, logged)	0.507	0.659
	(1.146)	(1.154)
Research Institutions (logged)	−1.450	−0.636
	(2.254	(2.169)
Percent Elderly	16.135	−3.994
	(30.691)	(30.339)
Unemployment Rate	0.778**	0.713**
	(0.283)	(0.285)
Nonstimulus Dollars (logged)	2.782**	2.835**
	(1.149)	(1.189)
Constant	−62.225*	−51.727
	(36.267)	(36.471)
R^2	0.25	0.23
Observations	150	150

a. Dependent variable is logged real grant dollars per 100,000 people. Data estimated using ordinary least squares. Robust standard errors are reported.

**$p < .01$ (one-tailed test); *$p < .05$ (one-tailed test;) ^$p < .10$ (one-tailed test).

First, the results offer support for the idea that Congress benefited from ARRA. If the president needed to use some stimulus spending in part to strike deals for passage of the act and then to maintain positive relations with Congress, he may have done so at the expense of his own electoral targeting of funds. Both models show a significant increase in stimulus grant funding for senators who serve on the Senate Appropriations Committee and those facing reelection. This result combines two important features of legislative influence—committee membership and electoral interest—that can directly or indirectly deliver federal funding. The contentious politics surrounding ARRA meant the president's strategy required targeting the states of key senators, not swing states. However, if legislators benefited from logrolling to garner votes for passage and assisting an executive seeking to avoid additional oversight, House members also should have benefited. The data show that to be the case. Specifically, states in which a majority of the House delegation is Democratic (the same party as the president during the years under analysis) saw huge benefits from the stimulus. For example, model 1 of table 5-1 suggests that states with Democratic majority House delegations saw about 215 percent more stimulus grant dollars than delegations dominated by Republicans. This finding makes sense given the majoritarian nature of the House of Representatives. Because of the strength of the Speaker of the House, the majority party, and a lack of supermajority rules on legislation, House majority members also should benefit from presidential deal-making efforts and concerns about oversight. There is no doubt that key legislative actors saw substantial benefits from discretionary stimulus grant funding. The president's efforts to meet the demands of Congress may help explain the lack of evidence of his targeting of swing states for receipt of funds.

Economic need was the chief motivation for ARRA, and the results show that economic need helps explain ARRA allocations. They reflect the interest of the administration and Congress in resolving the economic crisis through ARRA and are at odds with the idea of politicization of distributive policy. Much of ARRA was geared toward addressing one of the most pressing concerns during the recession: unemployment. Between March 2007 and March 2008, seasonally adjusted employment in the United States dropped by 5.9 million workers.[24] The results show that the stimulus directly targeted this problem. Every additional percentage-point increase in a state's unemployment rate translated to an increase of more than 70 percent in stimulus grant dollars. For the public, the unemployment rate is one of the most easily

---

24. Bureau of Labor Statistics, "Employment, Hours, and Earnings from the Current Employment Statistics Survey (National) [Seasonally Adjusted]" (http://bls.gov/ces/#tables).

observed and understood economic indicators, particularly during a recession. The labor market was also among the elements of the economy that took the longest to rebound. This result suggests that stimulus spending was responsive to this indicator.

I also include a measure of non-stimulus grant dollars received as a measure of broader state economic need or demand. The results show a significant relationship between non-stimulus and stimulus grant funding, suggesting that both non-stimulus and stimulus funds were allocated to satisfy similar needs. The structure of ARRA itself, in which stimulus spending was designed to be administered alongside non-stimulus spending, reflects an interest in coordinating the federal effort. In many cases, Congress explicitly wanted the spending to be mutually responsive. In a period of profound economic crisis, such an administrative strategy is to be expected. Federal agencies are charged with meeting needs in the areas under their jurisdiction. When those needs change, for whatever reason, so too must the agencies' efforts. The 2008–09 recession is a prime example of this.

The depth of the recession may also explain the limited presidential politicization of the stimulus. As President Barack Obama took office, the U.S. economy was in economic free-fall and that became the central policy issue during the first months of his administration. Need was growing; good public policy that targeted the weaknesses in the economy and the plight of citizens suffering the recession's worst effects was the only path forward. If one believes that politics played no role in the administration of ARRA, then the results—that funds targeted not swing states but those struggling economically—would be expected. Yet that belief would be naïve.

The results can also illustrate the actions of a president who was forced to modify his behavior to advance traditional political and electoral goals. Previous chapters show that presidents typically pursue their electoral interests through micro-level policymaking—by targeting federal funds to swing states. However, in the midst of the economic crisis, swing state strategy had to be secondary. The president was forced to devote primary attention to the collapsing macro-economy. If the economic situation were ignored, GDP continued to drop, and unemployment continued to rise, the president would face almost certain electoral defeat. As the recession deepened, the president's electoral interests were served by resuscitating the national economy. To that end, the president needed to do two things: target key congressional constituencies in order to pass ARRA and then deliver funds to those states most in need of help.

Beyond the political need to oversee economic recovery, there was a need to avoid funding schemes that were obviously politically motivated. Republicans wanted to illustrate that ARRA was a public policy failure that did nothing to resolve the economic crisis. As 2009 proceeded, job losses slowed and GDP turned positive. The ARRA-as-failure argument became less credible. For ARRA's opponents, it became much more appealing to illustrate the role of politics in the administration of the law. For much of 2010 and even into the presidential campaign two years later, Republicans in Congress and candidates for the GOP presidential nomination focused on the energy company Solyndra as an example of stimulus funding that was motivated by political relationships and resulted in a failure. In reality, Solyndra's failure was a single example in an otherwise largely successful loan guarantee program for green technology. Had presidential electoral politics dominated the distribution of stimulus funds, there may have been many more Solyndras, and the ensuing scandal would have cost the White House politically and eventually electorally. In this way, both the crisis and the politics surrounding the stimulus combined to modify the manner in which presidential electoral interests influenced the distribution of funds.

Beyond the Stimulus:
Standard Federal Funding during the Great Recession

The observations about the distribution of stimulus grant dollars raise a couple of questions about non-stimulus funding during the same period. Did the same presidential and congressional forces that affected stimulus funding influence other federal funding? Did the economic and political situation facing federal agencies in 2009–11 generate unique behaviors in distributing non-stimulus grant dollars? There is theoretical support for multiple answers to those questions.

Programs were not redesigned because of the recession and ARRA; in fact, for the most part stimulus funding was piled on top of existing agency appropriations. One might therefore expect agencies to operate according to standard procedures, which, as prior chapters demonstrate, are influenced by the president, Congress, and state demand. In that case, the distribution of non-stimulus funds should reflect many of the theoretical expectations and empirical results found in chapter 3. However, federal agencies and grant programs are not locked into procedures that prevent them from responding to the political, economic, and social conditions of the day. In fact, policy success, particularly with regard to federal funding, flows from the ability to change with changing needs, whether economic, political, or electoral. Given the additional demands that economic conditions placed on the federal government after 2009, one would expect some responsiveness in federal funding. Although ARRA faced a unique blend of challenges and demands, non-stimulus and stimulus funding shared some of the same political and policy challenges during the height and aftermath of the recession.

To provide answers to the questions posed above, I analyze non-stimulus funding during 2009–11 as I did stimulus funding in the previous section. In keeping with the state-year as the unit of analysis, there are 150 observations (50 states across three years). The data represent federal discretionary grant funding for 579,055 grants, totaling just over $218 billion. The estimation technique and choice of variables are identical to those discussed in the previous section. Table 5-2 presents the results of the analysis. The most striking result is that there is no statistical relationship between state electoral competitiveness and the distribution of non-stimulus grant funds—that is, fund amounts for swing, core, and lost cause states are indistinguishable from each other. This result is similar to the findings in the previous section regarding stimulus spending.

In contrast, congressional variables are associated with substantial effects. Being a member of the Senate Appropriations Committee, being a member of the Senate majority party (the party of the president), and having a House delegation with a majority of members from the president's party are all associated with increases in federal grant funding. Key legislative institutions, particularly those with partisan alignment with the president, benefit dramatically from executive branch allocation of grants. These results showing a congressional effect are similar to results found in previous chapters. However, one robust element of these results is that partisan alignment with the president proves a substantial benefit for legislators. That may be attributable to direct presidential efforts to benefit co-partisans or to the institutional dynamics of the legislative and executive branches during this period, specifically that Democrats control Congress and the White House for much of this period.

In addition, some key indicators of state-level need are significant and clarify the results. States with lower levels of gross state product and those with more research institutions receive substantially more federal funding. A state's economic need and capacity to demand federal funding affect its receipt of discretionary grant dollars. Although the variables of significance in this analysis differ, the results are similar to previous findings that state-level need is associated with federal funding.

Another measure of state need, particularly salient during this period of crisis, is the unemployment rate. However, the unemployment rate is negatively correlated with receipt of non-stimulus grant funds. This finding is interesting, particularly because it differs dramatically from that for stimulus funding.

Table 5-2. *Political Influence and Nonstimulus Grant Dollars, 2009–11*[a]

Variable	Model 1	Model 2
State competitiveness		
Swing State (0,1)	−0.705	−0.071
	(0.069)	(0.056
Lost Cause State (0,1)	0.002	
	(0.098)	
State-level congressional controls		
Senate Appropriations Committee (0,1)	0.145**	0.145**
	(0.051)	(0.051)
Appropriations Committee Election Year (0,1)	−0.218^	−0.218^
	(0.115)	(0.115)
Incumbent Senator Election Year (0,1)	0.139*	0.139^
	(0.092)	(0.091)
Competitive Senate Election (0,1)	0.120*	0.121^
	(0.088)	(0.089)
Senate Leadership (0, 1)	−0.117*	−0.117*
	(0.056)	(0.054)
Senate Majority Party Membership (0,1,2)	0.148**	0.147**
	(0.049)	(0.040)
House Delegation with President (0,1)	0.088*	0.088^
	(0.054)	(0.057)
House Cardinal (0,1)	−0.002	−0.002
	(0.060)	(0.058)
Intergovernmental controls		
Governor Election Year (0,1)	0.175*	0.175*
	(0.093)	(0.091)
Governor-President Party Alignment (0,1)	0.027	0.027
	(0.059)	(0.059)
Governor Election Year × Alignment (0,1)	−0.127	−0.127
	(0.117)	(0.116)
Controls and constant		
Real Gross State Product (logged)	−0.341**	−0.342**
	(0.109)	(0.111)
Roads (miles, logged)	−0.179*	−0.179**
	(0.072)	(0.073)
Research Institutions (logged)	0.298*	0.299*
	(0.160)	(0.158)
Percent Elderly	−9.215**	−9.228**
	(2.862)	(2.982)
Unemployment Rate	−0.080**	−0.080**
	(0.018)	(0.018)
Stimulus Dollars (logged)	0.013**	0.014**
	(0.005)	(0.006)
Constant	22.821**	22.829**
	(1.422)	(1.461)
R^2	0.59	0.59
Observations	150	150

a. Dependent variable is logged real grant dollars per 100,000 people. Data estimated using ordinary least squares. Robust standard errors are reported.

**$p < .01$ (one-tailed test); *$p < .05$ (one-tailed test); ^$p < .10$ (one-tailed test).

It suggests that while both stimulus and non-stimulus grant programs sought to deliver aid to needy applicants, each went about it with different criteria. Non-stimulus money flowed to meet more traditional needs while stimulus grant dollars targeted weaknesses in the labor market. Regardless of the recipients, the results in table 5-2, like those in table 5-1, show the critical role that state need/demand played in the distribution of non-stimulus dollars.

A question emerges: did President Obama simply fail to politicize the distribution of federal funds in the way that his predecessors did? A theoretical explanation and deeper look at the data may provide an alternative explanation. First, the data from 2009–11 likely *underestimate* the influence of presidential electoral interests. Why? Examination of federal fund distribution during president Obama's first term excludes 2012—his reelection year and the year when electoral interests should be most salient.[25] That year was excluded not because I chose to do so but because data were not available. If a president is seeking to maximize the benefits of playing electoral politics with federal spending, an election year should be critical. In fact, previous chapters suggest that the proximity of a presidential election has a substantial effect on the distribution of funds. In addition, if one is to believe that the economic recession as well as the president's electoral interests affected the distribution of all federal funding, there should be differences in the president's behavior across this time period. Any economy-induced limit on targeting funds to swing states would have been most sharp at the start of the Obama administration, when the recession was at its peak. Later on, there should have been greater freedom to use federal funds to advance electoral goals because of both the economic recovery and the salience of electoral interests.

The absence of data from 2012 presents a challenge for fully assessing the role of electoral interests in the distribution of funds during this period. However, one means of examining differences in the distribution of funds is to divide the data. I examine how non-stimulus funding in 2009 and 2010 differs from the same funding in 2011. Doing so presents three key advantages in examining presidential influence. First, previous chapters show that presidential electoral motives are more salient in the two years leading up to a presidential election. Second, starting in 2011, the House of Representatives

25. The same underestimation could explain the results from the stimulus data. However, in the case of stimulus spending, the answer to that question is elusive because access to 2012 data would not provide a sufficient answer. By 2012, almost all of the stimulus money had been spent. Any insight into the effect of salient presidential electoral interest would likely come from a *theoretical* exercise that asks whether offering stimulus funding at a later date would have led to greater politicization.

became majority Republican, introducing an inter-branch partisan dynamic that was absent in 2009–10. Third, by 2011 the recovery had begun in earnest. Economic need likely changed as every month in 2011 saw positive job creation. It is critical to examine whether political influence changed during this three-year period, and most important, whether any such changes are consistent with theoretical expectations about presidential influence.

Table 5-3 presents the results of the analysis of non-stimulus grant funding for each time period. Models 1 and 2 assess funding in 2009–10; models 3 and 4 assess funding in 2011. Models 1 and 2 offer findings similar to those in table 5-2. This result is largely expected, as those years represent two-thirds of the data from the previous analysis and are most distant from the upcoming presidential election. There is no statistical relationship between a state's competitiveness in presidential elections and grant funding. However, states with key legislative actors and those with greater economic need fare better in the receipt of discretionary grant funds.

Models 3 and 4 illustrate that there is a stark change in the way in which federal funds are distributed as a presidential election approaches.[26] Once again, estimates for state electoral competitiveness fail to reach statistical significance. However, the results *suggest* a difference. In Models 1 and 2 (grant funding in 2009 and 2010), although the estimates for the swing state variable are imprecise, they are in the negative direction, suggesting that swing states received *fewer* grant dollars. In Models 3 and 4, the estimates also are imprecise, but they are positive, suggesting that swing states received *more* grant dollars in 2011, as the presidential election drew near. While the finding is not definitive, it may indicate a change in the calculus that the president used in distributing funds.

It is important to clarify a few additional points about the findings in models 3 and 4 of table 5-3. Again, the year in which presidential electoral interests should be most salient, 2012, is missing from the dataset; ideally, the 2012 spending data would be included. If the claim made here is correct—that the proximity of the election and the benefits of the economic recovery would have given President Obama greater freedom and interest in playing electoral politics in grant funding after 2010—the 2012 data should help reinforce it. Finally, the lack of precision could be attributed, in part, to the reduced number of cases (fifty) in the 2011 dataset. Larger standard errors should be expected.

26. Three variables from models 1 and 2 do not appear in models 3 and 4. They denote states with Senate Appropriations Committee members up for reelection, Senate incumbents up for reelection, and competitive Senate elections. Because there are no Senate elections in odd-numbered years, there are no data to use to estimate the effects in 2011.

Table 5-3. *Changes in Political Influence over Nonstimulus Grant Dollars, 2009–11*[a]

Variable	2009–10		2011	
	Model 1	Model 2	Model 3	Model 4
State competitiveness				
Swing State (0,1)	−0.067	−0.079	0.088	0.031
	(0.0689)	(0.052)	(0.131)	(0.106)
Lost Cause State (0,1)	0.026		0.117	
	(0.104)		(0.201)	
State-level congressional controls				
Senate Appropriations Committee (0,1)	0.123**	0.125**	0.152^	0.145^
	(0.047)	(0.048)	(0.094)	(0.089)
Appropriations Committee Election Year (0,1)	−0.205*	−0.206*		
	(0.097)	(0.096)		
Incumbent Senator Election Year (0,1)	0.093	0.093		
	(0.081)	(0.081)		
Competitive Senate Election (0,1)	0.094	0.096		
	(0.077)	(0.077)		
Senate Leadership (0, 1)	−0.072	−0.069	0.001	0.003
	(0.056)	(0.055)	(0.159)	(0.163)
Senate Majority Party Membership (0,1,2)	0.114**	0.109**	0.169*	0.149*
	(0.048)	(0.040)	(0.094)	(0.079)
House Delegation with President (0,1)	−0.013	−0.018	0.222*	0.192^
	(0.065)	(0.065)	(0.123)	(0.144)
House Cardinal (0,1)	0.029	0.034	−0.116	−0.097
	(0.055)	(0.051)	(0.091)	(0.090)
Intergovernmental controls				
Governor Election Year (0,1)	0.105	0.103	0.352	0.417^
	(0.093)	(0.092)	(0.328)	(0.261)
Governor-President Party Alignment (0,1)	−0.077	−0.078	0.051	0.047
	(0.067)	(0.067)	(0.131)	(0.131)
Governor Election Year × Alignment (0,1)	0.009	0.009	−0.639	−0.639
	(0.110)	(0.109)	(0.387)	(0.380)
Controls and constant				
Real Gross State Product (logged)	−0.236*	−0.245*	−0.304	−0.321
	(0.118)	(0.114)	(0.218)	(0.219)
Roads (miles, logged)	−0.115	−0.113	−0.128	−0.126
	(0.075)	(0.074)	(0.140)	(0.135)
Research Institutions (logged)	0.229^	0.239^	0.220	0.231
	(0.171)	(0.169)	(0.298)	(0.291)

| | 2009–10 | | 2011 | |
Variable	Model 1	Model 2	Model 3	Model 4
Percent Elderly	–7.114*	–7.254*	–6.497	–7.115
	(2.717)	(2.794)	(5.550)	(6.029)
Unemployment Rate	–0.055**	–0.056**	–0.089^	–0.094*
	(0.017)	(0.017)	(0.047)	(0.041)
Stimulus Dollars (logged)	0.416**	0.410**	0.013	0.014
	(0.085)	(0.085)	(0.017)	(0.015)
Constant	14.844**	15.274**	21.725**	22.036**
	(2.237)	(2.212)	(2.661)	(2.735)
R^2	0.69	0.69	0.64	0.64
Observations	100	100	100	100

a. Dependent variable is logged real grant dollars per 100,000 people. Data estimated using ordinary least squares. Robust standard errors are reported.
**$p < .01$ (one-tailed test); *$p < .05$ (one-tailed test); ^$p < .10$ (one-tailed test).

Additional data would help clarify this point, but a change in the effect of presidential electoral interests on the distribution of funds could have a variety of explanations. In addition to the recovery and the increased salience of presidential electoral interests, presidential capacity may have played a key role. Every new president and administration face a learning curve, as (new) personnel grasp the reach and power of the president and the presidency. While President Obama brought on board several talented, experienced executive branch officials, a portion of his staff (broadly defined) was new to the job and to Washington and had little experience governing. President Obama shared those shortcomings. He entered the White House with no executive experience and very limited experience in the federal government. Such challenges mean that it takes time for a president to learn how to make the bureaucracy work for him.

One criticism of the learning curve theory emerges from the (correct) claim that appointees tend to serve short terms in office. Research by Dickinson and Tenpas indicates that often appointees serve only one to two years before departing.[27] However, short terms are not necessarily inconsistent with the idea of a learning curve. As new staff come to learn their roles and to

27. Dickinson and Tenpas (2002).

understand their power, they are able to implement processes that maximize that power and presidential influence. Choices made with respect to communication environments, policymaking structures, administrative environments, and agency hierarchies can offer a bit of continuity within a presidential administration. In addition, while a new administration leads to an immediate spike in "new blood," resignations from appointed positions often are staggered, allowing for continuity in procedures and levels of experience. Finally, the particular period of time in question is unique. The chief leaders of cabinet departments—the secretaries—have been incredibly stable during the Obama presidency. In fact, by one measure, the Obama cabinet has been the most stable since Franklin Pierce's cabinet, which had not a single resignation during his presidency (1853–57). Stability at the top of an agency surely allows for building expertise and stability in an administration.

In addition, regardless of how well a president comprehends his own power and that of his surrogates, personnel vacancies reduce presidential capacity. When any new president takes office, there are a large number of vacancies in politically appointed positions throughout the government—almost all of which are leadership, executive, and political positions. Vacancies are particularly high when there is a party change in the White House, as happened in January 2009. Because political appointees are able to pull the levers of control within federal agencies, their absence presents a true challenge for politically and electorally minded presidents. Moreover, in the absence of appointees, such roles are often taken on by "acting" individuals who are frequently career bureaucrats who may or may not be politically aligned with the incumbent administration. President Obama was notoriously slow at filling executive branch vacancies, as academics like law professor Anne O'Connell and media outlets like the *New York Times* have noted.[28]

The start of a new presidential administration introduces a new, often inexperienced chief executive who must govern a huge bureaucracy that he does not fully understand and has not fully staffed; that description applies exceptionally well to Obama in 2009. This administrative naïveté presents challenges for governing, but it also limits the president's ability to politicize public policy, particularly with micro-level grant allocations. However, as

---

28. Anne Joseph O'Connell, "Waiting for Leadership: President Obama's Record in Staffing Key Agency Positions and How to Improve the Appointments Process," Center for American Progress (April 2010) (www.americanprogress.org/wp-content/uploads/issues/2010/04/pdf/dww_appointments.pdf); Michael D. Shear, "Politics and Vetting Leave Key U.S. Posts Long Unfilled," *New York Times*, May 2, 2013 (www.nytimes.com/2013/05/03/us/politics/top-posts-remain-vacant-throughout-obama-administration.html?pagewanted=all&_r=0).

an administration wears on, the president and his staff gain knowledge and capacity. Political appointees take their posts. Presidential electoral interests become more salient. The politicization of public policy can be more fully realized, and the president is able to coordinate and advance his goals. Differences in politicization between 2009–10 and 2011 may have arisen in part because of the unique economic conditions in the former period. Yet such changes in new administrations are not unique or exceptional; they are routine and expected and may help to explain the distribution of federal funds during the first three years of the Obama presidency.

Conclusion

This chapter provides insight into a unique period in American history. As President Obama took office on January 20, 2009, the American economy was in shambles and conditions were worsening each day. The new president and his counterparts in Congress saw a path toward recovery, and that path was the American Recovery and Reinvestment Act of 2009. What became known as "the stimulus" entailed a huge injection of capital into the economy and came to be one of the most controversial pieces of legislation that President Obama signed. ARRA offered not only a huge flow of federal funding but also a distinctive policy environment that can be used to evaluate this book's central claim: that presidents influence distribution of federal funds to advance their electoral interests.

The analysis of stimulus and non-stimulus funds from the 2009–11 period shows some interesting findings. At first glance, the results are inconsistent with the expectation that presidents use federal funds to advance their electoral interests. Unlike in previous chapters, these data offer little support for the idea that the president targeted federal grants to swing states at the expense of non–swing states. However, that is not to say that the data from 2009–11 illustrate that presidential electoral interests no longer influenced federal funding. Instead, the results suggest that those presidential interests may be salient but may reflect a different calculus. Because the recession became the central policy issue to Americans, the president's electoral interests depended largely upon resolving the macro-economic crisis before other elements of electoral strategy could be considered and employed. The results reflect such considerations both for stimulus and non-stimulus money.

In the context of stimulus funding, the lack of political influence shows the importance of policy and political context in evaluating the administration of a law. ARRA gave the president and his surrogates exceptional discretionary authority. Despite that authority, it appears that the distribution of funds largely went to satisfy legislative needs and to do what it was intended to do: provide relief to those Americans struggling economically. Economic conditions were severe and the politicization of the stimulus likely would have come with dramatic political and electoral costs, regardless of policy success or failure. If political influence were also associated with policy failure, the costs to the president would have been incalculable. As a result, despite the opportunity for the president to inject electoral politics into the distribution of federal grants, he truly lacked the political ability to do so—at least in 2009 and 2010. Beyond the costs of politicizing the stimulus, the president faced additional limitations in the context of non-stimulus federal spending. The data offer some limited support for the claim that the president targeted swing states with non-stimulus federal grants. However, weaknesses in presidential capacity and staffing levels likely inhibited his ability to influence the distribution of grants for electoral purposes.

In broader terms, the analysis shows that the nature of presidential electoral interests can change, particularly in the context of crisis and policy environment. In 2009–11, the president focused on a policy that addressed a pressing national problem and that he felt was necessary to position himself for reelection, even though swing state targeting appeared limited. In addition, although the character of presidential interests may change depending on external policy forces, election proximity plays a critical role in informing and driving presidential behavior.

Any president comes to office with a set of plans that he would like to implement. Those plans often require adjustment. All presidents find a need to adjust political positions, policy goals, and administrative efforts in order to accommodate the primary goal, reelection. Some presidents face unique external forces that also affect the way in which they approach the job and pursue policy, electoral, and political goals. Just as John F. Kennedy did not expect to play a game of nuclear chicken with the Soviet Union and George W. Bush never anticipated being a wartime president, when Barack Obama declared his candidacy for president, he did not foresee governing during the worst economic crisis since the Great Depression. However, context and timing affect presidential behavior, and as 2009 began in the midst of a crisis, a new president responded in ways that differed from those of his predecessors.

6

A Web of Bureaucratic Control

Electoral interests drive presidents to influence the distribution of federal funds. Whether that influence involves targeting funds to swing states or advancing electorally strategic policy goals, presidents seek to get the most out of federal funding allocations. In addition, distributors—executive branch personnel with direct spending authority—have a critical role in helping presidents use the federal largesse as a campaign tool and thereby to realize their goals. This book shows that with a few (predictable) exceptions—namely those involving more insulated, independent institutions—distributors produce policy outcomes that are consistent with the president's goals.

This chapter essentially seeks to open a black box wrapped in red tape: political influence in the American bureaucracy. While it is clear that presidents influence federal fund allocations in electorally strategic ways, the precise processes and mechanisms by which they do it remain to be shown. The president is a lone individual charged with overseeing a bureaucracy that includes nearly 3 million civilian and 1.5 million military employees. One challenge that he faces is getting this burgeoning branch of government to respond in ways that support his electoral (and other) goals. Does the president's immediate staff contact distributive agencies and explicitly inform them of presidential preferences in allocations? Do presidents give political actors final decisionmaking authority? Or is the process more subtle and varied, with presidents relying on layers of contacts to diffuse information throughout the bureaucracy? In evaluating presidents' ability to engage in pork barrel politics, it is vital to understand the mechanisms that facilitate political or electoral control.

Too often, political scientists and other researchers studying political power and distributive influence find it efficient to illustrate statistical relationships without providing a full account of how they manifest. This book provides that account. This chapter and the next add essential detail to the description of presidential influence on federal spending given thus far. Using both systematic and qualitative sources, they paint a picture of how the bureaucracy functions and how political forces affect its function, providing insight into how agency personnel, design, and process intersect to invite political influence and produce policy. The discussion in this chapter is based on data from the 2007–08 Survey on the Future of the Government Service, which offers a look at how the government's highest-ranking career and appointed bureaucratic officials view the policy process, their role within it, and the forces that affect it.[1]

Administrative Control and Presidential Power

Personnel—both career civil servants and appointees—are the key to understanding how a bureaucracy works. Career civil servants are important actors in policymaking. Numbering in the millions, they make daily decisions that affect policy in myriad ways. Their roles vary from overseeing state offices of federal agencies to serving as directors of federal programs to providing customer service at local Social Security Administration offices. To varying degrees, these individuals enjoy civil service protections. Civil servants typically cannot be transferred, demoted, or fired without cause. Research on civil servants has examined their ability and efforts to develop autonomous spheres of power within government, often through traits such as personality and expertise.[2] Other forces that empower careerists include the complexity of tasks,[3] poor monitoring,[4] policy-motivated goals,[5] discretion,[6] and the design of bureaucratic institutions.[7] Using formal and informal tools, presidents work to ensure that civil servants make decisions consistent with presidential views.[8]

1. Lewis (2009).
2. Rourke (1984); Carpenter (2001); Wood and Waterman (1994).
3. Carpenter (2001).
4. Miller (1992; Wilson (1989).
5. Carpenter (2001); Gailmard and Patty (2007); Wilson (1989).
6. Huber and Shipan (2002); Ting (2012).
7. Fiorina (1977); Seidman and Gilmour (1986).
8. Nathan (1975).

Appointees are selected by the president for a variety reasons, often due to their loyalty and alignment with presidential goals. They are the president's surrogates in leadership and decisionmaking positions throughout the executive branch. They serve largely at the pleasure of the president. Given the size and diverse nature of the bureaucracy, political appointees help limit the president's organizational challenges, including shirking and drift.[9]

Presidents have broad institutional means of influencing the policy process within bureaucratic agencies, including personnel politicization, environmental politicization (detailed below), and centralization.[10] Personnel politicization is the process by which presidents increase the saturation (number) and penetration of political appointees within an agency.[11] Environmental politicization occurs when political actors ensure that communication and the workplace environment within an agency is subject to political pressure. Centralization is the process by which decisionmaking authority is transferred to higher-level political appointees, inside and sometimes outside agencies.[12] Each provides presidents greater opportunities to elicit responsiveness and control outcomes.

The location and strength of political institutions also have dramatic effects on policy. Throughout the twentieth century and often with Congress's assistance, presidents expanded presidential staff and organization.[13] They were thereby able to centralize decisionmaking in newly established White House institutions, including the White House Office, the Office of Management and Budget (OMB), and a host of other institutions inside the Executive Office of the President.[14] In addition, the White House developed policy-specific liaison offices for key groups, institutions, and issues to provide greater information sharing and control in those areas.[15] The growth of what scholars refer to as "the institutional presidency" expanded the reach of presidential power, facilitated White House development and coordination

---

9. Miller (1992).

10. Reorganization is another such tactic. Administrative reorganization empowers presidents to design decisionmaking and leadership structures in ways that enhance executive authority, empower appointees, and can determine policy outcomes (Arnold 1995; Lewis 2003; Pfiffner 1996; Seidman and Gilmour 1986). Reorganization, which often is large in scope, requires congressional approval; it is not discussed at length in this book.

11. Lewis (2008).

12. Rudalevige (2002).

13. Light (1995); Rudalevige (2002); Weko (1995).

14. Ragsdale and Theiss (1997); Wyszomirski (1991).

15. Tenpas (2000).

of policy, and placed greater authority in offices that were proximate to the White House both institutionally and physically.

Presidents not only augmented the power of the presidency, they also strengthened ties between the White House and government agencies. Presidents sought to transfer decisionmaking authority up the chain of command and into the hands of agency heads or cabinet secretaries or to the White House itself. Often justified as an effective means of improving communication and coordination, centralization also serves to decrease shirking and ideological drift and increase monitoring and presidential control of the bureaucracy.[16]

The result is that centralization offers presidents multiple ways to inject their political preferences into policymaking. One occurs when White House officials are directly empowered to make policy decisions, so that key political actors can use their authority to influence outcomes. Centralization and environmental politicization also can expand the institutional reach of the presidency by developing and using a highly political hierarchy to make policy decisions or convey presidential preferences and apply political pressure throughout the bureaucracy. In essence, the president does not need to pull the levers of power; he and his surrogates simply make clear which levers they want pulled.

Incentives for Political Control

Targeting political actors with distributive authority allows presidents the flexibility to maximize benefits (strategic fund allocations) and minimize costs (policy failure). To evaluate how presidents elicit responsiveness in policymaking institutions, it is critical to understand how differences among agencies affect presidential efforts to gain administrative control.

Presidential preferences over policy outcomes can vary dramatically across agencies because federal agencies administer policy in substantively different areas; accordingly, to evaluate the manner in which presidents approach political control, it is important to consider presidential goals in context. For example, the National Nuclear Security Agency (NNSA), a subunit of the Department of Energy, "ensures the nuclear warheads and bombs in the U.S. nuclear weapons stockpile are safe, secure, and effective in order to provide the nation with a credible nuclear deterrent."[17] The NNSA provides a service

16. Galvin and Shogun (2004); Moe (1985); Robinson and others (2007); Rudalevige (2002).
17. National Nuclear Security Agency, "Managing the Stockpile" (http://nnsa.energy.gov/ourmission/managingthestockpile).

that is essential to maintaining the security and military power of the United States, and performing its functions requires a high level of expertise. Using administrative tools to exert political control in such an agency not only could be disastrous for the president who chose to do so but would endanger the lives of Americans and others throughout the world. For the NNSA, presidents likely prefer expertise rather than politics to determine outcomes. Even a president seeking to gain political control in executive branch institutions would likely spare NNSA because any benefits from politicization would be far outweighed by the costs of loss of expertise.

However, while agency operations affect a president's decision to introduce politics into policymaking, presidents do not have to forgo administrative control across the board. Politicization of personnel and policy at the expense of competence or expertise can present both political costs and political benefits, which vary dramatically according to an agency's mission and the policy outcomes that the agency generates.

The NNSA deals with nuclear arms and potential Armageddon. On the other hand, the Delta Regional Authority does not have as tall an order to fill. The stated goal of the Delta Regional Authority is "to enhance economic development and improve the quality of life for the hard-working residents of the Delta Region,"[18] and it does so through the distribution of federal grants. While individuals in the Delta region depend on those grants to pursue greater economic opportunities, the costs and benefits of politicizing this agency differ dramatically from those of an institution such as NNSA.

The Delta Regional Authority provides a context in which the president can engage in politically strategic targeting of funds. When politics influences policy at this agency, the result is imperfect allocation of federal funds, largely to a specific region—a result that is unlikely to cause profound problems. In fact, as long as funds are distributed to eligible needy applicants, political influence may be difficult to identify, particularly when the consequences are so minimal. Compared with the NNSA, the Delta Regional Authority presents the president with a low-cost, high-benefit opportunity to politicize personnel and administrative structures.

In administering the government, presidents consider the risks and rewards of political control (concepts that vary across and even within agencies) in their overall political, electoral, and policy strategy. Generally, agencies that provide political and electoral benefits and carry low risks and/ or low costs from politicization become appealing centers for presidential

18. Delta Regional Authority, "About DRA" (www.dra.gov/about-us/default.aspx).

political and administrative control. In fact, presidents are uniquely positioned to identify, across and within agencies, potential costs and benefits and to maximize net benefits.

Extracting Electoral Benefits through Political Control

To examine more precisely how presidents influence not just broad spending policy but micro-level outputs, it is necessary to ask a few basic questions. Which agency staff make federal spending decisions? Are those key personnel political loyalists or expert bureaucrats? Which outside forces influence agency spending decisions and how?

To help answer those questions, I relied on the Survey on the Future of the Government Service, conducted from 2007 to 2008.[19] The survey sampled 7,448 federal executives across the government; 2,398 responded at least partially to the survey.[20] The data that I use here include the complete responses from 1,678 federal executives, of whom 11.1 percent (187) were political appointees, defined as individuals who are Senate-confirmed, Schedule C or non-career Senior Executive Service employees. The remaining respondents were career federal executives. In addition, the data include 1,031 respondents who noted that they were distributors; those respondents account for 63.8 percent of all respondents. The focus on federal executives, who often are intimately involved in decisionmaking at the highest levels, ensures that all respondents play critical roles in the administration of policy in the executive branch. The survey questions touch on a host of topics, including respondents' background, position, and qualifications, allowing for assessment of important issues such as expertise, political affiliation and loyalty, readiness to perform, and the extent of political pressure in policymaking. The survey is an exceptional source of data for testing questions regarding federal personnel and the role of politics in the administrative process. In addition to their broad usefulness, these data provide specific insights that serve the purposes of this study. For example, the survey asks whether respondents deal with federal spending policy:

19. The survey is a rich source of data from leaders within the executive branch of the U.S. government. Ideally, it would provide longitudinal (multiyear, repeated) data. However, the survey was conducted only once. Despite the one-time nature of the data, they still provide a keen look inside the executive branch and offer another forum in which to test questions critical to this study.

20. Details regarding the precise methodology used in the survey can be found in Clinton and others (2012).

Does your job deal directly *with decisions about:*

Procurement of the content of contracts with private firms? (Y/N)
Licenses or loans granted to private firms or citizens? (Y/N)
Grants to states and local governments, other organizations, or
    individuals? (Y/N)

This question allows the survey data to be divided according to "distributors"—those answering "yes" to one of the questions above—and "nondistributors." Differences in the experience of federal executives who deal with spending and that of those who deal with other types of policy illustrate whether presidential behaviors differ across areas of policy.

Federal Spending: The Decisionmakers

The president's appointment power allows him to politicize the executive branch in multiple ways. First, the president can select appointees based on political, work, and background characteristics that signal support for presidential interests. Second, he can influence the number of appointees in bureaucratic institutions. Third, he can give these actors substantial decisionmaking authority. The result is a multifaceted effort to enlist an army of appointees who are loyal, responsive, and politically sensitive.

The president's ability to affect personnel also extends to civil servants. Presidents can transfer individuals throughout the Senior Executive Service (SES) and reassign responsibilities, thereby moving responsive SES actors into more influential roles while rendering less responsive actors ineffective.[21] Moreover, when political appointees or White House institutions have influence or authority over agency hiring decisions, the administration can work to ensure that new hires in other areas of the civil service reflect presidential interests. Because civil servants can play key roles in federal spending, any power that political actors retain in staffing civil service positions can enhance electoral responsiveness. In the end, presidents and their surrogates wield broad powers to influence the character of the executive branch workforce through politicization of staffing decisions.

In the context of federal spending, such powers are important. Presidents realize that executive officials with spending power can deliver (or restrict) electoral benefits; therefore they identify those positions and work to ensure that the people who occupy them have personal and professional characteristics that signal greater responsiveness, such as political experience and

21. Lewis (2008); Wood and Waterman (1991, 1994).

alignment with the presidential ideology. In so doing, an election-driven president ensures that those administering distributive policy look fundamentally
different from other policymakers and better reflect his interests.

A look at political appointees offers some evidence on this point. It should
come as no surprise that political appointees, who almost always serve in key
leadership and decisionmaking roles in any administration, reflect the ideology
of the sitting president. In 2007, President George W. Bush oversaw a corps
of appointees who were quite conservative, unlike their career civil service
counterparts. With respect to self-reported ideology, 58 percent of appointees
reported being "somewhat conservative," "conservative," or "very conservative," while 32 percent reported being "moderate." Although ideology and
loyalty are not identical concepts, a president can be more confident of the
loyalty of ideologically aligned appointees than of ideologically opposed ones.

Beyond ideology, appointees reported more *political* experience. Over
56 percent of appointed respondents claimed to have had prior political experience (either in government, as a candidate or elected official, or through
work with a party). In fact, 20 percent of appointees reported prior experience working in the White House. Political experience, which implies that
potential appointees have greater knowledge of politics and an understanding
that political principals have expectations regarding appointees' behavior, is
essential for responsiveness.

That political appointees are ideologically aligned with the president and
politically experienced is not, of course, a recent discovery. It is expected.
However, confirming expectations can be informative and offer evidence that
data are valid on their face. The Survey on the Future of the Government Service provides additional evidence about the characteristics of appointees and
their relationship to federal spending. The data suggest that President Bush
was slightly more likely to assign conservative appointees to handle federal
spending than moderate or liberal appointees. The result is that, on average,
those making decisions on federal spending tended to be more in line ideologically with the president than other government employees.

The relationship between politics and federal spending goes further. Presidents do not simply ensure that appointed distributors are more conservative
or liberal; presidents also assign additional political appointees to areas of the
executive branch that administer spending policy. The survey asks all respondents (appointed and career) whether the number of political appointees in
their agency has increased. The underlying assumption is that presidents can
foster a more political environment by increasing the number of political
appointees in an agency. Distributive respondents reported statistically larger

increases than nondistributive respondents: 3.16 and 3.01, respectively, on a five-point scale.[22] This difference shows that those in areas that administered federal spending saw greater politicization of their agency than those in other areas. In addition, distributors' mean response was to report some level of increase in the number of appointees.

Together, those survey results suggest that because spending gives presidents access to electoral benefits, presidents are particularly sensitive to the number and characteristics of political appointees administering federal spending. They select ideologically aligned and politically experienced individuals to distribute federal dollars, and when possible, they increase the number of appointees overseeing federal spending. The results show White House recognition of the value and importance of appointees and the priority given to selecting them.

Yet the presidential interest in politicizing federal spending extends beyond appointees. Careerists play key roles in any administration and certainly do so in areas of federal spending. There are well-documented means by which political actors penetrate the civil service. The survey probes such issues, allowing insight into distributors' motives for entering government service and the manner in which they are recruited. One survey question asks:

Now thinking about your original decision to enter government service, how important were each of the following in your decision?

Enthusiasm for the party/person in power in the White House.
Personal request by a higher-level agency official.

Non-appointed (career) respondents selected answers on a scale of 1 to 5: "not important at all," "not too important," "moderately important," "important," and "very important" (1 = not important at all; 5 = very important). Although point estimates are statistically mixed, the results, reported in table 6-1, suggest that distributors were more likely than nondistributors to enter government service because of enthusiasm for the White House or because of a personal connection to someone selected by the White House. This finding is consistent with the expectation that because presidents seek political and electoral benefits, they try to assign supporters to distributive roles. It is often easy to deduce who in an applicant pool is enthusiastic about the president

22. Respondents were asked whether, since they had been in their current position, the number of political appointees or noncareer executives in their department or agency had changed. Responses ranged from 1 (decreased significantly) to 5 (increased significantly).

Table 6-1. *Motivations for Government Service*[a]

Decision to Work in Government	Distributors	Nondistributors
Enthusiasm for the party/person in the White House	1.45	1.36
Personal request by a higher-level agency official	2.06*	1.74*

a. The values represent the mean response to the question "Now thinking about your original decision to enter government service, how important were each of the following in your decision?" "Distributors" signifies a respondent who deals directly with federal grant allocations. Responses ranged from 1 = *Not important at all* to 5 = *Very important*. Number of distributors = 849; nondistributors = 493.

*$p < .05$ (one-tailed test), signifying a difference between distributors and nondistributors.

or the party in the White House. A candidate can easily convey such support through a résumé or interview by including volunteer work for political campaigns or affiliation with specific organizations that denote political alignment with the White House.

More convincing are the responses from nonappointed respondents who entered government work because of a "personal request by a higher-level agency official." Distributors were significantly more likely to have entered government service because of a personal request than nondistributors. Rather than trying to identify possibly responsive individuals in a broad applicant pool, agency officials can use personal networking and familiarity with individuals to target and recruit federal personnel. Such an effort would likely be far more effective at achieving responsiveness because personal familiarity with an individual reduces the risk of a hiring error.

The results in table 6-1 illustrate that politics affects executive branch personnel in two key ways. First, political motivations can affect an individual's decision to enter government service. People understand that the bureaucracy is a political institution, and support for a president may make a job in his administration more appealing. Second, the personnel system in the executive branch strategically identifies and recruits individuals who are likely to be responsive to the president and other executive branch principals. Although presidents want the entire bureaucracy to be responsive to their preferences, the results show that they pay particular attention to staffing positions that are most likely to lead to electoral benefits. Targeting the right kind of personnel gives presidents and their surrogates greater control over policymaking, particularly with regard to spending.

Federal Spending: Sources of Influence

Despite their best efforts, presidents face limits on their ability to politicize the bureaucracy. The supply of qualified loyalists is finite, and there can be statutory restrictions on the number of appointees allowed in an agency and on the president's ability to transfer appointees. Career staffing can be manipulated only to a certain extent. To overcome those challenges, presidents can use alternative techniques to generate greater responsiveness to their interests. For example, presidents can generate *environmental politicization* by structuring decisionmaking and communication hierarchies to allow political actors to have policy influence and to maintain an atmosphere in which political pressure and contact are pervasive. In this situation, careerists are constantly reminded of presidential or administration preferences and expectations regarding policymaking. Similar to politicization of personnel, environmental politicization allows senior, loyal, and responsive personnel to exercise policy influence or use strategic, political communication where responsiveness is lacking, particularly in areas that can deliver political or electoral benefits.

Fostering environmental politicization can be a highly effective means of eliciting responsiveness. Given the important benefits that federal spending provides, distributors' experience with political pressure and influence should differ from that of nondistributors. Environmental politicization through the application of political pressure is a more flexible tool than other methods of politicization because pressure can be effectively applied to specific individuals, groups of individuals, or entire agencies, depending on presidential need and intent.

The benefit and challenge of identifying influence by using data from the Survey on the Future of the Government Service is that because the sample consists of federal executives, every respondent has an influential role. However, policy influence is not necessarily equal in type or degree across all respondents. Variation exists with regard to level and scope of authority, across and within agencies. The survey offers a chance to examine that variation and identify both the sources of influence (who?) and the manner in which it manifests (how?).

One important benefit of using the survey to examine internal and external political and policy influence is the conservatism of the data. Federal executives and individuals in leadership positions in all spheres of life are prone to self-aggrandizement—that is, they may overestimate their own value and importance in responding to a survey. Several questions, however, ask respondents about the influence of *other* actors in the policy process. If self-aggrandizement is present, it would underestimate the influence of other actors, making their influence more difficult to identify. Another key benefit of the survey is that it asks federal executives directly about processes and behaviors within their institutions and in their daily working lives. These data allow a firsthand look into the avenues of influence within the bureaucracy. Specifically, in probing policy influence, the survey examines the role of key political and nonpolitical institutional actors. One question asks:

In general, how much influence do the following groups have over policy decisions in your agency?

White House
Office of Management and Budget
Political appointees
Senior civil servants
Congressional committees
Republicans in Congress
Democrats in Congress

The responses are given on a scale of 1 to 5: "none," "little," "some," "a good bit," "a great deal" (1 = none; 5 = a great deal). This question allows insight into how key actors in the executive and legislative branches affect "policy decisions" in particular. The appeal of this question is that it refers to *policy* influence specifically; referring to influence in general could lead to dramatic variation in respondents' interpretation of the term. The variety of groups surveyed provides a look at impact across and within branches and among political and nonpolitical actors.

Table 6-2 shows the average responses of career distributors and nondistributors to the question of policy influence. The results provide some interesting information about who influences policy and the different experiences faced by distributors. First, across the board, career respondents note that political actors in the *executive branch* wield tremendous policy influence. According to distributors, the White House, OMB, and political appointees have more influence than senior civil servants and substantially more influence than congressional actors (congressional committees, Democrats, and Republicans). The same result generally holds for nondistributors.[23] In fact, both distributors and nondistributors report that political appointees and OMB officials wield the most policy influence.

These results show that presidents delegate not only administrative functions but political influence, relying on both hand-selected appointees and

---

23. The one difference is that on average, nondistributors report that senior civil servants have slightly more policy influence than the White House.

Table 6-2. *Policy Influence of Institutional Actors*[a]

Institution	Distributors	Nondistributors
White House	3.87*	3.74*
Office of Management and Budget	4.15*	3.94*
Political appointees	4.30*	4.20*
Senior civil servants	3.84	3.77
Congressional committees	3.77*	3.52*
Republicans in Congress	3.48*	3.24*
Democrats in Congress	3.21*	2.99*

a. The values represent the mean response of career-level federal executives to the question "In general, how much influence do the following groups have over policy decisions in your agency?" Responses ranged from 1 = *None* to 5 = *A great deal.* Number of distributors = 947; nondistributors = 493.

*$p < .05$ (one-tailed test), signifying a statistical difference between distributors and nondistributors.

staff from the politically powerful sections of the Executive Office of the President. This finding sheds light on how they influence micro-level distributive policy. Table 6-2 shows that a network of executive actors allows presidential interests to invade a large, complex bureaucracy and affect outcomes.

In absolute terms, the career federal executives describe a politically powerful and influential president. However, when the experiences of distributors and nondistributors are compared, a view emerges of a president who also is politically sensitive to the benefits of federal spending. Table 6-2 shows that almost universally, distributors report significantly more policy influence from each category than do nondistributors. The only group for which the difference (between responses of distributors and nondistributors) fails to reach statistical significance is nonpolitical actors: senior civil servants.

The results also indicate that Congress is politically sensitive to the benefits of distributive public policy. Legislative actors seek greater policy influence among distributors than nondistributors, a finding that is in line with the view of the election-driven legislator who tries to influence the distribution of funds in order to improve his or her electoral odds. However, the findings in table 6-2 suggest that presidents do this in a more influential way.

In many cases, presidents and their surrogates can influence policy decisions within agencies, directly or indirectly. However, one challenge with respect to the survey question on policy influence is that it fails provide context. It is certain that political actors have policy influence, but it is less clear whether they obtain it directly through formal powers or through less direct means. What is likely is that policy influence manifests through a combination of direct administrative control and indirect political pressure. Political pressure can induce policy responsiveness and reduce shirking in areas where the president, White House staff, and other political appointees have a limited formal role in policymaking.

Measuring political pressure can be difficult. However, measuring contact is one way to gain insight into the degree of political pressure. If political actors seek to influence policymakers, they should contact them with some regularity. Although contact does not occur only to convey political interests, it is difficult to do so without contact. The survey asks respondents about contact with a wide variety of actors and institutions. This question reads:

How often do you have contact with:

White House
Members or staff of congressional committees
Republicans in Congress or their staff
Democrats in Congress or their staff
Political appointees in your department or agency

The responses are given on a scale of 1 to 5: "never," "rarely," "monthly," "weekly," and "daily" (1 = never; 5 = daily). The precision of this question helps to evaluate how often career executives deal directly with political actors.

Table 6-3 shows career federal executives' reported contact with political actors and institutions, once again dividing respondents according to whether they are distributors or nondistributors. The results show that distributors report greater contact with political actors (with the exception of the White House) than do nondistributors. This increased contact is true with respect to both legislative actors[24] and political appointees. This finding comports with the idea that distributors provide elected officials opportunities to participate in pork barrel politics.

These results not only demonstrate that distributors report more contact with political appointees than do nondistributors but also shed light on the extent of appointee influence. It is apparent from the results in table 6-3 (and was confirmed in separate tests) that career federal executives have

24. As mentioned previously, because the data include individuals who deal with more congressionally dominated types of spending, the contact with Congress is sensible. Respondents likely deal with distributive decisions on earmarking and on formula and block grants. In addition, because Congress requires reporting as part of the oversight process and often those dealing with budgetary matters have additional demands for reports, legislative institutions (committees and members' offices) would be expected to contact distributors more often.

Table 6-3. *Career-Level Federal Executives' Contact with Political Institutions*[a]

Institution	Distributors	Nondistributors
White House	1.67	1.74
Congressional committees	2.39*	2.22*
Congressional Republicans	2.27*	2.09*
Congressional Democrats	2.28*	2.11*
Political appointees	3.82*	3.65*

a. The values represent the mean response among career-level federal executives to the question "How often do you have contact with [institution]?" Responses ranged from 1 = *Never* to 5 = *Daily*. Number of distributors = 853; nondistributors = 498.

*p < .05 (one-tailed test), signifying a statistical difference between distributors and nondistributors.

significantly more contact with political appointees than with Congress or the White House.[25] In fact, the values of average responses in table 6-3 add substance to this claim. On average, career respondents report that contact with appointees occurs about weekly and contact with Congress occurs almost rarely.[26] These results suggest that contact occurs with more immediate supervisors rather than individuals at the highest levels of the executive branch. As further evidence of the structure of the communication environment, White House contact with distributors is not only indistinguishable from contact with nondistributors but also muted in absolute terms. On average, career respondents report that White House contact occurs slightly less than "rarely." That suggests that the president does not convey information directly to careerists; instead, he relies on political appointees to convey information.

These differences and the ubiquitous appointee contact likely emerge from a president's reliance on a complex, hierarchical network of surrogates to foster a politically charged flow of communication and information in which pressure is used to elicit responsiveness. Presidents face constraints because of the size of the executive branch and the number of policy decisions that they would like to influence. As a result, they rely on political appointees to

25. It would be difficult to rule out the role of congressional intervention filtering through executive branch institutions, except that congressional contact with the executive branch is muted. In an alternative scenario, the executive branch actors contacting federal executives are simply responding to efforts of Congress to politicize policy outcomes (and distributive decisions). However, this scenario is difficult to support when Congress's contact with the executive branch is limited.

26. The response value for "weekly" is 4, and the average response for distributors reporting contact with political appointees is 3.82 (3.65 for nondistributors). The response value for "rarely" is 2, and the average response for distributors reporting contact with legislative institutions ranges from 2.39 to 2.27 (2.22 to 2.09 for nondistributors).

Figure 6-1. *Communication Environment in the Executive Branch*

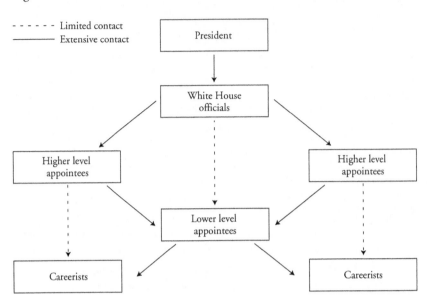

influence the distribution of funds rather than on direct White House intervention. In addition to being a resource-saving option, relying on appointees is appealing because they often have a more personal relationship with career executives. Because of that relationship, communication in conveying presidential needs may be more fluid. Figure 6-1 illustrates how a hierarchical communication structure may function. Presidents inform political appointees of their preferences; appointees subsequently inform other appointees and career personnel of those preferences, with the expectation of responsiveness permeating the communication environment.[27]

To assess whether the hierarchy illustrated in figure 6-1 truly exists, it is necessary to evaluate the communication environment surrounding political appointees, in particular the top and bottom of the structure. Table 6-4 shows political appointees' responses to the question on p. 146 about contact.

___

27. While figure 6-1 illustrates a communication environment within the executive branch, it is important to note that these forces do not exist in a vacuum. They are subject to forces outside the government, including constituencies like citizens, interest groups, policy organizations, corporations, and subnational governments.

Table 6-4. *Appointees' Contact with Political Institutions*[a]

Institution	Distributors	Nondistributors
White House	2.71	2.61
Congressional committees	3.24*	2.69*
Congressional Republicans	3.10*	2.59*
Congressional Democrats	3.00*	2.66*
Political appointees	4.68	4.55

a. The values represent the mean response among political appointees to the question "How often do you have contact with [institution]?" Responses ranged from 1= *Never* to 5 = *Daily*. Number of distributors = 94; nondistributors = 81.

*$p < .05$ (one-tailed test), signifying a difference between distributors and non-distributors.

The results offer evidence of the expected flow of communication within the executive branch. While differences between distributor-appointees and non-distributor-appointees are imprecise, the differences in level of contact across categories of political actors are clearer. Political appointees have more contact with the White House than career federal executives do (compare table 6-3 and table 6-4). Similarly, political appointees have contact with other appointees almost daily—significantly more often than careerists do. It appears from the results in tables 6-4 and 6-3 that the White House communicates more often with political appointees and that political appointees have substantial communication both within their own appointee network and with career federal executives. These results suggest once again that a strategic structuring of communication from political actors to careerists helps explain how and to what extent political preferences are conveyed from the White House throughout the bureaucracy.

By ensuring that the right individuals staff the bureaucracy and that they have the authority to make policy decisions, presidents are able to generate direct policy responsiveness. However, politicized staffing and the strategic assignment of decisionmaking authority provide other benefits for a president seeking responsiveness. Agency leaders can apply political pressure within agencies, contributing another means of eliciting policy responsiveness. Distributors are particularly subject to such control, given their ability to deliver key electoral benefits that presidents seek. On the other hand, contact with and policy influence from political actors can also be benign. The questions above do not offer a normative assessment of whether political actors are advancing technocratic policy goals or political and electoral interests. However, another section of the survey offers insight into careerists' interpretations of the purpose of contact and influence.

If career federal executives tend to advance policy-centered, mission-based goals and are resistant to or resentful of the politicization of policymaking, political pressure can make them unhappy in their jobs and may lead them to leave government service. One survey question asks respondents about the likelihood of leaving their job for a host of reasons, many of which reflect political pressure or influence. Specifically, the question asks

How important are each of these factors for your decision to stay or leave?

Problems with political appointees
Problems with White House
Policy disagreement with current administration
Problems with Congress

The responses are given on a scale of 1 to 5: "not important at all," "not too important," "moderately important," "important," and "very important" (1 = not important at all; 5 = very important).

Table 6-5 indicates that across the board, distributors were more likely than nondistributors to leave their jobs because of problems with political actors and institutions.[28] The results suggest that the environment in which distributive career personnel work is more politicized and challenging than that in which nondistributive staff work. Respondents also noted that the biggest political factor affecting their employment decision was an issue involving executive branch political actors: appointees.[29] Respondents identify such issues as a "problem" or a "disagreement." Most striking is that distributors report more problems or issues than nondistributors for each prompt from the question. The threat or possibility of exit means that such issues are a serious problem for respondents and that they are more intense in distributive policy areas.

A federal executive's decision to exit the government workforce allows presidential surrogates to fill the vacated position as they see fit and thereby enhance the political environment by selecting a more responsive individual. In fact, these results combined with those reported in table 6-1 suggest that political actors could drive individuals from distributive positions and then recruit more responsive replacements. Such a system of personnel replacement

28. The mean response suggests that career federal executives are unlikely to exit government service. This result comports with the idea that these individuals spend long careers in government and are comfortable with their positions, despite political pressure. That said, political pressure clearly affects their outlook at the margins in statistically significant ways.

29. In a separate analysis, the mean distributors' response to "Problems with political appointees" was the most extreme and statistically different from all other mean responses.

Table 6-5. *Career-Level Federal Executives' Workplace Challenges and Political Environment*[a]

Factor in leaving job	Distributors	Nondistributors
Problems with political appointees	2.45*	2.29*
Problems with the White House	1.96*	1.81*
Policy disagreement with administration	2.00*	1.90*
Problems with Congress	2.07*	1.82*

a. The values represent the mean response among career-level federal executives to the question "How important are each of these factors for your decision to stay or leave?" Responses ranged from 1 = *Not important at all* to 5 = *Very important*. Number of distributors = 848; nondistributors = 492.

*$p < .05$ (one-tailed test), signifying a difference between distributors and nondistributors.

would enhance the president's control over policy and increase his ability to extract electoral benefits from the system.

Because of the importance of federal spending to electoral interests, presidents and their surrogates intervene to ensure that federal executives who oversee federal spending are continually aware of the preferences and expectations of the leadership. Such political interference leads distributors to report a greater likelihood of exiting government service. These informal efforts at eliciting responsiveness—beyond personnel politicization and centralization—can have real effects on both the civil service and the outcomes that it produces.

Conclusion

The National Resource Conservation Service (NRCS) is an agency in the Department of Agriculture that illustrates the complexity of agency design and the challenges that face a president who seeks to politicize policy. NRCS falls under the purview of the secretary of agriculture and the undersecretary for natural resources and environment—both political appointees. In addition, the president appoints the NRCS chief and the chief oversees deputies. However, in addition to the central NRCS office, the agency operates offices in all fifty states. Although the state offices are charged with making critical decisions affecting their local jurisdiction, career federal executives run each office. Many of the services that the agency provides to the public are delivered through the state offices. As a result, the decentralized and professionalized (nonpolitical) nature of the agency and its state offices means that it can be challenging to inject politics into the administrative process, particularly in comparison with an appointee-heavy or centralized agency.

Presidents always want agency decisions to reflect their own preferences, however they define them. One way to enhance political responsiveness in an agency like the NRCS is to closely monitor agency decisions or to ensure that all final decisions pass through political appointees in the national office. Short of transferring powers directly to the White House or giving different agencies policy jurisdiction, presidents can encourage greater appointee intervention within agencies or increase the number of appointees in order to exact greater political control over policy. However, when agency decisionmaking rests in the hands of individuals likely to be less responsive to the president, alternative efforts like politicizing the communication environment can help presidents maintain control.

Rather than playing an active and direct role in the daily affairs of state offices, central agency appointees may use frequent contact to discuss with career executives the preferences of the administration and the most efficient means of achieving its goals. By constantly relaying information on administration priorities to career executives, appointees can convey the president's behavioral and policy expectations. As in any organization, the leadership can convey to staff its preferences and in an indirect way drive staff to promote leadership goals. In a federal agency, staff are reminded of whom they serve every time that they walk into their office as pictures of the president and department head are usually prominently displayed. Environmental politicization can be a highly effective means of promoting responsiveness, especially in institutions less likely to be responsive to the president.

Political control and presidential influence exist below the macro-level. Unlike broad approaches such as politicization and centralization, the mechanisms described here are unilateral and, more important, flexible. As a result, structuring internal decisionmaking to empower political actors and applying political pressure can be used in conjunction with broader, comprehensive efforts such as bureaucratic reorganization or in place of such techniques. The appeal of the mechanisms and methods described in this chapter is that often they do not require legislative authorization and they can be employed quickly and efficiently, often behind the scenes, away from the prying eyes of Congress and the public.

7

The Mechanisms of Presidential Spending Power

In the regular administration of public policy, the bureaucratic process is difficult to understand and navigate. When politics enters policymaking, the process becomes even more opaque. For personal, reputational, and often legal reasons, political officials have an interest in keeping private the details of how they influence and manipulate policy. Accordingly, throughout history, presidents and their appointees have claimed executive privilege, defended lawsuits, and even resigned in their efforts to keep the administrative process out of the public eye and the hands of Congress.[1]

Bureaucratic outcomes often are readily observable because government reporting—particularly in the context of federal spending—is public and pervasive. However, the internal machinations that produce those outcomes often are far less visible. Researchers studying public policy and administration often make inferences or assumptions based on observation of policy results and draw on theory to explain outcomes. I do so to varying degrees in the previous chapters of this book to demonstrate that electoral interests motivate presidents as well as Congress to influence policy. Each successive analysis works to analyze internal agency processes and to assess the mechanisms used by presidents to affect policy. However, it remains difficult to identify precisely how influence is exercised.

There exist multiple explanations of how presidents control the bureaucratic process and incorporate their own preferences into policy. One is that presidents and their surrogates intervene directly by instructing bureaucrats and appointees to make policy decisions that are consistent with their interests.

1. See Stack (2008).

For example, the secretary of the interior might call a policy administrator in the Bureau of Indian Affairs to explain the administration's expectations about the design of a specific housing program. Another explanation is that bureaucrats, understanding presidential preferences and realizing that there can be consequences for rogue bureaucrats and agencies that ignore those preferences, act strategically to avoid consequences; an agency would then operate on administrative autopilot, working to meet the president's goals with no need for intervention. In that case, an administrator in the Bureau of Indian Affairs would be well aware of the preferences of the secretary of the interior (and the president) and design policies that reflect their interests, knowing that they will pass any hierarchical approval process. In both cases, policy outcomes reflect what the president wants.

Employing Elite Interviews

The discussion in this chapter is based on elite interviews that I conducted during 2010–11 with individuals inside and outside government who deal with federal grants daily. Specifically, the respondents include federal bureaucrats and appointees, state bureaucrats and appointees, and interest group lobbyists, all of whom worked in the area of federal discretionary grant programs. These interviews help answer a critical question: what are the mechanisms used to exercise political influence in the federal grants process? Further, the interviews offer the first comprehensive look at the politicization of federal fund distribution not from a bird's-eye, statistical perspective but from inside the system. They provide a look at the complexity of the federal grants process and offer a detailed assessment of how political forces affect nearly every stage of grant making, ultimately shaping outcomes in ways that reflect presidential electoral interests.

Across the social sciences, researchers use elite interviewing to obtain greater detail about behaviors and processes in order to find the causes of various phenomena. Research on executive branch politics and public policy frequently employs this useful research tool because it offers both methodological and empirical benefits. Methodologically, elite interviews are resource efficient in that they can target empirical topics and extract critical information in a short period of time. In addition, interviews—unlike large datasets—allow for clarification and deeper empirical exploration when necessary. In many ways, elite interviews allow access to data that lie beyond the reach of systematic analysis. Firsthand insight into processes at the individual level gained through interviews can help researchers confirm or disconfirm findings or conclusions from quantitative analysis, build or refine hypotheses, and/or aid in making causal arguments. Given the complex and often seemingly impenetrable nature of executive branch policy and political processes, elite interviews are common in this area of research.

Despite the benefits that elite interviewing brings to the study of social sciences, this technique, like many others, faces methodological challenges that if not addressed can lead to empirical limitations. Generally, similar types of concerns are encountered in collecting and analyzing both quantitative data and interview data, including selection effects, the trade-off between depth (concept validity) and breadth (generalizability), and response validity.

Sample modification and expansion is a technique commonly used to overcome many of the methodological challenges associated with elite interviewing, but the manner in which it is used is critical. For the purposes of this study, I employ a similar technique—across-group sample diversification—in a unique way to improve its methodological strength.[2] Across-group sample diversification is a simple method used to choose whom to interview. With this method, the interviewer identifies several diverse groups of respondents who are involved in or connected to the process or phenomenon of interest and conducts interviews within each group. By relying on various groups, the researcher deals with respondents who have different motives, perspectives, and priorities and thereby extracts data from heterogeneous but related sources, within a specific context. This construct allows the interviewer to limit the impact of distortion, overcome selection effects, and have greater ability to balance concept validity and generalizability.

In any study of the U.S. bureaucratic process that covers federal spending policy, scholars must focus on the agencies of the executive branch, which play central roles in the administration of funding and can provide a wealth of knowledge and insight on the topic. For this analysis, I designed a sample that includes individuals working in federal grant programs across various issue areas and agencies and further diversified federal agency respondents by including both career bureaucrats and appointees.

However, federal bureaucratic institutions are not the only actors relevant to this area of policy. Interest groups—organizations that seek to advance their interests through lobbying, media outreach efforts, and information sharing and exchange—often have roles to play in determining federal spending policy. They can influence both congressionally dominated spending programs,

2. Appendix 7A, at the end of this chapter, provides a detailed discussion of the methodology employed in this chapter.

including formula and block grants, and executive-controlled spending, such as discretionary grants and procurement.[3] Interest groups play an important role in presenting elected officials and policymakers with information on policy efforts, implications, and how policy proposals will affect constituents and stakeholder groups. Interest groups make it their business to gather such information, which often is difficult or cost prohibitive for the government to ascertain on its own, and make it available to interested parties, including the legislative and executive branches.[4] Interest groups and federal bureaucrats have very different loyalties, interests, and perspectives, each of which is crucial to understanding the grants process.

In the policymaking process, interest groups are not simply information providers. They also play a more dynamic, self-interested role, as policy demanders. Many groups have a national network and serve a body of dues-paying members. These groups often communicate which areas need policy attention (or here, federal funding) and actively use the resources of the network to help their issue-based constituency reap policy benefits.

Interest group respondents provide real benefits for a research project like this. First, they do not face the same (legal or informal) limitations on their ability to discuss the policy process that government employees do. Second, because interest group lobbyists are external actors, they play a unique role in the process. This unique role offers a different perspective from that of other participants in the policymaking and federal grants processes. In an effort to counterbalance respondent biases from inside government institutions, I interviewed interest group lobbyists to gather the most reliable information from sources outside of government.[5] Similarly, government sources help balance bias among nongovernment sources.

The dynamic role of interest groups demonstrates the importance of examining policy demanders as well as policy suppliers when conducting elite interviews in the area of executive politics. To that end, grant applicants serve as the core group of policy demanders in this analysis. While there are many types of grant applicants, a recurring type is the state government agency. Each year, state agencies seek funding through discretionary grant programs.[6] In fact,

---

3. Freeman (1965); Gais, Peterson, and Walker (1982); Heclo (1977); Lowi (1969); Peterson (1992); Polsby (1978); Schattschneider (1960).

4. See McCubbins and Schwartz (1984) for an example.

5. Appendix 7A offers a more detailed discussion of the inclusion of interest group lobbyists into the sample.

6. In some programs, state agencies serve as direct demanders of federal funds. In others, they serve as intermediary institutions through which private or municipal applicants apply for funds.

several federal grant programs *require* that funding requests originate with state government agencies.

State agencies are an appealing data source for three reasons. First, states have similar experiences in navigating the federal policy process and face similar institutional rules when applying for grants. While differences exist across states in terms of their ability to spend time and resources on pursuing federal funds, such variation is muted when compared with that among other policy demanders.[7]

Second, state agencies are consistent demanders of federal grants. Often, states seek the same federal funding opportunities each year. Given that consistency and their dynamic needs, states are a more appealing demander than local governments, private citizens, or other entities that may not seek grants as frequently. The regularity in the states' pursuit of federal grants also allows the researcher to make longitudinal comparisons.

The third reason, which is related to the consistency of state demand, is that state agencies develop experience over time and maintain institutional knowledge about the grants process. State agency employees often serve long careers in the same issue area, and many tend to work in the same position with similar responsibilities for a number of years. The result is a more knowledgeable, better functioning, experienced bureaucracy. Accumulated knowledge allows state bureaucrats to build a comprehensive, clear, long-term understanding of the policy process. These individuals can thus identify the loci of power in the process, explain how the process has changed, and assess which influences have a real impact on policy outcomes.

In sum, this study relies on data from three types of respondents who play the most critical and consistent roles in the policy process. Each respondent type offers a perspective that complements or supplements that of the others. Specifically, the sample is composed of respondents from federal agencies that supply grants, state agencies that demand them, and interest groups that play intermediary or joint roles. While each individual offered unique insights, all respondents participated in the federal grants process.

Observing Political Influence in the Federal Grants Process

The sample design described above ensures that the elite interviews provide rich data that address and allow a clear assessment of the key research questions

---

7. For example, county and municipal governments exhibit much broader variability in terms of staff and revenue than do state governments. Even broader variation—in terms of time, experience, monetary resources, and access to institutional support—exists among private citizens seeking funds.

in this chapter: Do presidents influence policy outcomes (grant allocations) to support their electoral interests? If they do, precisely how do they extract benefits and control micro-level outcomes?

To address those questions, I conducted twenty-four elite interviews with career (eight respondents) and appointed (three respondents) staff at federal grant-making agencies; with interest group lobbyists who deal with federal discretionary grants (seven respondents); and with bureaucrats from swing and non–swing states who actively apply for federal discretionary grants (six respondents). All of the respondents had positions with their respective employers that involved federal discretionary grant policy.[8] All interviews were conducted between summer 2010 and spring 2011. Respondents worked in various programs and issue areas; in several instances, however, federal government, state government, and interest group respondents were directly or indirectly linked by the same grant program. Respondents' tenure ranged from less than one year to more than 30 years. Interviews, which were generally open ended, explored similar aspects of the grants process. Interviews lasted between 35 minutes and two hours; with the exception of one interview, they were conducted in person.[9] Appendix 7A outlines the precise interview methodology.

The interviews explored a host of topics with each respondent type. Broadly, the interviews explored the political influence of elected officials on the grants process; specifically, the questions probed direct and indirect ways that the White House, political appointees, the Office of Management and Budget (OMB), and Congress seek to advance their political and electoral interests. I asked respondents to describe how the federal grants process works, to detail their role in it, and to identify which actors have decisionmaking authority, influence on the process, and influence over outcomes. Other questions queried the effects of changes in agency and department leadership, presidential administrations, party control of Congress, and legislative leadership.[10]

The interviews demonstrate the myriad ways in which presidential interests are not only conveyed but implemented throughout the policy process.

---

8. Many also dealt with other areas of federal policy and even other areas of spending. However, each interview focused on their role involving discretionary grants.

9. Because respondent anonymity is required by the Vanderbilt University Institutional Review Board, I am unable to identify the individuals interviewed or the agencies, organizations, or states from which they come. Instead, I simply note whether each is a federal appointee, a federal career employee, a state bureaucrat, or an interest group lobbyist. In some instances, I interviewed individuals who worked for a federal agency but at a subnational office; those respondents are identified as such.

10. Appendix 7B includes a basic framework of all questions asked of each type of respondent. While each interview was organic and often explored different areas depending on responses, each interview covered at least the questions listed in the appendix.

Ultimately, respondents noted that political influence—particularly presidential influence—on the grants process is substantial and manifests itself in many ways.[11] Presidents and their surrogates can affect outcomes directly, through their decisionmaking authority, and indirectly, through program and criteria design, OMB oversight, and strategic communication environments. The interviews illustrate that conventional views of how presidents and Congress influence distributive policy (that is, by making a phone call or sending a letter) are misguided and elementary. In reality, political influence is exercised in a complex, multipart process that affects administrative decisionmaking in unique and pervasive ways.

I focus on respondents' views in five key areas that reflect the president's ability to manipulate the federal grants process and personnel for political or electoral gain: first, the power of political appointees in the federal grants process; second, control of the development of formal, informal, and discretionary grant criteria; third, the role of the Office of Management and Budget and its satellite offices within agencies and cabinet departments in the federal grants process; fourth, the limited role of Congress in the distribution of funds; and fifth, the nonpolitical nature of the federal grants process.

The Power of the Appointee in the Grants Process

Information obtained from the elite interviews is presented here to describe the precise mechanisms that political appointees use to influence the federal grants process and its outcomes. Often, political scientists conceptualize presidential control and appointee influence as a linear process whereby elites ensure that their preferences override the rules of technocratic policy administration. However, even though the president and his surrogates can and do intervene directly in grant policy decisionmaking, they also have indirect and less publicly transparent ways of affecting outcomes.

THE INDIRECT IMPACT OF POLITICAL APPOINTEES. Political appointees can have an indirect influence on outcomes by fostering a communication and

11. Throughout this chapter, an effort is made to incorporate direct quotations into the text. The ideal would be to have an abundance of quotations, but the reality is that it was difficult to do so for multiple reasons. First, many respondents were uncomfortable with audio taping, making it necessary to take notes by hand. As appendix 7A notes, that led to a more open discussion. At times, respondents were uncomfortable with my taking down specific quotations when I felt that they would be useful, preferring instead that I paraphrase their words. Finally, the Vanderbilt University Institutional Review Board barred me from using any quotations that would allow for identification of the office, program, agency, department, or policy area in which the respondents worked. In many cases the anecdotes, discussions, and quotations involved information that would violate that requirement. As a result, I paraphrase rather than quote respondents' comments.

administrative environment that makes policy expectations clear to career civil servants. By generating those environments, appointees can induce responsiveness to presidential preferences and priorities.

Almost all respondents reported that political appointees and even the president himself set clear public policy priorities and objectives that policy outcomes are expected to reflect. At the presidential level, policy priorities are painted with a broad brush; the army of political appointees, who serve at the pleasure of the president, conveys administration objectives about micro-level policy. An appointee heading a subnational office of a federal agency explained that "the president and the [cabinet] secretary set clear priorities that are easy to follow." In fact, a senior careerist in a federal agency who deals predominantly with the distribution of federal funds explained that it was quite clear that the tone for policymaking was set in the White House but that cabinet secretaries could make small adjustments. Both respondents noted that priorities from on high are considered controlling; while lower-level and subnational appointees have some discretion, the decisionmaking hierarchy in both the agency and the department is top-down in nature.

The communication of administration objectives through appointees is pervasive and observable by most players in the federal grants process. One federal careerist described a process that his agency employs for each discretionary funding program: Often Congress offers an agency broad discretion with respect to the objectives and goals of a program or the development and design of the program itself. Next, in developing the procedures for each project, careerists, who deal with different aspects of the program, meet as a group with a political appointee. The appointee makes the administration's objectives and preferences clear, either in advance of or during the meeting, and the career administrators are then charged with operating within that framework. In fact, one career staffer explained that because administration preferences are so important, longer-serving, more loyal, and more trusted appointees are in charge of the process. As careerists build better and longer-lasting relationships with appointees, the careerists understand clearly the information being conveyed and the preferences that they are expected to advance. In several instances, federal government respondents described a similar process in their own agencies.

One subnational federal agency appointee detailed precisely the information dynamics of influence. He noted that contact between central agency appointees (and their immediate staff) and subnational appointees occurred at least daily, by telephone, e-mail, or fax. His office received a flow of briefings from the White House, the department leadership, and the department's

White House liaison regarding the administration's priorities. In addition, agency and department appointees travel frequently to observe the administration of policy within subnational units. In-person visits are critical events for the subnational appointee. The visits allow the national office appointees to convey the administration's preferences and monitor how funding programs are being administered.

Respondents inside and outside the bureaucracy described an information environment in which presidential preferences are conveyed to key actors in the process. One interest group official dealing mainly with federal grant policy noted that while career bureaucrats or lower-level appointees contacted the interest group seeking potential applicants for funds, the directive to do so clearly came from higher up the chain of command. According to this respondent and several other interest group officials, such behavior was most notable in advance of elections, when administrative environments and distributive outcomes changed considerably. That the information environment changes in advance of presidential elections suggests that electoral concerns affect the behaviors of political actors in the executive branch.

State bureaucrats expressed frustration with the overarching impact of administration preferences. One state bureaucrat who had served in multiple state agencies over the course of her career explained the necessity of communicating with appointees at the federal agency in order to facilitate the success or at least an understanding of the federal grants process. That need exists in the context of competitive federal grants in particular. Either senior state civil servants or state appointees have regular contact with federal appointees to learn the interests and preferences of the administration in regard to given programs.

Moreover, across interviews with state bureaucrats and interest group officials, it became clear that a bifurcated information system exists in many grant programs. There is a formal, publicly available body of information for each grant program that often is contained in a request for proposals (RFP), which details the program's funding range, eligibility criteria, purpose, and application procedure. However, other information exists that embodies the actual goals of the funding program and the objectives (political or otherwise) that the administration hopes to achieve. That information, as an official with a state-based, grant-centered interest group explained, is acquired by fostering and maintaining relationships and an information-sharing environment with key federal agency actors.

Fostering a communication environment that emphasizes presidential preferences and priorities is one means by which presidents and their surrogates influence public policy. However, that does not necessarily mean that the pressure applied to achieve those priorities translates into electorally strategic influence.[12] Several of the interviews shed light on how presidential objectives can be pursued in electorally strategic ways.

One political appointee who headed a subnational office of a federal agency explained that the distribution of funds can be manipulated in a preemptive manner. He explained that often programs are designed at the central level within a federal agency and their design incorporates administration priorities. Those priorities may be purely policy oriented, he noted, but "issue-based priorities can favor certain states." An interest group official similarly noted that some agency priorities preclude certain areas, states, and regions. As a result, when grant programs incorporate administration priorities, they can affect the distribution of funds in clear, predictable, and strategic ways.

Those two respondents clearly noted that policy priorities can affect the geographic distribution of funding. A single policy priority cannot target all swing states exclusively. However, developing objectives that benefit or preclude states based on population or other demographic characteristics, prominence of the industrial or the service sector, natural resource endowments, or other reasons can bias the geographic distribution of federal funds in critical and strategic ways. This approach allows presidents or their surrogates to develop funding programs that institutionalize an electoral strategy cloaked in a publicly presentable, issue-centered, non-electoral justification.

For example, the formal published description of a grant program may suggest that eligibility is fairly universal, but the administration's emphasis within the program may narrow its scope and thereby have a serious effect on distribution of funds. For example, during the 1990s and 2000s, in response to an amendment to Superfund laws, the Environmental Protection Agency began to focus on "brownfield" cleanup to transform polluted land into economically usable space.[13] Because environmental pollution of all kinds exists in all fifty states, the resulting program formally applied to a broad range of areas. However, in response to the Brownfields law, the Bush administration made "mine-scarred lands" a priority.[14] With the new emphasis on the sites of former mineral mines, eligibility for environmental cleanup funds narrowed

12. For example, during the George W. Bush administration, faith-based initiatives became a presidential priority. While that effort could be construed as an electoral tool, it is not clear how it could be used to advance electoral goals in the manner described in this study (by gaining support in swing states at the expense of other states).

13. See *Small Business Liability Relief and Brownfields Revitalization Act*, P.L. 107-118, 115 Stat. 2356, January 11, 2002.

14. Environmental Protection Agency (2005).

dramatically because mineral mines are not geographically universal. Although mine site cleanup certainly achieves noble goals, particularly for the residents of affected areas, this administration priority had distributional and electoral implications. Mineral mine sites exist in several key swing states, including Pennsylvania, Ohio, West Virginia, Nevada, and Colorado, among others.[15] In this case, the administration sought to apply a broad grant program in a narrow subset of areas that could provide key political benefits to the president.

I gained additional leverage about the phenomena discussed in this chapter from the observations of respondents who had participated in the federal grants process for several years. The ability to observe change (or stability) over the long term can provide great insight into the bureaucratic process. Almost universally, respondents noted that the transition from one president to another causes dramatic changes in the priorities and focus of agencies, in the administrative procedures governing the federal grants process, and in the information environment. One long-serving career civil servant in a federal agency explained that while a change in president can dramatically affect policy and distributive outcomes, so too can a change in agency leadership. She noted that such changes had little effect on the day-to-day operation of an agency because of the stability of the civil service but that real effects were felt in funding preferences and demands for the entertainment of new ideas. Another career bureaucrat noted that discretionary programs can face dramatic redesign under new leadership for a variety of reasons, some of which are political in nature.

The interest group respondents also noted the effects of managerial changes in federal agencies. Most interest group officials and state bureaucrats noted the absolute need to foster relationships with federal agency officials, which can be strengthened in formal and informal ways. One interest group lobbyist went on to describe the relationship as being helpful in terms of understanding administration priorities. However, he explained that during the transition and adjustment period caused by leadership changes, lobbyists and other interest group officials rely on their relationships with careerists and on the stability of the civil service to understand fully the nature of a new administration's priorities.

The information environment demonstrates clearly the means by which presidents can affect even micro-level policy. The constant flow of communications regarding administration goals and preferences down and up a complex chain of command can accomplish two tasks. First, it serves as an effective

15. No interviews were conducted with respondents dealing with this issue; it is used only as an illustrative anecdote.

monitoring mechanism, whereby individuals closer to the president are constantly informed about the behavior, productivity, and effectiveness of individuals working throughout the administrative apparatus of government. This process helps enhance accountability and limit shirking and drift. Second, the flow of communications (and more important, their frequency) ensures that appointees at the lowest levels and career staff are constantly informed of the interests of the president, of how well their performance reflects those interests, and of any changes or adjustments in preferences that affect outcomes. In this way, lower-level actors are kept informed of administration priorities, and it is also is made clear that they are expected to incorporate those priorities into policy. This construct begins to shed light on how the preferences and interests of one individual—the president—are effectively communicated through an enormous bureaucracy.

THE DIRECT INFLUENCE OF POLITICAL APPOINTEES. In addition to conveying administration priorities and objectives, political appointees often have a more direct role in the execution of federal grant policy and agency allocations. Administrative procedures affect outcomes. In fact, one long-serving careerist in a federal agency said that it was clear that the nature and adjustment of administrative procedures can have a direct and meaningful impact on policy outcomes. Many agencies' structures empower political appointees to be the final arbiter in the allocation of grants. In agencies that do not have such structures, appointees often have the ability to modify administrative procedures in a way that gives them decisionmaking authority. One senior career official in a federal agency explained that the role of appointees in making the final allocation decision "honestly depends on whether they care." She went on to note that some appointees arrange processes so that they play a substantial and critical role in allocations. Others, however, are comfortable delegating that power to career staff in order to focus on other priorities. That "lack of caring" may not reflect an appointee's discretionary decision but the priorities of the White House vis-à-vis that agency or issue area.

What results is decisionmaking that varies depending on appointee interest and initiative and the existing structures within the administrative process. A long-serving senior lobbyist for a Washington-based interest group explained that his decades of experience in lobbying multiple agencies demonstrated that the influence of appointees is not felt equally in all agencies. However, in what became a chorus of similar responses among interest group officials within and outside Washington, he noted that the tone set by an appointee or a new administration had a direct effect on the access of a lobbying organization, which can have real distributive consequences.

When appointees take an active role in distributive decisionmaking, their impact can have political and electoral implications. A national interest group grant manager centered in Washington described an initiative in which she sought funding assistance for her group's members and subnational sister organizations. A federal agency worked closely with an interest group to identify applicants—affiliated with her organization—to distribute funds for a pilot program. The respondent explained that the agency delivered these funds almost exclusively to swing states. When I pressed the respondent about whether that distributive behavior was unique, the question was met with humor and an additional example of another funding program in which federal dollars were funneled to a particular swing state in advance of a presidential election. In fact, in this case the agency had asked the respondent to identify prospective applicants in that state because it was the target for the program.

From the perspective of appointees, the ability to influence outcomes is clear. A federal appointee in charge of an agency's subnational office noted that he could simply change or veto distributive outcomes directly but that his ability to influence was broader. He noted that he could indirectly apply pressure to career staff by highlighting certain distributive preferences. Although this appointee explained that while that power structure was not unique to his subnational office, he resisted such actions because they could complicate the important working relationship between him and his staff.

However, an appointee's deference to careerists' policy recommendations is not a universal behavior; in fact, it can lead to an internal conflict for a political appointee. Another subnational federal agency head explained, "I am torn between serving the president and being part of a customer service system." He estimated that he defers to staff in about 95 percent of cases; however, he said, the national office delivers a steady stream of information and demands and "there is a need to make central office suggestions a priority." This appointee found the need and hierarchical motivation to step into the allocation decisionmaking process and exercise his own discretion. Serving as the formal and final decisionmaker on grants passing through this subnational office, he was positioned to affect outcomes when necessary. A careerist in a federal grantmaking agency noted that appointee involvement in final allocation decisions can occur for a host of reasons but that "clearly the process can be political."

The power of appointees to serve as the locus of authority was clear across respondents in federal and state governments and interest groups. However, the reach of their power and the character of their influence can vary. One senior careerist at a federal agency explained that while the appointed agency head had the formal authority to approve allocations, the approval process was simply a formality—a fact attributed to the bipartisan and technical nature of that agency's policy area.

Other federal careerists noted the myriad and institutionalized ways in which appointees exercise their decisionmaking authority over federal grant allocations. As noted above, a careerist explained that in his agency the appointee has the opportunity to make his objectives clear in the program design stage and encourages—even if tacitly—the implementation of those objectives. Another career program director described a similar process in her agency but also noted that the appointee has veto power over proposed allocations. That power is a blunt instrument of administrative influence. Rather than giving the appointee the ability to make micro-level adjustments in allocations as described in other agencies, this agency essentially allows the appointee an up-or-down vote on allocations.

Not all decisionmaking is as blunt, however. Another long-serving career program director explained that a career program staffer prepares different sets of proposed allocations and formally presents them to the appointee, who then chooses the allocation scheme that he or she prefers. While the ability to present a set of proposed allocations could place discretionary power in the hands of the career staffer, the program director explained that the staffer has a feel for what the appointee prefers and those preferences are institutionalized ex ante. Essentially, it would be a waste of work hours for the staffer to propose allocations that are inconsistent with the appointee's preferences because those proposals are unlikely to be chosen. Furthermore, besides the ability to choose a proposal, the appointee retains the authority to "tweak" allocations. The respondent explained that such tweaking is uncommon, attributing it not to a lack of administration influence but once again to the fact that appointee preferences are already institutionalized in the process.

A federal agency appointee heading a subnational office noted an additional way that the central office can target funds geographically. There is pressure for subnational units of federal agencies to spend (distribute) all of their allocated funds because if the funds are not distributed, they are returned to Washington. However, they are not sent to the Department of the Treasury; they are transferred back to the central office of the agency. The agency head is then free to redistribute those excess or unspent funds to subnational offices as he or she sees fit. That power, which can facilitate a geographically targeted distribution scheme, presents at least the opportunity for one of the president's surrogates to influence the distribution of grants directly.

A challenge in evaluating presidential influence over micro-level policy is understanding how one individual charged with leading a massive bureaucratic organization can affect outcomes at the individual level in a manner consistent with the president's needs. The design, decisionmaking hierarchy, and information environment of administrative agencies clearly facilitate and in many cases institutionally ensure that presidential interests become the interests of those throughout the system. Appointees are able to capitalize on formal and informal mechanisms to provide the president critical electoral and political benefits.

Criteria: A Cornerstone of Control

Criteria are an important part of the federal grants process. They outline eligibility requirements, which serve to qualify or disqualify prospective applicants. The creation of criteria can entail immense power to influence or determine the allocation of federal funds. Two types of grant criteria are crucial to understanding policy outcomes: formal, published criteria and informal or discretionary criteria.

Formal Criteria: Grant Making in Black and White

The development of formal criteria often is a political process. Political appointees often position themselves at the center of the criteria design process in order to craft grant programs in strategic ways. A Washington-based interest group grant manager explained that because appointees can design criteria to benefit or preclude certain applicants, they can use criteria in strategic ways. The respondent noted that relations with the administrative agency and its appointees are always careful because criteria can be designed or redesigned to punish or reward certain recipients, organizations, or geographic areas.

Career and appointed federal government respondents also described the breadth of power that political appointees wield in designing criteria. As agency executives committed to administration priorities, appointees use their authority to ensure that programs and ultimately the distributive outcomes that they produce reflect such priorities. Several interest group officials also spoke candidly of the distributional power that appointees exercise by controlling criteria design. One lobbyist explained that frequently the distributional impacts of criteria can be observed in outcomes.

For example, a large number of areas throughout the country could be eligible for broad-based grants to improve waterways. However, if criteria are designed to give priority to the Great Lakes region, funds can go to states that are critical in presidential elections, including Minnesota, Wisconsin, Michigan, Ohio, Indiana, and Pennsylvania.[16] That criteria design almost always

16. This anecdote is used for illustration; it was not provided by the respondents referred to in this paragraph.

involves and at times is reserved for political actors suggests that it is a critical way to control administrative decisions and influence policy outcomes.

Even subnational offices of agencies often employ appointee-designed criteria. One subnational federal appointee explained that he has final approval of criteria at the subnational level; other criteria are created at the central office and almost always require central office appointee approval. He explained that the manner in which programs are designed and priorities are implemented through program design ensures that certain groups and states are better positioned to receive funds. Another appointee noted that some programs include criteria with immense distributive implications: "one concern [is] that the process is too formulaic . . . [it] works for one or two recipients and essentially becomes an entitlement."

A Washington interest group grant manager observed that appointees also can affect the rules and process governing how an agency or program designs criteria. One way that appointees affect that process is to inform career staffers of the administration's desires and objectives for a given program and then charge them with designing the program and its criteria within that framework. In describing this process, one federal bureaucrat explained that staffers must present the pre-influenced criteria to the appointee for final approval. At that stage, approval is typically a formality, as the appointee's (and/or administration's) preferences have already been incorporated.

Informal Criteria: Pulling Back the Curtain on Grant Making

Despite the importance of controlling criteria design, control is not always absolute or precise. Many interest group lobbyists and administration officials explained that grant program criteria and evaluation processes do not always result in outcomes that align exactly with the objectives of political appointees. For these situations, political appointees wield additional power over the process through the development and exercise of informal or discretionary criteria.

Interest group lobbyists noted in several interviews that just as important as understanding the formal criteria listed in RFPs is awareness of the subtext or informal criteria. Applicants' chances of success are enhanced if they understand how the formal criteria or other characteristics and details are actually evaluated. Of greater importance, these respondents noted that political appointees typically determine, apply, and fail to disclose publicly or transparently the nature of informal criteria.

One interest group official who dealt with grant applications at the state level explained that one agency maintained liaisons who served as key information distributors to relevant interest groups and stakeholders. However, with recent budget reductions, several liaison positions had been cut. The respondent was concerned about the group's ability to compete effectively for federal funds without the liaisons. He explained that while reading the criteria in an RFP served to start the application process, understanding which criteria would receive the most attention and how agency leadership would evaluate them was essential to obtain funding. He further noted that changes in agency leadership frequently led to changes in both formal and informal criteria and in expectations of applicants. The liaison relationship was critical if applicants wanted to be informed of changes immediately rather than discover them through trial and error. This liaison example reveals the important role that political appointees play in designing, interpreting, and evaluating grant criteria. Eliminating such positions—whether because of fiscal constraints or an appointee's decision—helps mask the influence of informal criteria.

In addition to informal criteria, appointees often apply discretionary criteria in evaluating grants in order to assist specific applicants or groups of applicants. Use of these criteria empowers appointees to make exceptions to the peer review process. Many grants are evaluated through a peer or administrative review process under which a group of individuals evaluates, scores, and ranks proposals based on quality.[17] Rankings result in recommendations that are then forwarded to political appointees and/or senior career administrators who may approve, disapprove, or in some cases make adjustments to the recommendations. A grant manager for an interest group explained that even in the face of the peer review process, appointees distribute funds to certain recipients and geographic areas. While this claim was striking, several other respondents corroborated the point, noting the ability and actions of appointees to override certain peer or administrative review processes.

A long-serving state bureaucrat explained that he not only had experienced the peer review process as an applicant but also had participated in the process as a reviewer. He noted that although recommendations frequently were accepted and adhered to, that practice was not universal. He explained that after he and his peers ranked proposals, the political appointee in charge of the program played two key roles in the review process. First, the appointee was able to set the cut-off score, below which proposals would not be funded. Second, the appointee could determine outcomes by changing the ranking of applications after the peer review process concluded. Although it was not

17. These panels often include individuals from federal agencies, state agencies, policy experts, stakeholders, and citizens in order to take diverse views into account.

exercised in a dramatic fashion, administrative discretion did affect some out-comes. The respondent noted that the ranking of some proposals was raised or lowered and that in a few cases, proposals that were not well-regarded by agency staff found their way to the final distribution list. This respondent could not recall specifically who benefited from the adjustments but noted that the institutional actors responsible for such decisions—appointees and the OMB—are political.

Central office appointees also use their discretion to affect outcomes at the subnational level. Both subnational and central office appointees can add administrative or discretionary points to application scores to enhance the competitiveness of certain proposals. A career staffer at a federal agency's sub-national office explained that administrative points added to scores by central and subnational appointees are handled differently. The respondent said that while the motivation can be political, the appointee devises a nonpolitical public justification—such as reputational considerations—in case a Freedom of Information Act request is filed requesting materials from the review pro-cess. Administrative points added by central agency appointees are not made public, but they can lead to real changes in the distribution of funds. The respondent explained that nonetheless, the role of politics was at the mar-gins and that all funding decisions—peer reviewed or appointee influenced—assisted applicants with real needs.

Another subnational federal agency head echoed that account, noting that the central agency leadership can influence subnational funding allocations. The respondent explained that while discretionary criteria and administrative points can be used for political influence, his office typically relied on them to boost proposals that are more competitive at the national review stage[18] and to overcome formal criteria that target a small, select subset of applicants. While this appointee described his office's approach to the use of discretionary crite-ria or administrative points as magnanimous, he noted that criteria designed at the national level certainly affected how and where funds were distributed. The respondent explained the different uses of discretionary criteria at the subnational and national levels were often a competition between apolitical and political efforts, respectively.

In sum, presidential preferences can affect outcomes through the design and manipulation of administrative criteria. Not only are appointees empow-ered to create the criteria on which grant allocations are evaluated, they have

---

18. Some grant programs require a review at both the local and regional levels and a subsequent review at the national level.

additional paths of influence to use when those criteria result in policy outcomes that are inconsistent with their goals. Appointees are able to adjust scores, rankings, and outcomes related to the peer and administrative review processes to advance or hinder certain applicants, thereby allowing presidential preferences to filter down and influence distributional outcomes at the micro-level in critical ways.

OMB: A Checkpoint on the Road to Presidential Influence

The Office of Management and Budget has long been recognized as important to the efforts of the White House to advance the goals and preferences of the president. The federal grants process is not spared from those efforts. In fact, federal grants fall under the purview of OMB for multiple reasons. First, OMB oversees fund allocations for fiscal reasons. Second, OMB often serves as an information clearinghouse for federal agencies, ensuring that published communications such as RFPs and grant criteria are consistent with the legal and political expectations of the administration. OMB's role as an information control center can dramatically affect both the administrative process and policy outcomes. Specifically, OMB and its satellite offices within departments and agencies affect communications flowing into (such as those from Congress) and out of bureaucratic institutions. OMB is therefore positioned to be highly influential in determining administrative and distributive policy. Third, as the budgetary arm of the White House, OMB affects distributive outcomes in direct and formal, yet politically strategic ways.

Outgoing Communications

Senior career staff within agencies almost universally noted in interviews that OMB contact is a critical aspect of their jobs. One staffer explained that it is absolutely essential for her office to get to know OMB staff and understand their priorities because OMB is such a key player in the administration of funds and the flow of communications. It became clear from this discussion that efficiency is gained by understanding and possibly preemptively incorporating OMB preferences and expectations into outcomes.

Every federal agency respondent noted, to some degree, contact with and the influence of OMB in their daily working relationships because of the statutory and political authority that OMB regularly asserts. One senior careerist explained that every published document from his office required not just OMB approval but editing. In fact, his cabinet department's OMB extension office reviewed all proposed publications. He detailed clearly the various procedures that the office used to monitor publications. In some cases, a document would be submitted and then returned with proposed changes. Other times, after a document is submitted, OMB edits and publishes a final version without first returning it to the agency. Final versions were not always changed in dramatic ways, but he noted that "some were unrecognizable."

Another long-serving career program director described OMB's broader role as regulator of the information environment within an agency. She explained that in her agency, OMB clearance was needed for all publications, grant criteria, and even distributive decisions. For example, each document was reviewed and edited as deemed necessary by OMB officials. However, as the respondent detailed, OMB effectively influences public policy outcomes at all stages of the process. Another career-level agency official observed that its influence included the ability to outline or detail the precise processes used to distribute funds so that OMB has substantial influence on who gets what and when.

Incoming Communications

The influence of OMB extends beyond control of the information disseminated by an agency to include strict control of the information coming into an agency as well. Because so much of the literature on distributive politics examines the role of Congress, one might imagine that Congress seeks to influence federal grant allocations by contacting agency staff directly. Accordingly, I sought to evaluate the level of contact that career staff had with Congress. In general, respondents noted that OMB handles contact with "the politicals."

One senior career federal bureaucrat explained that agency policy prevents staffers from discussing program details with members of Congress and their staff. In fact, if an individual receives a phone call from Capitol Hill, he must immediately transfer it to the department's OMB staffers to handle the inquiry. Any information in that call deemed necessary or important to agency operations is relayed to agency staff only through the internal OMB office.[19] OMB, of course, decides what is necessary or important.

This institutional dynamic increasingly centralizes power in multiple ways. First, it ensures that all information being distributed by the agency comes from or flows through a common source, ensuring tight, consistent messaging. Second, it provides a buffer between Congress and agency staff, thereby limiting congressional influence on agency decisionmaking. Thus, OMB, one

---

19. Any information that must be relayed to Congress also has to flow through the OMB office on its way to Capitol Hill.

of the president's most useful political institutions, serves as an information gatekeeper for federal agencies.

Distributive Outcomes

Like presidents, legislators have a substantial interest in directing federal funds to key constituencies. Given Congress's oversight and appropriations roles, direct contact from Capitol Hill could easily intimidate bureaucrats into responding to congressional rather than presidential preferences. A communication buffer staffed by the OMB, which is part of the Executive Office of the President, ensures greater executive branch control over distribution. In some cases, Congress cannot even *suggest* to career staff how funds should be distributed unless that information is conveyed by administration officials.

The long-serving state bureaucrat mentioned above who had sat on federal peer review panels in the past noted the power of OMB from the distributive perspective. He explained that both his first-hand experience within the review process and his relationships over the years with many federal government officials had revealed that OMB does not function as just a blind budgetary check that compares bottom lines; it has more specific powers. In particular, after the peer review process produces a ranking of grant applications by quality scores, OMB can change the order in which proposals are funded in many programs, thereby influencing the timing, location, and likelihood of funding. Given OMB's position as a political liaison, its authority over federal fund allocations can have substantial political and electoral implications.

The effects of OMB were also felt outside Washington and beyond the federal government. Even for state bureaucrats, OMB influence is not just administrative in nature. A state bureaucrat noted that because monitoring of funds is fairly pervasive, contact with OMB is quite frequent. However, beyond such checks, the political nature of OMB shows itself as a new administration takes office, when OMB's behavior and expectations of state grant recipients can change dramatically. However, of greater importance, the respondent noted that OMB can change certain reporting requirements to reflect the preferences and priorities of the incumbent president. For example, during the recent recession, the administration—through OMB—increased the emphasis on reporting job creation through federal funding, even changing the accounting practices for measuring job creation multiple times. Although that requirement did not have distributional implications, it highlights the highly political nature of OMB.

The respondents described OMB as a powerful institution within the executive branch, which, along with its subsidiary offices within departments and agencies, strictly controls the flow of information in and out of distributive institutions and has a direct impact on federal fund allocations. The Office of Management and Budget limits Congress's influence on and facilitates presidential control of federal agencies, thereby enhancing the ability of the White House to affect micro-level public policy decisionmaking.

Limitations on Congressional Leverage

Congressional influence on the distribution of funds has been well catalogued in many areas; however, as discussed in the previous chapters, there is a lack of evidence of congressional influence on discretionary federal grants. That does not necessarily reflect a weakness in Congress's power; it can be due instead to the institutional design of the grant programs being analyzed. Nonetheless, congressional influence serves as a primary alternative hypothesis of this study and one that was extensively explored in the elite interviews that I conducted. Generally, federal bureaucrats noted a lack of contact with Congress in terms of legislators seeking funds for their constituents. One senior careerist explained that for the most part, his dealings with Congress concerned reporting requirements and upcoming appropriations legislation. He noted that legislative impact on the distribution of funds was seen not with general grant programs but with legislative earmarks. With some regularity, legislators include earmarked appropriations in legislation or in committee reports; in most cases, agencies are required or expected to honor those congressional requests. In such situations, a given portion of funding is set aside for that specific purpose. However, despite the media attention given to earmarking, it consumes a very small portion of discretionary funding and has little impact. Respondents largely noted that except for earmarking, their contact with Congress was essentially nonexistent.

As further evidence of the limited influence of Congress within federal grant-making agencies, state bureaucrats often do not seek help from Congress when applications are under review. In fact, one state bureaucrat noted that it is far more effective to contact relevant interest groups that maintain positive relationships with federal agencies. State grant applicants often build and foster relationships with contacts who improve both their understanding of the grants process and their likelihood of success. That those contacts rarely include members of Congress demonstrates the lack of legislative influence within administrative agencies.

State bureaucrats provided additional insight into the limited role of Congress. One would expect that because state bureaucrats apply for funds for select constituencies and federal legislators seek to claim credit for providing funds, legislators might encourage state bureaucrats to seek federal funding opportunities for their mutual benefit. However, interviews with state bureaucrats demonstrated that they have little or no contact with members of Congress in that or any other respect. These bureaucrats did note that pressure to seek funding comes from state legislators and the offices of governors, particularly because federal funds help balance state budgets. Generally, state bureaucrats suggest that while state and local officials understand the beneficial implications of pursuing federal grants, members of Congress make little effort to persuade state bureaucrats do so.

As mentioned, interaction between many agencies and Congress occurs through OMB, not through direct contact. This system ensures that contact with agencies is made through political appointees and that legislators have limited influence within agencies. In fact, the constancy that federal bureaucrats observe across transitions in party control of Congress is evidence of the limits on direct legislative influence. Two senior careerists in federal agencies explained that because their contact with Congress was so infrequent (and in the case of one individual, restricted), changes on Capitol Hill had little impact on them. One suggested that even though communications from Congress flow to OMB officials within his cabinet department, the information flowing from those officials to the program staff remains fairly constant. Such an observation is important. Different parties have unique demands for federal programs. For example, Republicans want EPA to be weak and passive, while Democrats prefer the agency to be more robust and aggressive. Such differences between parties are true among a host of federal agencies and policy areas. Alternatively, that steadiness may demonstrate that the OMB officials within the government effectively shelter bureaucratic staffers from legislative demands and influence.

The constancy of information flow, even in the face of transitions in Congress, could mean that the political party that seizes the majority may make no new demands on federal agencies, allowing them to continue to operate without political pressure. That may be the case for some agencies that are less subject to partisan politics. However, many agencies and policy areas face specific, partisan demands, and the respondent mentioned above served in one such agency.

However, OMB's control of the information environment in federal agencies does not mean that Congress lacks influence. Although Congress cannot simply apply pressure directly to federal bureaucrats, it does work with key executive branch institutions to seek influence. Given the inter-institutional nature of the legislative process and the cooperative nature of policymaking, it is safe to assume that in specific cases, OMB accepts some legislative requests and actively encourages bureaucrats to respond to them. Yet unless the source of such a request is clearly discussed by OMB and the bureaucrat, the latter observes political pressure and influence only from OMB. In that context, civil servants are unable to distinguish the original source of influence. Respondents noted that the Office of Management and Budget applies political pressure; however, that pressure does not reflect White House interests only. Instead, OMB pressure may involve some combination of presidential interests and congressional policy preferences that are approved by the administration.

The relationship between interest groups and Congress can illustrate the existence or extent of legislative influence on the federal grants process conceived more broadly. Generally, interest group lobbyists and grant managers said that their relationship with Congress had two aspects: information sharing and appropriation seeking. One lobbyist explained that because his organization is a leading voice in a given policy area, Congress relies heavily on the information that it provides. The organization has a broad network of members and experts that provide a comprehensive understanding of public policy issues, and it maintains a level of expertise that Congress cannot match. In a similar way, Congress frequently conveys legislative proposals to the interest group and discusses the possibility of their success in upcoming sessions of Congress. The relationship that this lobbyist describes is a traditional one, long profiled in the political science literature, that has remained stable in the context of contemporary policy.

In terms of interest in specific appropriations, Congress has profound influence on federal grant policy. Interest group respondents explained that they frequently work closely with Congress to increase—or at least maintain—funding levels, particularly for federal grant programs. One interest group grant manager explained that because of the effectiveness of interest groups and their policy expertise, federal agencies often contact them to lobby Congress for their own appropriations. While federal agencies serve policy communities, they do not have a constituency in the same sense that interest groups do. Moreover, these organizations can mount effective information and grassroots campaigns to secure funding. Federal agency staffers also saw the relationship between agencies, interest groups, and Congress as a crucial force in securing funding. In this context, Congress is a critical player.

An interview with a subnational federal appointee demonstrated the congressional role most clearly. This appointee oversaw the subnational region from which his "cardinal" hailed—that is, the subnational region included the congressional district of the House Appropriations Subcommittee chair, who had jurisdiction over the appointee's agency. Such an institutional alignment should give a member of Congress the best opportunity to exercise legislative influence on executive branch fund allocations. However, the appointee stated that he had encountered no attempts by the cardinal to influence the distribution of funds to that congressional district or to influence any other matters. Rather than seeing the proximity of the cardinal as a source of political influence or a challenge, the appointee found it to be a perk: the appointee had greater access to the individual charged with shepherding the appropriations bill that funds his agency. He found the relationship to be beneficial.

This relationship distinguishes Congress's two roles in fiscal matters. Often the legislative branch's appropriation power is conflated with distributive power. It is true that legislators often are successful in securing funding for their constituencies, but that is true only in specific contexts—for example, with respect to legislative earmarking, block grant and formula grant programs, and contact with the Office of Management and Budget and other political appointees. However, for discretionary funding programs, legislative influence is not as pervasive. Although Congress does have some opportunity to influence outcomes, other preferences factor into the distribution of funds. It is important, therefore, to distinguish the appropriator from the distributor. Congress serves as the appropriator for all programs, and the responses of interviewees in this study showed a keen awareness of that appropriator role in their dealings with the legislative branch. With regard to the funding programs analyzed in this volume, the executive branch and particularly the political appointees within it play the role of distributor.

The interviews with lobbyists and bureaucrats paint a picture of a weakly influential legislative branch and help to clarify some uncertainty in chapters 2 and 3 of this book. In evaluating the effect of Congress, I note that it is unclear whether the statistical evidence of an impact is due to the direct actions of legislators or to those of executive branch actors working to keep Congress happy. The communication system and behaviors described above strongly suggest the latter. Because the White House limits contact between Congress and career bureaucrats and because appointees play such pervasive and influential roles, it appears that congressional effects occur because of indirect legislative and direct executive action. Executive branch actors ultimately pull the strings in response to legislative requests because of a realization that Congress plays policymaking and oversight roles in a system of separated powers.

Thus, Congress is limited in its ability to influence the distribution of federal discretionary grants. Most agencies have little contact with federal legislators or their staffs. Instead, much of the communication between the branches flows through specific channels, often officials affiliated with the White House. That effectively limits the ability of the legislature to directly influence administrative agencies. What the results of these interviews and the systematic data presented earlier suggest is that the executive branch functions as it should. The president is the chief executive, who, in concert with his appointees and the employees of the federal government, administers the law within the bounds that Congress sets. Often those bounds include discretionary authority that empowers members of the executive branch to make critical decisions about the execution of the law, including the distribution of funds. Stories in the press, anecdotes in history, and even studies in political science focus on the role of Congress. The role and influence of executive branch actors—especially, the president—may be surprising given the popular attention paid to Congress in the area of spending policy. However, it is entirely consistent with the design of government, the structure of statutes, and the interests and motivations facing presidents and their appointees.

The Nonpolitical Nature of the Federal Grants Process: A Commentary

The results from the systematic analyses in this book do not suggest that federal grants give the president unfettered opportunities for exercising political and electoral influence. Instead, the findings provide evidence that an electoral strategy in the allocation of funds is observed at the margins. While federal discretionary grant dollars are spread all over the United States, states that are electorally important to the president receive disproportionately more funding. The results of the elite interviews conducted as part of this study also support that finding.

A senior career-level federal bureaucrat best put this finding into perspective. He explained that there is no doubt that external forces influence grant allocations and that some of those forces are political in nature. However, he noted that despite the influence of politics and efforts to direct funds in specific ways, the "people who get grants are all in need." Even when political or electoral forces influence outcomes, agencies do not deliver benefits to those who do not need them; instead they deliver them with the expectation that the funds will be both beneficial to recipients and politically or electorally beneficial to principals.

That needs exist everywhere allows individuals involved in public policy—and specifically in federal grants—to work effectively within a political framework. An interest group grant manager explained that even when politics influences the system and programs are designed to have biases, it is easy to identify people in need in the targeted areas. In fact, the respondent noted that need in her policy area is substantial and universal and that the demand for assistance *always* outpaces supply. Politics does not enhance the shortfall, she explained; it simply directs the funds used to mitigate the effects of the shortfall. She described a situation in which the administration chose to target certain states for federal grants and noted that even under that scenario, there existed no shortage of prospective needy applicants in the targeted states.

Every respondent had a keen awareness that he or she was working to administer policy in a system influenced by politics. Rather than creating discontent, that fact was accepted as part of the job. Further, the role of politics did not limit respondents' ability to help those in need. Instead, several respondents, including state bureaucrats, federal bureaucrats, and political appointees, claimed that 90 to 95 percent of grants were allocated on the basis of technocratic rather than political reasons. That estimate is consistent with the results of the systematic data analysis reported in previous chapters.

Despite an institutional framework that allows political actors to influence outcomes or at least internalize specific preferences in the system, those whom I interviewed believed that needs were being met by the assistance that they provided. In fact, both needs and the ability to help meet needs emerged as a driving force in the work ethic of respondents. They did not perform their jobs in a stereotypically bureaucratic, mechanical, monotonous manner. Instead, these respondents saw the human aspect of their work, realizing that in most cases, their decisions affected the lives of real people. Respondents clearly understood that need—sometimes serious or dire need—existed and that the federal government was charged with helping citizens. However, as they saw it, when the government is called into action, so too is politics. This perspective was nearly universal despite the diversity among interviewees. I interviewed individuals—young and old, Democrat and Republican, liberal and conservative—at the start and toward the end of their careers and found, despite expected differences, a generally uniform view on this point.[20]

Respondents also demonstrated bureaucratic innovation—a concept often deemed paradoxical. A senior career official in a federal agency explained that in an effort to meet growing and changing needs, her agency constantly

20. While I never asked individuals directly about their ideological predisposition or partisan affiliation, many volunteered that information during the course of the interview or it was easily observable based on responses.

focuses on modifying program details to accommodate changes. She describes this process not as an internal administrative effort, but one that integrates staff, policy experts, prospective applicants, and key stakeholders in the community. The goal is to get the program "right" in the sense that it effectively meets the needs of the policy community.

Another senior career official in the federal government detailed a similar process in his agency. He explained that previously, allocations were made on a first-come, first-served basis. However, it became clear over time that this procedure helped states that are more efficient in applying for funds—a characteristic not necessarily correlated with need (or, frankly, politics). The program was eventually redesigned to level the playing field and serve those in greatest need. This respondent further explained that short-term events can lead to short-term, need-based responses. He noted that while the economic recession placed greater demands on his agency (and many others), there was no corresponding increase in regular appropriations. Rather than trying just to maintain the status quo, he and his colleagues worked actively to modify programs to help more people more effectively. That effort revealed a responsive and responsible aspect of discretionary programming. While the malleability of programs can be and is exploited for political purposes, it can also be used to help those facing hardship.

The nonpolitical nature of the federal grants process can be seen in the efforts of individuals besides those who work in the Washington offices of federal agencies. Officials on the ground and in the field constantly work to understand local needs, changes in those needs, and ways in which agencies can respond. The network of policymakers and policy shapers includes a web of federal and state government officials and national and local interest groups that try to stay informed of citizen needs. An interest group official at the state office of a national organization explained that he and his colleagues go into communities to help spread information about funding opportunities and even to help individuals with grant preparation. He explained that some applicants truly struggle to prepare materials for grants. His organization's expertise and experience with the complex grant process can help deliver increased grant funds to those in need whose lack of understanding of informal criteria and other factors could put them at a disadvantage.

Responding to and meeting local needs drives the behaviors of those at subnational offices of federal agencies—even at the appointee level. An interview with one such appointee revealed that a large part of his job involves holding (or being invited to) town hall meetings at which he and his staff mount an information campaign to spread the word about funding opportunities. He also noted that he and his staff recognize a serious problem involving applicants in the grants process. Those applying for funds typically were struggling with their needs or faced enormous time constraints in dealing with their needs. As a result, prospective applicants often had limited time and training to complete the onerous amounts of paperwork required to apply for funds.

His staff implemented a twofold solution. First, they worked to streamline the application process to make it less intimidating for prospective applicants. Second, in addition to making staff available to help with grant preparation, they modified the evaluation process to take into account resource limitations among applicants. That change allowed staff to meet the needs of applicants based not on the perfection of a grant proposal but on the thorough identification of real need. What this discussion revealed was that a political appointee—one who acknowledged that political demands enter the policy process and influence outcomes—still saw his role as an assistance provider to the community and that despite serving at the pleasure of the president, he worked to help communities and provide public goods.

There is no doubt that presidential politics plays an influential role in the distribution of federal grants. Although this book focuses on the political and electoral forces that affect fund allocations, it must be noted that the system is not purely political, stripped of technocratic and need-based considerations. Instead, bureaucrats at the state and federal levels, interest group officials, and even political appointees understand that while political principals must be satisfied, the core part of the policy process involves service to the public.

Conclusion

Often there exist competing views of political influence in policymaking. These views differ about the source of influence (the president or Congress) as well as about whether influence is direct (through decisionmaking) or indirect (through, for example, the application of political pressure). This chapter shows that none of these explanations is false. Instead, they offer an incomplete account of the realities and complexities of exercising policy influence and political control, omitting a tremendous amount of detail regarding how politics works within the administrative process. Presidents and their appointees effectively control even minor details of policymaking within the burgeoning central government. Moreover, this analysis helps explain why scholars and observers of the executive branch often mischaracterize or underestimate the role of the election-driven president in manipulating policy. The often opaque and always strategic approach of presidents and their surrogates to exercising political influence ensures that the mechanics of the process lack transparency. Only (and particularly) the outcomes are for public consumption.

Political actors in both the executive and legislative branches have specific and unique opportunities to influence outcomes. Presidents rely substantially on political appointees and the Office of Management and Budget to affect policy in key ways. Both tightly control information environments within federal agencies. While OMB functions as a bureaucratic buffer from external political influence, appointees foster a communication environment that continually keeps bureaucratic actors informed of administration priorities and preferences. Political appointees and OMB also affect distributive outcomes in other indirect ways, such as through strategic program design and criteria creation, and in more direct ways by formalizing their role in the policy decisionmaking hierarchy.

This chapter identifies and details the key mechanisms in the grants process that facilitate political influence and control, filling a substantial gap in the literature and overcoming some of the weaknesses of previous research in this area. In addition, it illustrates how political control can have distributional implications that can easily conform to political elites' electoral interests. In the process, a picture of an electorally driven, micro-policy-oriented, highly political president emerges. The permanent campaign that many scholars believe that presidents conduct also affects the administration of public policy. Bureaucrats and appointees in the federal government, state government employees, and interest group lobbyists are aware that in the quest for federal funding, presidential elections play a role. As a result, the character, motivation, and overall scope of presidential power is seen in a different light.

Appendix 7A

This appendix provides an overview of and details on the methodological approach to elite interviewing used for this book. It covers design, identification/sampling, and instrumentation. In many cases, the amount of detail that could be provided was limited by the requirements of the Vanderbilt University Institutional Review Board.[21]

Design

As detailed in chapter 7, I conducted interviews with three types of subjects: federal agency employees (bureaucrats and appointees), state bureaucrats, and interest group officials. Respondents were drawn from a series of issue areas; however, in several cases, interviewees across respondent types were connected by issue areas.

Between August 2010 and June 2011, I conducted a total of twenty-four interviews with eleven federal agency employees, six state bureaucrats, and seven interest group officials. Most federal agency employees worked in the central office of an agency; however, three respondents (two appointees and one career bureaucrat) worked in a subnational office of a federal agency. All interest group officials (lobbyists and grant managers) worked in the Washington, D.C., office of their institution's national headquarters, with one exception: one interest group grant manager worked at a multistate office of an interest group.

Interviews at the state level included respondents from swing, core Democratic, and core Republican states. Among all respondents, two individuals had worked for their institution for less than one year; seven respondents, for one to three years; five respondents, for four to nine years; and ten respondents, for ten years or more.

Interviews typically lasted between 45 and 60 minutes. The shortest interview was 30 minutes; the longest lasted just over two hours. Initially I asked respondents to allow me to tape their interview, but I very quickly found that most respondents were uncomfortable with that request and declined. Moreover, I found that respondents who declined the recording in the middle of the interview were initially more guarded in their responses. In those cases, as the interview proceeded, the "recording effect" abated and information became more accessible. After the fourth interview, I stopped asking to

---

21. Part of this research was conducted at Vanderbilt University.

record interviews and relied on handwritten notes. In all cases, I clarified and analyzed my notes as soon as possible after the interview.

Nearly all interviews were conducted in person; only two were conducted by telephone. One respondent requested a phone interview because of scheduling conflicts; the other requested a phone interview for weather-related reasons. All other interviews were conducted face to face. Each was conducted in either the office of the respondent or a nearby conference room, with one exception. At the request of the respondent, one interview began in a Starbucks restaurant and continued on a subway train because of a scheduling conflict. Each interview was conducted one on one, with one exception. One senior federal agency employee asked to be interviewed together with a subordinate whose job dealt directly with the interview topic.

All interviews were guided by a similar set of questions and topics to be discussed. However, all interviews were open ended, and often other, related topics were explored, depending on the responses given and the avenues that the respondent wished to take. Respondents were guided back to the relevant topic if the discussion became too tangential. Sometimes respondents veered in unexpected directions, revealing important information.

Identification/Sampling

I identified prospective respondents first by using a list of all federal agencies and grant programs compiled for this study. The list encompassed the institutions that allocated all federal discretionary grants between 1996 and 2008. Not every agency allocated grants in every year of that period; however, most agency behavior with respect to funding was similar from year to year. I did not disregard agencies that failed to allocate funds in *every* year, but all agencies identified as a possible research site were frequent or universal distributors.

I eventually narrowed the list to twelve agencies on the basis of issue diversity and institutional location and structure. I included ten cabinet institutions and two independent institutions; however, all federal agency respondents ultimately came from cabinet institutions. Next, using each agency's website, I was able to identify which individuals dealt most closely with federal discretionary grants.[22] I contacted each prospective federal agency respondent through his or her government e-mail address, using my own Vanderbilt University e-mail address.

---

22. In some instances, such resources were insufficient and I relied on the *Federal Yellow Book*. When both methods failed, I e-mailed the career staffer most closely identifiable with federal fund distribution and requested the contact information of the proper individual.

After scheduling interviews, I next identified interest groups that dealt with federal grants in the agencies for which the federal agency respondents worked. Relevant, issue-based national interest groups often were easily identifiable, but in some cases I used congressional reports, published agency reports, and media accounts to identify interest group sources. I used staff directories available online to identify key prospective respondents in those organizations. I subsequently contacted each via e-mail.

Next, I chose states on the basis of their presidential electoral competitiveness, including swing states, Democratic core states, and Republican core states.[23] I then identified relevant state agencies in those states, which often were issue-based institutional complements of the federal agencies in which interviews were to be conducted. Using online staff directories, I identified key prospective respondents at those state agencies who dealt most frequently with federal grant programs. I contacted those individuals and requested interviews via e-mail.

The sampling technique used in this study was purposefully non-random. However, the sampling did meet study goals. First, within a respondent type, respondents dealt with different issue areas; however, respondents of different respondent types often were involved in similar policy areas. Second, interviewees of each respondent type were sampled. Third, respondents at the state level were drawn from states whose presidential electoral competitiveness varied.

Instrumentation

As mentioned, interviews were open ended, and while they explored similar themes, institutional processes, and political dynamics, each played out very differently. I sought to explore predetermined topics. However, exploring those topics could be difficult, depending on the respondent's comfort and willingness to answer questions. Typically, respondents were quite open and forward in responding. In certain cases, it was clear when respondents were uncomfortable and guarded. I then attempted to elicit answers; if my attempts were unsuccessful, I veiled the question for use later in the interview.

Although the interviews were open ended, the Vanderbilt University Institutional Review Board required and subsequently approved a set of sample questions for each respondent type that had to be offered to each respondent. The questions served as a topical guide more than a strict questionnaire, as

23. Because of privacy restrictions imposed by the Vanderbilt Institutional Review Board, I am unable to identify which states were used. However, the states were small to medium-size in terms of population.

respondents often explored and offered insight into different, related, and important areas of inquiry. The sample questions are found in appendix 7B.

In designing the sample interview instrument for this study, I found that it was important to be sensitive to the institutional position of the respondent with respect to the information being requested. For example, federal agency officials might be unwilling to discuss explicit questions about the influence of the White House, the Office of Management and Budget, or political appointees. Similarly, state bureaucrats and interest group officials might be unwilling to answer questions that probe how personal connections within an agency benefit their grant proposals. Such topics were either presented delicately or approached using veiled questions. For example, a federal bureaucrat might be unwilling to state that OMB can change grant allocations; however, he or she might be more willing to respond to a series of questions asking about OMB's contact with, oversight of, and role in decisionmaking at the agency. Such techniques were used frequently during the interviews and produced useful information from nearly every respondent.

Finally, it is important to note that respondents were informed in a consent form that they had the right to decline to answer any questions. In only two cases did respondents decline, a response that in both cases was due to poor wording of the question in the context of that interview. To try to overcome such issues, I explained to all respondents that privacy requirements prevented the revealing of any personally identifying information in reporting results. I noted that if I were a journalist, the information would be considered on background or not for attribution; I would simply identify their respondent type. Often that explanation satisfied respondents. However, on a few occasions, respondents requested that portions of the interview be done off the record. In the end, flexibility in instrumentation and responsiveness to interviewees' preferences and needs were the most straightforward means of obtaining information.

Appendix 7B
Proposed Survey Questions for Each Respondent Type

Federal Grant Managers

1. Please describe the processes by which grant applications move through your agency.
2. Please describe your role in the grant application process.
3. Do there exist procedures that "fast track" applications?
4. Describe the grants process in terms of the structure of your agency.
5. After your role, which actors process applications next?
6. Who has final approval over grant allocations?
7. How often are your recommendations accepted?
8. How much contact do you have with
   a. applicants?
   b. senior agency staff?
   c. agency and department heads?
   d. the Office of Management and Budget?
   e. White House staff?
   f. Congressional member/committee staff?

Interest Group Lobbyists

1. Please describe your role in the federal grants process.
2. Please describe the ways in which you aid clients seeking support from the government.
3. Who are the individuals most responsible for the success/failure of grant applications?
4. What other means do clients use to enhance their success before federal agencies?
5. Do political appointees in agencies work closely in the federal grants process?
6. Who has final approval over federal grants?
7. Does the White House have contact with the relevant actors in the federal grants process?
8. Do political appointees have such contact?
9. Does the Office of Management and Budget have such contact?
10. Does Congress have such contact?

Local Officials

1. Please describe your role in the federal grants process.
2. Are there any specific individuals or offices in federal agencies that you deal with directly?
3. Are there any procedures to use or individuals to talk to that can fast track an application?
4. What is your office's success rate at applying for federal grants?
5. During your tenure in this office have formal or informal application procedures changed dramatically across presidential administrations?
6. Has your success in the grants process changed dramatically across presidential administrations or over time?
7. When your applications are being considered do you contact any federal agency officials on a regular basis?
8. Do you contact any other local officials on a regular basis?
9. Do you contact any officials in a Congressman's or Senator's office on a regular basis?
10. Do state agencies rely on the help from any interest groups in advancing their success in terms of the federal grants process?

8

Conclusions and Implications

Presidents are election-driven individuals who use the formal and informal tools of their office to advance their electoral interests. They engage in a basic, strategic, and widely used behavior among elected officials: pork barrel politics. Presidents wield extensive spending authority and direct federal dollars to swing states in advance of elections as swing states represent a critical constituency that decides whether candidates win or lose presidential elections. Discretionary spending power serves incumbent presidents as a campaign tool to further their reelection efforts and the efforts of their same-party successor.

Presidents have the motive, means, and opportunity to engage in pork barrel politics. However, political scientists often view such behavior as beneath or beyond the president—as a tool reserved for legislative actors. Because of Congress's role as chief appropriator and members' manageable constituencies, the literature focuses on their desire and ability to target funds in strategic ways. In a similar way, presidents capitalize on delegated spending power to motivate a broad bureaucracy to be responsive to their interests, including electoral interests. White House officials, the Office of Management and Budget, and political appointees serve as an army of responsive surrogates using their leadership positions to ensure that policy outcomes reflect presidential preferences. These political actors use a host of tools and mechanisms to help satisfy the president's penchant for pork. These include direct efforts such as distributive intervention, budgetary oversight, and personnel politicization as well as informal means such as the manipulation of funding criteria, strategic design of grant programs, and the application of political pressure. What results is a complex system of political tools that empower presidents to behave in electorally strategic ways.

This book illustrates the comprehensive and successful efforts that presidents and their surrogates mount in order to achieve electorally strategic policy responsiveness from their administrations. I offer two claims that deviate from standard research on the presidency. First, presidents are *primarily* election-driven individuals. This view challenges arguments that such motives are ancillary. It also extends research on presidential elections and the permanent campaign to include an examination of the effects of electoral interests on public policy. Second, presidents are able to influence and determine policy even at the micro-level more effectively than Congress can. This perspective insists on a reexamination of theories of presidential behavior and demonstrates the significant distributional consequences when presidential electoral interests drive policy administration.

What We Know: The Effects of Electorally Strategic Policymaking

It is well understood among the Washington establishment that presidential spending authority is a critical power that allows the White House to generate policy that will deliver political and electoral benefits to the president. Discretionary grants—totaling about $100 billion annually—provide an ideal context for testing theories of presidential policymaking and electoral behavior. I capitalize on this area of federal spending to show that presidential electoral preferences substantially influence both *where* and *when* these funds are distributed.

This book illustrates the myriad ways in which presidents—even though they serve as head of a large, diverse bureaucracy—effectively influence policy at the micro level, particularly in the area of distributive policy. Straightforward, well-publicized, easily interpreted presidential electoral preferences are easily conveyed throughout the bureaucracy. With respect to distributive policy, it is simple to communicate preferences about which key states should be targeted. Presidents can use political appointees effectively in a wide variety of capacities. The president's handpicked surrogates have numerous ways to influence fund distribution for political or electoral gain. These include strategically structuring decisionmaking, creating grant criteria, applying political pressure, and controlling the information environment surrounding civil servants. This book shows that presidents also influence micro-level policymaking by strategically selecting executive branch personnel—both appointed and career staff. The findings also highlight a critical aspect of these presidential efforts. Staffing decisions are particularly sensitive to presidential preferences for positions that have distributive authority—power with electoral implications.

Presidents and their appointees are broadly effective at using their spending authority and power over bureaucratic processes to engage in pork barrel politics. However, this electorally strategic policy control is not uniform across the executive branch. Instead, specific institutional designs, such as insulated independence and politicization, condition presidential control and policy responsiveness to electoral interests. The findings in this book show that the design of federal agencies has both policy and distributional consequences that can have electoral implications as well.

A unique contribution of this research is that it illustrates the power of the executive branch and specifically presidential preferences in an area widely believed to be the purview of Congress. However, this book does not suggest that Congress is powerless to influence funds but that in the context of discretionary grants, legislative power is severely limited. Presidents and appointees enjoy and capitalize on discretionary spending authority. However, the president realizes that *Congress giveth and Congress taketh away*. Presidents know that their ability to engage in pork barrel politics largely depends on the delegation of power, and to preserve that power, presidents ensure that the congressional actors most directly charged with determining discretion benefit from pork.

What We Think: A Reexamination of Presidential Behavior

Political scientists, journalists, and pundits have long examined why elected officials behave as they do. In the context of presidential behavior, disagreements about presidential motives lead to various explanations. A robust, theoretically rich examination of presidential incentives helps in understanding the calculus by which presidents think and ultimately act.

Presidential Motives and Incentives

Sidney Blumenthal was right. In 1992, he explained that presidents face a "permanent campaign." As quickly as presidents finish their inaugural address, step inside from the West Front of the Capitol Building, and submit their first nominations to the Senate, they begin running for reelection. Presidents distinguish themselves as consummate campaigners. They devote extensive staff, time, travel, planning, strategy, and resources to their reelection and the election of their same-party successor. Many have looked at presidential campaigns as just that: campaign activity.

In the context of policymaking, the president is seen as differently focused. The literature often describes the "national" president, one with a unique vantage point in the American political system and policymaking arena. This narrow and misguided view of the unique "national" president emerges from four assumptions about presidential behavior that fail to withstand theoretical (and as demonstrated in this book, empirical) scrutiny. Presidents almost obsessively focus on swing states, ensuring that presidential constituencies are substantially smaller than the national constituency. The institutional design of the Electoral College requires presidents to think differently about their constituency and the ways in which they can connect to it.

As mentioned above, the concept of a president with electoral interests is not new, nor is it an original idea that presidential elections focus on swing states. However, the literature is schizophrenic in describing presidential interests. Work on the permanent campaign describes a president focused on electoral interests on the campaign trail, frequently engaging in a swing-state strategy. However, work on the president as policymaker or as administrator shows a different, macro-oriented, national president. Rarely do these two views of the president meet in research on the presidency. This book takes that step, showing that the same incentives that drive presidents on the campaign trail also motivate presidents in the Oval Office as they forge policy.

The theoretical discussion and the subsequent empirical support demonstrate that scholars of the presidency must move away from the view of the president as a unique national actor too busy or disinterested to let electoral interests affect policymaking. Nor should researchers assume that campaign behavior is reserved for the campaign. Instead, the role of electoral interests is critical in evaluating presidential behavior broadly. Presidential behavior is election centered and constituency oriented and employs the profound resources of the executive branch to affect policy at all levels. Particularly in the context of a common electoral behavior—pork barrel politicking—presidents are uniquely positioned, substantially empowered, and fiscally endowed to direct federal money to key constituencies at critical times.

The Effect of Electoral Institutions on Presidential Incentives

The institutional design of the Electoral College provides insight into the nature of pork barrel spending in presidential politics and has given rise to a central debate in the study of distributive politics. Scholars often clash over the proper constituency that elected officials should target with government revenue. The conflict, often labeled the swing-versus-core debate, centers on the effectiveness of targeting marginal (swing) voters in an effort to change minds or base voters in an effort to stimulate turnout. This debate continues to generate substantial theoretical and empirical scholarship in the legislative arena. However, in the context of presidential politics, the design of the Electoral College provides an easy solution to an often complex theoretical issue. Clearly, funneling government revenue (or campaign time, energy, and resources) to core states offers the president no marginal benefit. A Democratic president who purchases advertising time or targets federal grant allocations to the Baltimore media market will win Maryland's ten electoral votes. However, a Democratic president is just as likely to win those ten votes without that resource expenditure. Essentially, targeting funds to core presidential constituencies has no payoff because whether a candidate wins a state by 1 percent or 70 percent, he receives the same electoral benefit: that state's electoral votes. Instead, a president must (and does) focus energy, resources, and pork barrel spending on swing states in the hope that those expenditures will move electoral votes from his opponent's column to his own.

This evaluation of presidential elections and the impact of the Electoral College system supports the swing hypothesis at the interstate level. However, it does not settle questions about resource targeting at the intrastate level. When a campaign targets funds to a swing state, where are those funds directed *within* that state? Some evidence suggests that the funds are (and should be) targeted to core constituencies. This book is silent on this point, as the unit of analysis (the state) cannot provide an effective empirical evaluation of the question. Efforts to use these data to examine fund allocations below the state level face serious theoretical, empirical, and methodological challenges.

Yet, from a theoretical perspective, the targeting of core voters within swing states has merit (see Chen 2009 for empirical evidence of this point). In the aggregate, presidential elections strive not for turnout but for the strategic combination of state-level successes needed to total 270 electoral votes. However, at the state level, campaigns spend a tremendous amount of time on turning out core constituencies in an effort to affect the final vote tally in the state. Democratic candidates rely on public employee unions, conservation groups, college organizations, and women's rights groups to turn out their voters to support the party's standard bearer. Republican candidates rely on church groups, family values organizations, chambers of commerce, and groups focused on individual liberties and federalism to generate enthusiasm among their members and sympathizers. Bringing higher numbers of partisans to the polls within swing states may be the key to winning not just the state but the day.

The Electoral College may institutionalize a unique and bifurcated campaign focus for presidents. It may induce presidents to implement an interstate swing strategy and an intrastate core strategy in order to maximize effectiveness. This book has provided substantial evidence that swing states benefit significantly when strategic presidents seek to advance their own electoral interests. However, more work should and must be done in order to evaluate presidential strategy more comprehensively. By examining presidential resource allocation strategy in a systematic way, research can offer a complete view of presidential electoral behavior both across and within states.

Federal Spending Power in Other Areas

The analysis of federal discretionary grants provides an ideal setting for assessing questions of presidential power and electoral interests, political control, and the president's role in public policy. However, the focus on federal grants in this project demonstrates one part of a broad area of presidential power: spending authority. Discretionary spending authority offers presidents substantial influence in the policy process and extends far beyond grants. Contracts and procurement, licenses, cooperative agreements, and government insurance provide presidents a host of other opportunities to affect distributive outcomes. The focus on a singular area of presidential spending power allows for a detailed, systematic, and nuanced analysis of the people and processes that define and determine policy outcomes. This book has offered such analysis for grants and provides insights that likely extend to other areas of discretionary authority.

Other research can extend this analysis by applying the same or similar questions to other areas of spending. Some research has taken this step (see Taylor 2008), but much more can be done. This area of policy has tremendous potential for making great strides in understanding the connection between presidential elections and the administration of public policy. Such analysis would provide important information regarding presidential power. Similar findings that suggest that presidential electoral interests influence the distribution of funding sources such as cooperative agreements or contracts would illustrate the broad scope of presidential pork barrel politics. If such behavior extends across discretionary spending areas, it would demonstrate that the federal funds available to incumbents are greater than this analysis shows. Alternatively, if the electorally strategic allocation of federal funds is restricted to grant distribution, it will facilitate another important avenue of research into presidential policy power and administrative control. Such a finding would suggest that the ability to exploit discretionary authority for electoral gain is not uniform. Instead, some intervening factor(s) condition presidential power or incentives. Understanding how differences in personnel and processes across these spending areas affect outcomes will shed greater light on which bureaucratic structures and policymaking procedures condition presidential spending power. This project provides evidence of such conditionality within one area of spending, but the analysis can be improved through extension into other areas.

The Normative Implications of Presidential Pork Barrel Politics

Equity and fairness, in the abstract, are quintessential American values. Often citizens support public policy based on those values. At the same time, however, they also expect their elected representatives to do everything that they can for their constituents. As a result, West Virginians enjoy beautifully manicured roads, while other states may not—an outcome to which few West Virginians would likely object. Many Americans believe that all states are created equal, but as long as they themselves benefit, they do not oppose some states being more equal than others.[1] The benefactors of pork often strongly support it, while those facing shortfalls prefer a more equitable system.

One question that naturally arises from the study of pork barrel politics concerns the normative implications of the practice. When presidents engage in pork barrel politics, they target large sums of federal discretionary grant dollars to swing states at the expense of other states—a behavior that is robust across political parties and over time. The result is a bias in the allocation of government revenues that favors certain Americans simply because they reside in a particular state or because a presidential election is coming up. Is such political manipulation of public policy detrimental to the administration of government? Does it deny citizens equitable access to relief?

To evaluate the normative effects of the discretionary allocation of funding, it is critical to put influence into context. This study illustrates clearly the ways in which presidents divert funds to swing states at key times. Yet presidents and their appointees do not take money from needy constituencies, citizens, and groups and redirect that money to groups with abundant resources. Such a scenario would represent not only a failure of policy but a failure of the moral intent of federal assistance. In reality, the president's strategic efforts to influence fund allocations are aided by copious needs and limited resources. Almost universally, the demand for grant funding far outpaces the supply. As a result, even the most scientific, need-based, automatic, nonpolitical allocation of federal funds results in some needy applicants being

---

1. To paraphrase a celebrated line from George Orwell's 1945 book *Animal Farm*.

denied assistance. For example, widespread demand exists for a Department of Energy grant program intended to assist low-income families in making energy efficient improvements to their homes. Families in Wisconsin may be just as needy as families in North Dakota for improvements that allow their homes to withstand the winters in the upper Midwest. Yet not all needs across or within those states can be met. There may be only enough funding to help a portion of those who can use assistance. Appropriations, not the behavior of the president or the executive branch, determine how much need can be met. Presidential politics determines the allocation of the funds appropriated to meet that need.

Moreover, the effects of political (or electoral) influence exist at the margins. Only a portion of federal government funding is allocated for political rather than need-based reasons. In the Department of Energy example, some families in Wisconsin with slightly less need may receive funds at the expense of certain North Dakotans with slightly more need. Thus, some of the unmet need is shifted from Wisconsin to North Dakota. However, what the system does not produce is a perverse means of distribution whereby wealthy Wisconsinites receive subsidies while impoverished North Dakotans freeze. The marginal impact of presidential electoral interests ensures that outcomes generally meet needs and serious policy failure is avoided.

To attain the bureaucratic ideal, federal funds would have to be allocated strictly on the basis of need and the likelihood of the allocation achieving program goals. If a federal program had 1,000 grants to award, the 1,000 neediest individuals would receive funds, regardless of their state of residence, representation in Congress, or alignment with the party of their governor. However, policy in the United States is designed, developed, approved, and implemented in a political system. It should come as no surprise that political values and interests affect outcomes. In fact, one means of ensuring accountability is through politicization of the policymaking process. By permitting elected officials to participate in all stages of the process, politicization allows voters to punish the officials responsible for policy failures or reward them for success. The system institutionalizes a form of democracy and accountability that might be lost in a system devoid of the influence of political actors. Political influence, as described throughout this volume, therefore is a consequence of the design of the U.S. system of government. However, *consequence of design* should not be conflated with a mistake or an error. Taken to its logical extreme, presidential electoral interest in the distribution of federal funds could result in profound policy failure. If all $100 billion in annual discretionary federal grants was directed to Ohio, Florida, New Hampshire,

Pennsylvania, Virginia, and a few other highly competitive states, many citizens elsewhere would suffer as their needs went grossly unmet. However, institutional mechanisms in the democratic system allow for the correction of such an unbalanced outcome. Congress could redesign federal spending programs to restrict the president's power; oversight investigations could be launched into every federal agency that participated in the inequitable distribution of funds; and voters in uncompetitive states could voice their disapproval in presidential elections.[2] What would result is a democratic backlash penalizing the president's behavior. As it is, presidents generally protect themselves from any such backlash by incorporating their preferences in policy implementation in a more measured and marginal fashion.

That voters and democratic institutions allow presidents to behave in this way may have one of two explanations. First, presidents may behave in electorally strategic ways that voters and elected officials fail to notice. This scenario suggests the measured nature of presidents' electoral efforts. However, in a system with such heavy oversight and reporting requirements and in which data on the distribution of federal funds are public, voters and institutions would take note if those efforts led to profound misallocations of funds. Presidents are able to engage in such behavior without being detected not because the behavior is imperceptible but because its effects are generally innocuous.

Second, the media and political elites are well aware that the executive branch uses its spending power for political and electoral gain, even if the details of how it does so are unknown. Voters also expect politicians to use their power and authority for political gain. Therefore presidents may engage in pork barrel politics without creating a democratic backlash because citizens and other elected officials are comfortable with their behavior and, by failing to respond, tacitly approve it.

That is clearly the case for members of Congress. Legislators are known and expected to engage in pork barrel politics. Whether citizens agree or disagree with the practice, it does not engender a visceral negative response. In fact, while citizens may be bothered by the practice in the aggregate, they often are pleased when their own representatives do it. That approval is evidenced by legislators' public bragging—credit claiming—for bringing home the bacon. Essentially, in a democratic system, citizens may expect

2. While this study accepts the premise that non–swing states' electoral outcomes are a foregone conclusion in a presidential election, that may not be the case in the face of a profound abuse of office for electoral gain—particularly in states that are victimized by it. Voters also could rise up during the primary process to penalize incumbent presidents and party candidates for such abuses.

their elected officials to behave in political ways; in fact, in some cases, they may prefer them to do so. As long as their political actions fall within certain bounds of acceptability, citizens tacitly allow the behavior. Safety valves to prevent political abuses are in place, but they are reserved for exceptional actions. As long as presidents affect grant allocations at the margins and need is generally met (given resource constraints), this type of presidential behavior will be allowed to continue.

There may be one means by which the normative effect of pork barrel politicking can be measured. Through analysis like that presented in this book and even analysis on legislative pork, one can identify the constituencies that receive a boost in federal benefits above the baseline. Using that information, one could take on the intimidating task of examining documents produced to meet federal reporting requirements during the funding close-out process. By identifying projects that fail, remain unfinished, go over budget, or do not meet standards, researchers could identify which states, congressional districts, counties, and so forth have higher failure (or truly, non-success) rates. Determining whether those rates are correlated with the politicization of funding may be one step toward deciding whether pork barrel politics produces normatively negative and financially costly outcomes. However, despite the findings of such a study, it is still likely that elected officials—regardless of inefficiencies or failures—would strive to deliver additional funds to key constituencies.

What Can Be Done: Addressing Presidential Influence

If presidential pork barrel politicking is a normative ill in the system, could policy changes reform the practice? To affect presidential behavior—specifically exercising influence on federal fund distribution for electoral gain—either presidential powers or incentives must be manipulated. Policies and/ or institutional reforms can be enacted that elicit different behaviors and ultimately influence the nature of distributive outcomes. However, in evaluating any proposed systemic changes, it is vital to assess the likelihood of those changes as well as their consequences.

Limiting Discretion

Presidents' ability to influence the distribution of federal funds depends primarily on their discretionary spending power. That power, delegated by Congress, allows the executive branch to make allocation decisions involving large sums of money. One means of limiting presidential influence in this area is to limit presidential discretion by withdrawing the executive branch's authority to design programs, criteria, and evaluation procedures as well as to make allocation decisions. By reducing discretion, Congress regains power over those facets of the funding process.

Congress is unlikely to restrict presidents' discretionary spending authority, however, for two reasons. First, presidents are not passive recipients of discretionary authority. As a key player in the legislative process, presidents use their discretion as a bargaining chip in their negotiations with Congress in exchange for their signature on a piece of legislation. Because of the chief executive's role in creating and approving legislation, Congress cannot simply reduce discretion unilaterally. Given the electoral benefits associated with their spending power, presidents would be especially protective of it and resist any congressional effort to reclaim it.

Moreover, Congress may not want to reclaim the spending authority that it typically delegates to the chief executive. Discretion is critical for Congress. Powers are delegated to the executive branch because Congress lacks the time, staff, and expertise to codify funding procedures for all types of federal spending. Areas where Congress wields extensive spending power, such as formula and block grant programs, require extensive internal negotiation—a task that would become unwieldy if it were expanded to all areas of federal funding. In short, while the delegation of spending authority empowers presidents to use funds in electorally strategic ways, it also benefits Congress.

Even if the president were to accept having his discretionary authority restricted and Congress could effectively handle the dramatic increase in its policymaking and administrative responsibilities, the change still would not remove politics from policy. Rather than depoliticizing federal fund distribution, restricting presidential discretion would simply redirect the opportunity to exercise political influence to Congress. The president's ability to target funds to swing states would be quite limited; however, members of Congress would be able to direct federal dollars to *their* key constituencies. The literature on distributive politics describes the manner in which legislative interests influence allocations and which characteristics of legislators lead to greater funding (for example, seniority, partisanship, committee assignment, electoral vulnerability). In fact, Lee and Oppenheimer (1999) demonstrate that when Congress designs legislative formulas, states with the smallest populations receive the greatest benefit, as a low-cost way of gaining senators' support and building the coalitions necessary for passage of legislation. Under that scenario, small-population states like Wyoming, South Dakota, and Alaska receive disproportionate benefits. On the other hand, because larger portions of the U.S. public live in targeted areas (swing states), more people benefit when a president exercises influence.[3] While presidential discretion is unlikely to be restricted, doing so would do little to strip politics from federal fund allocations. It would simply empower a different branch, composed of a higher number of elected officials, to make distributive decisions.

Insulating away Influence

Another way to limit presidential electoral influence on the distribution of funds involves insulating bureaucratic institutions from such influence. The empirical evidence presented in this book illustrates that insulated adminis-trative design can effectively limit presidential power. Specifically, the presi-dent's ability to extract distributive benefits and advance his electoral interests is limited in independent agencies with lower levels of politicization and in independent commissions. New agencies can be designed to include commis-sion features such as fixed and staggered terms for commissioners and party-balancing requirements, among others. Alternatively, new independent agen-cies can be created with a restricted number of political appointees relative to staff size. In addition, existing cabinet agencies can be redesigned in order to incorporate the same characteristics. Such institutional reforms would give agencies the structural characteristics that limit presidential influence.

The legislative process ensures that insulating institutional reforms are unlikely to be adopted. Presidential approval is required to create new agencies and redesign or reorganize existing agencies, and the White House is unlikely to support any curtailing of presidential power intended to limit presiden-tial spending authority and influence over distributive outcomes. Evidence of such resistance can be seen in recent presidential efforts aimed in the opposite direction: *de-insulation*. As mentioned previously, President George W. Bush sought greater administrative power during the creation of the Department of Homeland Security in 2003. In fact, part of the reorganization process involved transferring the Federal Emergency Management Agency (an inde-pendent agency) to the cabinet. In addition, President Bush sought to *increase* the number of political appointees in the new department rather than main-tain or decrease it. In 2012, President Obama's request for greater reorgani-zation authority under the Consolidation Authority Act sought to transfer independent institutions—including the Small Business Administration, the Export-Import Bank, the Overseas Private Investment Corporation, and the

---

3. For example, after the 2000 election, 125 million Americans lived in states that were decided by 10 percentage points or fewer.

U.S. Trade and Development Agency—into a new cabinet department. That effort sought to remove the insulating structures of the institutions and transfer them to the part of the executive branch in which presidents wield the most pervasive political and electoral influence. These presidential efforts demonstrate that institutional reforms that aim to *increase* insulation are unrealistic.

Although reforms to increase the insulation of agencies are incredibly unlikely to occur, they could be effective if they were implemented. The empirical evidence presented in previous chapters suggests that independent commissions and less politicized independent agencies effectively buffer presidential influence—that is, in those institutions, presidents are generally unable to manipulate outcomes in order to advance their electoral interests. In those particular institutions, there is no systematic relationship between state electoral competitiveness and the receipt of federal grants.

This study also shows that congressional influence too is restricted in more insulated federal agencies. Congress's institutional, political, and electoral interests tend not to affect distributive outcomes in independent commissions and less politicized independent agencies. In fact, congressional interests are more likely to be satisfied through the distribution of funds from cabinet agencies. Insulation thus creates a paradoxical institutional incentive for Congress: congressional interests are advanced by granting the president control over federal fund distribution. Limiting insulation of agencies not only pays dividends for the election-driven president but substantially benefits legislators seeking additional federal funding. This incentive structure also decreases the likelihood that reforms can be enacted. Surely presidents would resist efforts to insulate federal agencies, but the evidence presented here suggests that Congress should also resist insulation.

Finally, insulating federal agencies from presidential influence would not necessarily purge policymaking of politics. This study analyzes the influence of presidential electoral interests (as well as a host of congressional interests) on agencies, but it does not examine the role of other political actors in independent agencies and commissions. Interest groups may play powerful roles within independent institutions, and expanding the number of those institutions might simply expand the role of different actors across broader areas of policy. Once again, insulating agencies may not expunge political influence. It is more likely to transfer it to different actors and institutions.

Reforming the Electoral System

Another way to limit presidents' distributive discretion would require changing presidential incentives. The institutional design of the Electoral College induces presidents to target attention and resources to swing states. To stop or modify that behavior, one option is to reform the process by which presidents are elected. Various proposals have been made to eliminate the Electoral College and replace it with a different system, and each proposal would affect presidential candidates' and presidents' quest for electoral success in different ways. Two of the most common proposals involve dramatic changes in the way that votes are counted. Under one, the Electoral College system is largely kept in place, but states apportion their votes in different proportional ways.[4] Under the other, the presidential electoral system would be transformed into a national plebiscite, and the winner of the national popular vote would become president.

The likelihood of either of these proposals coming to fruition is also low. The first would require either a constitutional amendment or broad legislative efforts at the state level. Amending the Constitution is an onerous process that is rarely used and is especially burdensome for reforming the political process. In addition, states are unlikely to transform the manner in which their electoral votes are allocated, particularly if doing so negatively affects the state party in power. For example, Democrats frequently control a supermajority of both houses of the state legislature in Massachusetts, and Massachusetts is a core Democratic state in presidential elections. The Democratic Party–controlled state legislature is unlikely to reform its electoral vote allocation system in a way that delivers some of those votes to a Republican presidential candidate. State legislative unwillingness to reform the system reduces the likelihood of such changes occurring through either a constitutional amendment or state legislation.

Even if states were willing to convert their electoral vote allocations to an alternative system, it would likely be short-lived. For example, if a Democratic state switched to a more equitable allocation system, one result could lead to a rapid reversion to a winner-take-all system: a Republican winning the White House because of that Democratic state's system. That could happen in a host of ways. For example, consider what would happen if a state like Rhode Island—reliably Democratic in presidential elections—opted to allocate its electoral votes to whichever candidate won the popular vote nationwide. In a close presidential election, Rhode Island could cast the decisive electoral votes for the Republican nominee for president, despite a Democrat winning more

---

4. One proportional proposal requires all electoral votes to be allocated proportionally according to the percentage of each state's popular vote that each candidate wins. Another requires two electoral votes to be allocated to the candidate who wins the state, while all other votes are allocated proportionally.

popular votes in the state. In this situation, one could imagine the Rhode Island legislature—with a supermajority of Democrats—trying to change its electoral laws between Election Day and the date on which electoral votes are cast. Or alternatively, the legislature would likely revert to the traditional, winner-take-all system of allocating electoral votes for the next presidential election. While adopting a more proportional or democratic means of allocating electoral votes is an admirable ideal, the politics and possible consequences of that action make it untenable in the short-term or unsustainable in the long-term.

The second type of reform—a national plebiscite—requires a constitutional amendment and faces the same institutional stumbling blocks for passage. Not only would several states be unwilling to support a constitutional amendment because it would empower the other party, Congress would be hesitant to initiate the amendment process for the same reasons.

Similarly, rational legislative actors in key states would resist such reforms because they could lead to a reduction in the level of grant funding. Besides that, the reforms would entail less campaigning from presidential candidates and fewer campaign dollars flowing into those states. Perennial swing states are likely to be especially resistant to any proposal—legislative or constitutional—that seeks to change or eliminate the Electoral College.

If an effort to reform the Electoral College did succeed, how would it change presidential preferences and what would be the effect on distributive policy outcomes? The precise effects of electoral reform would, of course, depend on the details of the new system. It is likely that swing states would become less of a target for presidential candidates. For example, if the system were transformed into a national plebiscite, states would no longer be the unit of focus for campaigns; instead, campaigns would mount a broad effort to increase voter turnout, particularly among core voters. The focus of a presidential campaign would be to target areas that were ideologically aligned with the candidate's party and his or her values. Presidential candidates might target areas that displayed more partisan homogeneity or those with higher population densities so messaging efforts could reach more people more efficiently. There are strategies to target key constituencies that increase the likelihood of electoral success based on the institutional structure of the presidential election process—however reformed. The result would not remove electoral politics from distributive policymaking; instead, reforms would most likely redirect political influence to a new set of recipients. Wisconsin, Pennsylvania, and New Mexico would no longer be the target of presidential campaigns. Instead, Republicans may target funds to Texas, Tennessee, and Louisiana while Democrats target New York, New Jersey, and California. Under a more complex political strategy, Republicans may target upstate New York and the gold coast of Connecticut, while Democrats target Houston and New Orleans. Targeting would shift, but key constituencies would be targeted nonetheless. Presidential influence on the distribution of discretionary federal grants would remain even in the face of institutional reforms intended to stop it.

A Final Note

Electoral institutions could be reformed, agencies could be redesigned, spending legislation could be rewritten. Any such efforts are unlikely to be undertaken, their goals would be difficult to achieve if they were, and they would not put an end to the politicization of policymaking if they succeeded. Political manipulation of federal spending for electoral gain is an attribute of the U.S. political system and one that citizens do little to resist or reform. Is there a more equitable ideal by which funds can be distributed? Absolutely. Is it achievable? Absolutely not.

This book illustrates the reach of presidential power, the consequences of presidential incentives, and the implications of those incentives for public policy. It is not, however, an indictment of presidential influence on distribution of federal funds. The targeting of federal funds for electoral gain is an institutionalized characteristic of the U.S. democratic system and one that is more a fact of life than a point of contention. As long as Americans charge their elected officials with the design and implementation of public policy, politics will influence outcomes. And as long as they elect a president to administer an executive branch upon which they place substantial demands, two predictions can be made with certainty: presidents will remain powerful, and pork barrel politics will continue as usual.

References

Abramowitz, Alan I., Brad Alexander, and Matthew Gunning. 2006. "Incumbency, Redistricting, and the Decline of Competition in U.S. House Elections." *Journal of Politics* 68 (1): 75–88.

Alesina, Alberto, and Howard Rosenthal. 1989. "Partisan Cycles in Congressional Elections and the Macroeconomy." *American Political Science Review* 83 (2): 373–98.

Altfeld, Michael, and Gary Miller. 1984. "Sources of Bureaucratic Influence." *Journal of Conflict Resolution* 28 (4): 701–30.

Amemiya, Takeshi. 1984. "Tobit Models: A Survey." *Journal of Econometrics* 24 (1-2): 3–61.

Anagnoson, J. Theodore. 1982. "Federal Grant Agencies and Congressional Election Campaigns." *American Journal of Political Science* 26 (3): 547–61.

Ansolabehere, Stephen, David Brady, and Morris Fiorina. 1992. "The Vanishing Marginals and Electoral Responsiveness." *British Journal of Political Science* 22 (1): 21–38.

Arnold, R. Douglas. 1990. *The Logic of Congressional Action.* Yale University Press.

———. 1995. "Pork Barrel." In *The Encyclopedia of the United States Congress,* vol. 3, edited by Donald C. Bacon, Roger H. Davidson, and Morton Keller, pp. 1569–71. New York: Simon and Schuster.

Balla, Steven J. 1998. "Administrative Procedures and Political Control of the Bureaucracy." *American Political Science Review* 92 (3): 663–73.

Balla, Steven J., and others. 2002. "Partisanship, Blame Avoidance, and the Distribution of Legislative Pork." *American Journal of Political Science* 46 (3): 515–25.

Barron, David J., and Todd D. Rakoff. 2013. "In Defense of Big Waiver." *Columbia Law Review* 113 (2): 265–346.

Baumgartner, Frank D., and Bryan D. Jones. 1993. *Agendas and Instability in American Politics.* University of Chicago Press.

Bendor, Jonathan, Serge Taylor, and Roland Van Gaalen. 1985. "Bureaucratic Expertise versus Legislative Authority: A Model of Deception and Monitoring in Budgeting." *American Political Science Review* 79 (4): 1041–60.

Berry, Christopher, and Jacob Gersen. 2010. "Agency Politicization and Distributive Politics." Harris School of Public Policy, University of Chicago.

Berry, Christopher, Barry Burden, and William Howell. 2010. "The President and the Distribution of Federal Spending." *American Political Science Review* 104 (4): 783–99.

Bertelli, Anthony, and Christian Grose. 2009. "Secretaries of Pork? A New Theory of Distributive Public Policy." *Journal of Politics* 71 (3): 926–45.

Bickers, Kenneth N., and Robert M. Stein. 2000. "The Congressional Pork Barrel in a Republican Era." *Journal of Politics* 62 (4): 1070–86.

Biden, Joseph. 2009. "Remarks by the Vice President at the First Recovery Plan Implementation Meeting." White House, Office of the Vice President. February 25.

Blumenthal, Sidney. 1992. *The Permanent Campaign.* New York: Touchstone Press.

Bureau of Economic Analysis. 2012. "GDP by State (Millions of Dollars)." Department of Commerce.

Calmes, Jackie. 2006. "In Search of Presidential Earmarks." *Wall Street Journal,* February 21.

Cameron, Charles. 2000. *Veto Bargaining: Presidents and the Politics of Negative Power.* Cambridge University Press.

Canes-Wrone, Brandice. 2001. "The President's Legislative Influence from Public Appeals." *American Journal of Political Science* 45 (2): 313–29.

———. 2006. *Who Leads Whom? Presidents, Policy, and the Public.* University of Chicago Press.

Canes-Wrone, Brandice, and Kenneth W. Shotts. 2004. "The Conditional Nature of Presidential Responsiveness to Public Opinion." *American Journal of Political Science* 48 (4): 690–706.

Carpenter, Daniel P. 2001. *The Forging of Bureaucratic Autonomy: Reputations, Networks, and Policy Innovation in Executive Agencies: 1862–1928.* Princeton University Press.

Carsey, Thomas, and Barry Rundquist. 1999. "Party and Committee in Congressional Policy Making: Evidence from the Domestic Distribution of Defense Expenditures." *Journal of Politics* 61 (4): 1156–69.

Census Bureau. 2001. "Population Estimates for the U.S., Regions, Divisions, and States by 5-Year Age Groups and Sex: Time Series Estimates, July 1, 1990 to July 1, 1999 and April 1, 1990 Census Population Counts." Department of Commerce.

———. 2011a. "The Federal Assistance Award Data System." Department of Commerce.

———. 2011b. "Intercensal Estimates of the Resident Population by Five-Year Age Groups, Sex, Race and Hispanic Origin for States and the United States: April 1, 2000 to July 1, 2010." Department of Commerce.

———. 2012. "Estimates of the Resident Population by Selected Age Groups for the United States, States, and Puerto Rico: July 1, 2011." Department of Commerce.

Charnock, Emily, James A. McCann, and Kathryn Dunn Tenpas. 2009. "First Term Presidential Travel from Eisenhower to George W. Bush: The Emergence of an 'Electoral College' Strategy." *Political Science Quarterly* 124 (2): 323–39.

Chen, Jowei. 2009. "When Do Government Benefits Influence Voters' Behavior? The Effect of FEMA Disaster Rewards on U.S. Presidential Votes." University of Michigan.

Chubb, John E. 1985. "The Political Economy of Federalism." *American Political Science Review* 79 (4): 994–1015.

Clayton, Cornell W. 1992. *The Politics of Justice: The Attorney General and the Making of Legal Policy.* Armonk, N.Y.: M.E. Sharpe.

Clinton, Joshua D., and David E. Lewis. 2008. "Expert Opinion, Agency Characteristics, and Agency Preferences." *Political Analysis* 16 (1): 3–20.

Clinton, Joshua, and others. 2012. "Separated Powers in the United States: The Ideology of Agencies, Presidents, and Congress." *American Journal of Political Science* 56 (2): 341–54.

Cohen, Jeffrey E. 1995. "Presidential Rhetoric and the Public Agenda." *American Journal of Political Science* 39 (1): 87–107.

Cook, Corey. 2002. "The Contemporary Presidency: The Permanence of the 'Permanent Campaign': George W. Bush's Public Presidency." *Presidential Studies Quarterly* 32 (4): 753–64.

Cooper, Joseph, and William F. West. 1988. "Presidential Power and Republican Government: The Theory and Practice of OMB Review of Agency Rules." *Journal of Politics* 50 (4): 864–95.

Cooper, Phillip. 2002. *By Order of the President: The Use and Abuse of Executive Direct Action.* University of Kansas Press.

Dickinson, Matthew, and Kathryn Dunn Tenpas. 2002. "Explaining Increasing Turnover Rates among Presidential Advisors, 1929–1997." *Journal of Politics* 64 (2): 434–48.

Dixit, Avinash, and John Londregan. 1996. "The Determinants of Success of Special Interests in Redistributive Politics." *Journal of Politics* 58 (4): 1132–55.

Doherty, Brendan J. 2007. "The Politics of the Permanent Campaign: Presidential Travel and the Electoral College, 1977–2004." *Presidential Studies Quarterly* 37 (4): 749–73.

———. 2010. "Hail to the Fundraiser in Chief: The Evolution of Presidential Fundraising Travel, 1977–2004." *Presidential Studies Quarterly* 40 (1): 159–70.

Duncan, Philip D., and Christine C. Lawrence. 1997. *CQ's Politics in America 1998: The 105th Congress.* Washington: CQ Press.

Eisner, Marc A. 1991. *Antitrust and the Triumph of Economics: Institutions, Expertise, and Policy Change.* University of North Carolina Press.

Environmental Protection Agency. 2005. "Mine Site Cleanup for Brownfields Redevelopment: A Three-Part Primer."

Epstein, David. 1997. "An Informational Rationale for Committee Gatekeeping Power." *Public Choice* 91 (3): 271–99.

Epstein, David, and Sharyn O'Halloran. 1999. *Delegating Powers: A Transaction Cost Politics Approach to Policy Making.* Cambridge University Press.

Federal Highway Administration. 2008. "Highway Statistics 2008: Public Road Length—2008 Miles by Functional System." Department of Transportation.

Fenno, Richard. 1978. *Homestyle: House Members in Their Districts*. Boston: Little, Brown.

Ferejohn, John. 1974. *Pork Barrel Politics: Rivers and Harbors Legislation 1947–1968*. Stanford University Press.

Fiorina, Morris. 1977. *Congress: Keystone to the Washington Establishment*. Yale University Press.

———. 1981. *Retrospective Voting in American Elections*. Yale University Press.

Fisher, Louis. 1975. *Presidential Spending Power*. Princeton University Press.

Freeman, John Leiper. 1965. *The Political Process: Executive Bureau–Legislative Committee Relations*. New York: Random House.

Gailmard, Sean, and John Patty. 2007. "Slackers and Zealots: Civil Service, Policy Discretion, and Bureaucratic Expertise." *American Journal of Political Science* 51 (4): 873–89.

Gais, Thomas L., Mark A. Peterson, and Jack L. Walker. 1982 "Interest Groups, Iron Triangles, and Representative Institutions in American National Government." *British Journal of Political Science* 14 (2): 161–85.

Galvin, Daniel. 2010. *Presidential Party Building: Dwight D. Eisenhower to George W. Bush*. Princeton University Press.

Galvin, Daniel, and Colleen Shogun. 2004. "Presidential Politicization and Centralization across the Modern-Traditional Divide." *Polity* 36 (3): 477–504.

Gasper, John T. and Andrew Reeves. 2011. "Make It Rain: Retrospection and the Attentive Electorate in the Context of Natural Disasters." *American Journal of Political Science* 55 (2): 340–55.

Gilligan, Thomas W., and Keith Krehbiel. 1987. "Collective Decisionmaking and Standing Committees: An Informational Rationale for Restrictive Amendment Procedures." *Journal of Law, Economics, and Organization* 3 (2): 287–335.

Gordon, Sanford. 2010. "Executive Control vs. Bureaucratic Insulation: Evidence from Federal Contracting." New York University, Department of Politics.

Greene, William. 1993. *Econometric Analysis*. New York: Macmillan.

Grunwald, Michael. 2012. *The New New Deal: The Hidden Story of Change in the Obama Era*. New York: Simon & Schuster.

Hamman, John A. 1993. "Bureaucratic Accommodation of Congress and the President: Elections and the Distribution of Federal Assistance." *Political Research Quarterly* 46 (4): 863–79.

Hammond, Thomas H. 1986. "Agenda Control, Organizational Structure, and Bureaucratic Politics." *American Journal of Political Science* 30 (2): 379–420.

Heclo, Hugh. 1977. *A Government of Strangers: Executive Politics in Washington*. Brookings.

Hetherington, Marc J. 1996. "The Media's Role in Forming Voters' National Economic Evaluations in 1992." *American Journal of Political Science* 40 (2): 372–95.

Hoover, Gary, and Paul Pecorino. 2005. "The Political Determinants of Federal Expenditure at the State Level." *Public Choice* 123 (1): 95–113.

Howell, William G. 2003. *Power without Persuasion: The Politics of Direct Presidential Action*. Princeton University Press.

Huber, John, and Nolan McCarty. 2004. "Bureaucratic Capacity, Delegation, and Political Reform." *American Political Science Review* 98 (3): 481–94.

Huber, John D., and Charles R. Shipan. 2002. *Deliberate Discretion? The Institutional Foundations of Bureaucratic Autonomy.* Cambridge University Press.

Hurwitz, Mark S., Roger J. Moiles, and David W. Rohde. 2001. "Distributive and Partisan Issues in Agriculture Policy in the 104th House." *American Political Science Review* 95 (4): 911–22.

Jeffrey, Terence P. 2010. "Leading Conservative Senator: Congress Has a Right, and Duty, to Earmark." CNSnews.com. March 14 (www.cnsnews.com/news/article/62746).

Kagan, Elena. 2001. "Presidential Administration." *Harvard Law Review* 114 (8): 2245–385.

Kernell, Samuel. 1993. *Going Public: New Strategies of Presidential Leadership.* Washington: CQ Press.

Kiewiet, D. Roderick, and Mathew D. McCubbins. 1991. *The Logic of Delegation.* University of Chicago Press.

Koszcuk, Jackie, and H. Amy Stern. 2005. *CQ's Politics in America 2006: The 109th Congress.* Washington: CQ Press.

Krause, George A. 1999. *A Two-Way Street: The Institutional Dynamics of the Modern Administrative State.* University of Pittsburgh Press.

Kuklinski, James. 1978. "Representativeness and Elections: A Policy Analysis." *American Political Science Review* 72 (1): 165–77.

Lacey, Marc. 2000. "Gore Puts Limits on Politicking by the President." *New York Times,* October 28.

Larcinese, Valentino, Leonzio Rizzo, and Cecilia Testa. 2006. "Allocating the U.S. Federal Budget to the States: The Impact of the President." *Journal of Politics* 68 (2): 447–56.

Laswell, Harold. 1936. *Politics: Who Gets What, When, and How.* Whittlesey House, McGraw-Hill.

Lee, Frances E. 2000. "Senate Representation and Coalition Building in Distributive Politics." *American Political Science Review* 94 (1): 59–72.

———. 2003. "Geographic Politics in the U.S. House of Representatives: Coalition Building and Distribution of Benefits." *American Journal of Political Science* 47 (4):714-28.

Lee, Frances, and Bruce Oppenheimer. 1999. *Sizing Up the Senate: The Unequal Consequences of Equal Representation.* University of Chicago Press.

Levitt, Steven D., and James M. Snyder Jr. 1995. "Political Parties and the Distribution of Federal Outlays." *American Journal of Political Science* 39 (4): 958–80.

Lewis, David E. 2003. *Presidents and the Politics of Agency Design: Political Insulation in the United States Government Bureaucracy 1946–1997.* Stanford University Press.

———. 2008. *The Politics of Presidential Appointments: Political Control and Bureaucratic Performance.* Princeton University Press.

———. 2009. "The Survey on the Future of Government Service." Vanderbilt University, Center for the Study of Democratic Institutions.

Light, Paul C. 1995. *Thickening Government.* Brookings.

————. 1999. *The President's Agenda: Domestic Policy Choice from Kennedy to Clinton*, 3rd ed. Johns Hopkins University Press.

Loveless, Bill. 2004. "DOE Officials Hit Battleground States to Dole Out Awards One by One." *Inside Energy with Federal Lands*. October 18: A4.

Lowi, Theodore J. 1969. *The End of Liberalism: Ideology, Policy, and the Crisis of Public Authority*. New York: Norton.

Lugar, Richard. 2010. *Lugar: Eliminating Earmarks Cuts No Spending*, press release, November 16, 2010 (http://web.archive.org/web/20110106222457/http://lugar.senate.gov/news/record.cfm?id=328587&&).

Mann, Thomas, and Norman Ornstein. 2000. *The Permanent Campaign and Its Future*. Washington: American Enterprise Institute.

Mayhew, David. 1974. *Congress: The Electoral Connection*. Yale University Press.

McCubbins, Mathew D. 1985. "The Legislative Design of Regulatory Structure." *American Journal of Political Science* 29 (4): 721–48.

McCubbins, Mathew D., and Thomas Schwartz. 1984. "Congressional Oversight Overlooked: Police Patrols versus Fire Alarms." *American Journal of Political Science* 28 (1): 165–79.

McCutcheon, Chuck, and Christina L. Lyons. 2009. *CQ's Politics in America 2010: The 111th Congress*. Washington: CQ Press.

Mebane, Walter, and Gregory Wawro. 2002. "Presidential Pork Barrel Politics." Working Paper. University of Michigan, Department of Political Science.

Miller, Gary J. 1992. *Managerial Dilemmas*. Cambridge University Press.

Moe, Terry M. 1982. "Regulatory Performance and Presidential Administration." *American Journal of Political Science* 26 (2): 197–224.

————. 1985. "Control and Feedback in Economic Regulation: The Case of the NLRB." *American Political Science Review* 79 (4): 1094–1116.

————. 1989. "The Politics of Bureaucratic Structure." In *Can the Government Govern?*, edited by J. E. Chubb and P. E. Peterson. Brookings.

————. 1993. "Presidents, Institutions, and Theory." In *Researching the Presidency: Vital Questions, New Approaches*, edited by George C. Edwards III, John H. Kessel, and Bert A. Rockman. University of Pittsburgh Press.

————. 1999. "The Presidential Power of Unilateral Action." *Journal of Law, Economics, and Organization* 15 (1): 132–79.

Moe, Terry M., and William Howell. 1999. "A Theory of Unilateral Action." *Presidential Studies Quarterly* 29 (4): 850–71.

Moe, Terry M., and Scott Wilson. 1994. "Presidents and the Politics of Structure." *Law and Contemporary Problems* 57 (2): 1–44.

Nathan, Richard P. 1975. *The Plot That Failed: Nixon and the Administrative Presidency*. New York: Wiley.

————. 1986. *The Administrative Presidency*. New York: Macmillan.

National Center for Education Statistics. 2012. *Digest of Education Statistics, 2011*. Department of Education.

Neustadt, Richard E. 1960. *Presidential Power*. New York: Macmillan.

Nzelibe, Jide. 2006. "The Fable of the Nationalist President and the Parochial Congress." *UCLA Law Review* 53 (5): 1217–73.

Obama, Barack. 2009a. "White House Releases State-by-State Numbers; American Recovery and Reinvestment Act to Save or Create 3.5 Million Jobs." White House, Office of the Press Secretary. February 17.

———. 2009b. "Statement on Recovery and Reinvestment Agreement." White House, Office of the Press Secretary. February 11.

———. 2009c. "Remarks at the American Recovery and Reinvestment Act Implementation Conference." White House. March 12. See Gerhard Peters and John T. Woolley, *The American Presidency Project* (www.presidency.ucsb.edu/ws/index.php?pid=85855& st=infrastructure&st1=#axzz2jglDfPRf).

Office of Personnel Management. 2012. "FedScope: Federal Human Resources Data." (www.fedscope.opm.gov/employment.asp).

Peterson, Mark A. 1992. "The Presidency and Organized Interests: White House Patterns of Interest Group Liaison." *American Political Science Review* 86 (3): 612–25.

Peterson, Paul E., and Jay P. Greene. 1994. "Why Executive-Legislative Conflict in the United States Is Dwindling." *British Journal of Political Science* 24 (1): 33–55.

Pfiffner, James. 1991. *The Managerial Presidency.* Pacific Grove, Calif.: Brooks/Cole.

———. 1996. *The Strategic Presidency: Hitting the Ground Running,* 2nd ed. rev. University Press of Kansas.

Pika, Joseph A., and John Anthony Maltese. 2006. *The Politics of the Presidency,* 6th ed. rev. Washington: CQ Press.

Polsby, Nelson. 1978. "Interest Groups and the Presidency: Trends in Political Intermediation in America." In *American Politics and Public Policy,* edited by Walter Dean Burnham and Martha Wagner Weinberg. MIT Press.

Ragsdale, Lyn, and John J. Theiss III. 1997. "The Institutionalization of the American Presidency: 1924–92." *American Journal of Political Science.* 41 (4): 1280–318.

Randall, Ronald. 1979. "Presidential Power versus Bureaucratic Intransigence: The Influence of the Nixon Administration on Welfare Policy." *American Political Science Review* 73 (3): 795–810.

Ripley, Randall B., and Grace A. Franklin. 1984. *Congress, the Bureaucracy, and Public Policy.* Chicago: Dorsey Press.

Robinson, Scott E., and others. 2007. "Explaining Policy Punctuations: Bureaucratization and Budget Change." *American Journal of Political Science* 51 (1): 140–50.

Rottinghaus, Brandon. 2006. "Rethinking Presidential Responsiveness: The Public Presidency and Rhetorical Congruence: 1953–2001." *Journal of Politics* 68 (3): 720–32.

Rourke, Francis Edward. 1984. *Bureaucracy, Politics, and Public Policy.* New York: Little, Brown.

Rudalevige, Andrew. 2002. *Managing the President's Program: Presidential Leadership and Legislative Policy Formation.* Princeton University Press.

Rundquist, Barry, and Thomas Carsey. 2002. *Congress and Defense Spending: The Distributive Politics of Military Procurement.* University of Oklahoma Press.

Rundquist, Barry, Jeong-Hwa Lee, and Jungho Rhee. 1996. "The Distributive Politics of Cold War Defense Spending: Some State-Level Evidence." *Legislative Studies Quarterly* 21 (2): 265–81.

Schattschneider, E. E. 1960. *The Semisovereign People: A Realist's View of Democracy in America.* New York: Holt, Rinehart, and Winston.

Seidman, Harold. 1998. *Politics, Position, and Power: The Dynamics of Federal Organization.* Oxford University Press.

Seidman, Harold, and Robert Scott Gilmour. 1986. *Politics, Position, and Power: From the Positive to the Regulatory State.* Oxford University Press.

Shaw, Daron R. 2006. *The Race to 270: The Electoral College and the Campaign Strategies of 2000 and 2004.* University of Chicago Press.

Shaw, Daron R., and Brian Roberts. 2000. "Campaign Events, the Media, and the Prospects of Victory: The 1992 and 1996 U.S. Presidential Elections." *British Journal of Political Science* 30 (2): 259–89.

Shor, Boris. 2006. "Presidential Power and Distributive Politics: Federal Expenditures in the 50 States: 1983–2001." University of Chicago, Harris School of Public Policy.

Snyder, James, and Barry R. Weingast. 2000. "The American System of Shared Powers: The President, Congress, and the NLRB." *Journal of Law, Economics, and Organization* 16 (2): 269–305.

Solomon, John, Alec MacGillis, and Sarah Cohen. 2007. "How Rove Directed Federal Assets for GOP Gains." *Washington Post,* August 19.

Stack, Kevin. 2008. "The Story of *Morrison* v. *Olson*: The Independent Counsel and Independent Agencies in Watergate's Wake." In *Presidential Power Stories,* edited by Curtis Bradley and Christopher Schroeder. Foundation Press.

Stein, Robert M., and Kenneth N. Bickers. 1994. "Congressional Elections and the Pork Barrel." *Journal of Politics* 56 (2): 377–99.

———. 1995. *Perpetuating the Pork Barrel: Policy Subsystems and American Democracy.* Cambridge University Press.

Stern, H. Amy. 2001. *CQ's Politics in America 2002: The 107th Congress.* Washington: CQ Press.

Stewart, Joseph, and Joseph S. Cromartie. 1982. "Partisan Presidential Change and Regulatory Policy: The Case of the FTC and Deceptive Practices Enforcement: 1938–1974." *Presidential Studies Quarterly* 12 (4): 568–73.

Taylor, Andrew J. 2008. "The Presidential Pork Barrel and the Conditioning Effect of Term." *Presidential Studies Quarterly* 38 (1): 96–109.

Tenpas, Kathryn Dunn. 2000. "The American Presidency: Surviving and Thriving amidst the Permanent Campaign." In *The Permanent Campaign and Its Future,* edited by Norman J. Ornstein and Thomas E. Mann. Brookings.

Tenpas, Kathryn Dunn, and Matthew J. Dickinson. 1997. "Governing, Campaigning, and Organizing the Presidency: An Electoral Connection?" *Political Science Quarterly* 112 (1): 51–66.

Ting, Michael. 2012. "Legislatures, Bureaucracies, and Distributive Spending." Columbia University, Department of Political Science.

Tobin, James. 1958. "Estimation of Relationships for Limited Dependent Variables." *Econometrica: Journal of the Econometric Society* 26 (1): 24–36.

Wayne, Stephen. 1978. *The Legislative Presidency.* New York: Harper and Row.

Weko, Thomas J. 1995. *The Politicizing Presidency: The White House Personnel Office, 1948–1994.* University Press of Kansas.

Wilson, James Q. 1989. *Bureaucracy: What Government Agencies Do and Why They Do It.* New York: Basic Books.

Wiseman, Alan E. 2009. "Delegation and Positive-Sum Bureaucracies." *Journal of Politics* 71 (03): 998–1014.

Wood, B. Dan. 1990. "Does Politics Make a Difference at the EEOC?" *American Journal of Political Science* 34(2): 503-30.

Wood, B. Dan, and Richard W. Waterman. 1991. "The Dynamics of Political Control of the Bureaucracy." *American Political Science Review* 85 (4): 801–28.

———. 1994. *Bureaucratic Dynamics: The Role of Bureaucracy in a Democracy.* Boulder, Colo.: Westview Press.

Wyszomirski, Margaret. 1991. "The Discontinuous Institutional Presidency." In *Executive Leadership in Anglo-American Systems,* edited by Colin Campbell and Margaret Wyszomirski. University of Pittsburgh Press.

Zaller, John. 1992. *The Nature and Origins of Mass Opinion.* Cambridge University Press.

Index

Abraham, Spencer, 32
Accountability, 4, 164, 196
Across-group sample diversification, 155
Agency-level allocations, 9, 68–107;
agency characteristics as variables,
78–80, 100; annual fund allocations
as unit of analysis, 70, 76–77; and
burrowing of staff, 75; cabinet institutions, extent of presidential power in,
85–89, 97, 98, 104–05; cabinet institutions vs. independent commissions in
allocations to swing states, 81–85; and
cabinet stability under Obama, 130;
congressional influence on, 80, 93–96,
97–98, 101, 174–78; data analysis to
test hypotheses, 76–80; external vs.
internal policy traits, 70; full use of
allocation, 15; future research needs
on, 99; and ideology, 75–76, 79–80,
104–05; independent commissions
as resistant to influence, 81–85, 93;
independent institutions, extent of
presidential power in, 89–93, 97, 106–
07; independent variables of interest,
78, 100–01; innovation in, 179–80;
insulated independence, 72–73, 78–79,
81–85, 91, 93, 97, 102–03; and mission of agency, 75; myth of agency
homogeneity, 69–71; OMB role in, 18,
83, 159, 173–74; and politicization,

73–75, 79, 97, 104–05, 130–31; and
presidential discretion, 71–72; reorganization of agencies, 135; responsiveness to presidential electoral interests,
80–96; responsiveness to presidential
preferences, 31, 71–76, 161, 170–71;
and staff-level homogeneity within
an agency, 75. *See also* Appointees;
Bureaucracy; Career civil servants
Agriculture Department, 151
Alesina, Alberto, 35
Alternative energy grants, 32
American Recovery and Reinvestment Act
of 2009 (ARRA), 9, 108–32; analysis of stimulus spending (2009–11),
118–23, 131–32; congressional influence on, 114–15; and economic need,
115–17, 120–22, 124–26; enactment
and purpose, 1–2, 108–11, 131; how
it works, 2, 110–18; and non-stimulus
spending, 117–18, 123–31, 132; and
presidential power, 111–14
Appointees: authority in federal grants
process, 7, 18, 159–67; contact
between central agency appointees
and subnational appointees, 160–61,
165–66, 168, 170; contact with political institutions, 148–49; and design
of grant programs, 14, 167; direct
impact of, 164–67; and evaluation

CPSIA information can be obtained at www.ICGtesting.com
Printed in the USA
BVOW08s2253121115

426915BV00001B/23/P